East Asian Democratization

East Asian Democratization

Impact of Globalization, Culture, and Economy

Robert W. Compton, Jr.

PRAEGER

Westport, Connecticut
London

Library of Congress Cataloging-in-Publication Data

Compton, Robert W., 1964–
  East Asian democratization: impact of globalization, culture, and economy /
Robert W. Compton.
      p.   cm.
  Includes bibliographical references and index.
  ISBN 0–275–96446–9 (alk. paper)
    1. Democratization—East Asia.   2. East Asia—Politics and government.
  3. Globalization.   I. Title.
  JQ1499.A91C65   2000
  320.95—dc21   00–022346

British Library Cataloguing in Publication Data is available.

Library of Congress Catalog Card Number: 00–022346
ISBN: 0–275–96446–9

First published in 2000

Praeger Publishers, 88 Post Road West, Westport, CT 06881
An imprint of Greenwood Publishing Group, Inc.
www.praeger.com

Printed in the United States of America

The paper used in this book complies with the
Permanent Paper Standard issued by the National
Information Standards Organization (Z39.48–1984).

10 9 8 7 6 5 4 3 2

In order to keep this title in print and available to the academic community, this edition
was produced using digital reprint technology in a relatively short print run. This would
not have been attainable using traditional methods. Although the cover has been changed
from its original appearance, the text remains the same and all materials and methods
used still conform to the highest book-making standards.

To my family, who paid dearly for my frequent absence.

For Joyce, my loving wife, and our beautiful children,
Kelly, Christopher, Kayla, and Colin,
who have the blessing of living in a prosperous democracy.

Contents

Figures and Tables

East Asian
Democratization

1

The Problem
of Asian Democracy

I, for one, did not entertain any doubts as regards the transitory
nature of the mob violence. [President Eisenhower's visit to Japan
had to be canceled.] Public opinion has consistently opposed fanat-
icism, both of the Left and Right, and the larger body of our nation
is anxious that a stable Government should exercise a strict control
over the extremist elements which agitate in collusion with foreign
Communists. I am certain that most of these misguided elements will
in time be cured of their juvenile radicalism as our country continues
to advance steadily towards a true democracy.

> Shigeru Yoshida, Prime Minister of Japan
> (quoted from Yoshida 1962: 290)

INTRODUCTION: CULTURE RECONSIDERED

As Asian leaders envision governance for the 21st century, they must
embrace the ultimate reality of globalization and economic modernization. The recent departures of Ferdinand Marcos (the Philippines) and
General Suharto (Indonesia) and the decline of dominant party systems
in South Korea, Japan, and Taiwan—seemingly a permanent fixture on
the Asian political scene—harbingered the dawning of a more fluid and
perhaps even tumultuous dawn for Asia in the 21st century. Throughout
the 1980s and onward, leaders throughout East Asian nations[1] experienced the new opportunities and constraints placed on them by the increasingly rapid shifts in global security arrangements and globalized
domestic economies. The end of the Cold War signalled the loss of U.S.
acceptance of authoritarian political systems as a bulwark against com-

munism; and the rapid economic growth, brought about in part due to globalization, led to changing domestic political culture. Economic growth and modernization created a significant middle class throughout East Asia which questioned the existing political systems.

Without a doubt, most Asian nations benefited from a global economy because of their export-oriented strategy toward growth. However, the Asian "economic flu" which began in 1997 serves as a portentious reminder that no country, especially Asian countries which derive a large percentage of their gross national product (GNP) through trade, could become complacent and expect continuous economic and political stability. As a well-beaten cliche notes, no nation is an island. However, with an increasingly interdependent and globalized world, this phrase reflects a completely new reality which slowly erodes and perhaps corrodes the nexus around which a society functions. Political and economic expectations and the cultural underpinnings of Asian political systems currently exist in a state of flux, as if the plate tectonics of Eastern and Western social systems meet.

As Asian nations defined their political and economic existence, either after years of colonization or periods of sustained foreign threat (in the cases of Japan and Thailand), culture played an important role in the construction of economic and political reality. Culture set the paradigm under which political power could be exercised legitimately (Aronoff 1983; Pye 1985). Yet, so many social scientists have become enamored by the quantifiable indicators of political and economic development, including the trappings of economic modernization consisting of economic growth, urbanization, and the like. However, these indicators tell us only part of the story, and it is a sketchy picture at best. Even for indicators of political modernization—the extent to which political parties compete for power and the existence of modern apparatuses of government, including the military and a bureaucracy—the cultural milieu in which these institutions and actions take place provides a more comprehensive picture of political change. Therefore, comparative politics should remain sensitive to a cultural and historical context.

Cultural and historical context implies "local" in contrast to "global." In this book, the importance of local and global forces complement each other. Despite global pressures for information-based, internationalized national economies based on a standardized division of labor among countries, local conditions persist. For example, the globalization process began centuries ago, even when the United States began its economic modernization. Yet, while the U.S. effort at industrialization remained anchored in the British experiences with technology, the political development of the United States diverged. The United States did not develop a monarchy or create a political system embedded in traditionalism. Instead, as Alexis de Tocqueville so aptly noted, an American sense of egalitarianism lay at the core of the country's economic and political systems.

The experiences of Asian nations with the twin forces of globalization and local political culture reveal a similar pattern of distinctiveness. In other words, Asia may look more like the United States 50 years from now, but in many ways it will remain very different. Keep in mind that empricial observations suggest that even the culturally similar United States and United Kingdom to date have developed a myriad of different economic and political practices, all within the specific cultural context. Some scholars minimize the impact of culture in providing the contextual framework for organizing politics and economics, and thereby become remiss in drawing the important linkages between economics and politics within a cultural framework. Leaders in the East Asian context, for example, realize the intricate nexus around which the exercise of power takes place. Specifically, the export-driven economies in the region are cultural constructs in the sense that leadership—whether Japan's Yoshida Shigeru, China's Mao Zedong, or Singapore's Lee Kuan Yew—relies on cultural values to create economic and political legitimacy. Culture, in this context, has symbolic merit in assisting these leaders in statecraft.

Despite these empirical examples, social scientists, economists, and policy analysts remain unconvinced that culture affects political and economic construction. For example, during the recent economic crisis that swept through the region, analysts targeted "Asian cronyism," mismanagement, and a failure to embrace market forces as the primary cause of Asia's problems. Yet, prior to the recent crisis, these factors clearly operated in the economic environment. How did these evidentiary factors remain concealed during the years of rapid economic growth? For Asian nations to become successful, is it as simple as saying that they need to adopt democracy and market principles?

Given the past experiences with authoritarianism in the political arena and state intervention in economics, to what extent can many of these Asian nations change and adopt "liberal democracy" and "market principles" of economic organization? The answer to this question is locked in understanding the past historical and cultural underpinnings of power. Because the divergent development patterns of East Asia contrasted with Europe and the United States, exploring ideas of Asian culture can advance the state of political development theory. This work examines the impact of culture on economic development and political development in the context of Asian nations. What sense can be made of the historical patterns of economic and political development in East Asian nations? Is this relevant to the current conditions under which democratization takes place? And lastly, how do external and internal factors, such as culture, economic globalization, and the end of the Cold War affect the trajectory of political development? This book seeks to explain the emerging patterns of Asian democracy through an analytical tool based on political cutlure. A coherent synthesis of various perspectives reflects the complexity of the "Asian Political Development Model" presented in Chapter 4. Cultural theories and developmental state and political elite literature comprise the theoretical impetus of a search for this model. A comprehensive approach for explaining democratic consolidation in the Asian context requires sensitivity to culture, economics, and politics. By drawing on historical patterns of Asian political development, this examines the linkages between economic modernization and democracy through a cultural lens. The unfolding patterns of East Asian political liberalization, within the cultural context of traditional and modern sources of power, make this inquiry timely and pertinent.

At the core of this work is a reexamination of the relationship between modernization and political development through a cultural framework. This work represents a response to the general stagnation in political development theory, which has recently addressed inadequately or even ignored the role of culture in modernization and political development. To better explain and describe political development and its future direction, culture lies at the center of this research. It builds on the emerging debate about the trajectory of modern history (Fukuyama 1992) and on the controversies surrounding the future shape of democracy in Asia (Huntington 1994, 1996; Fukuyama 1992, 1995; Mahbubani 1992, 1995; Neher 1994a; Jones 1994; Funabashi 1993; Deyo 1987).

CULTURE AS FRAMEWORK

Analysis and review of early works on modernization and political development lead one to conclude that they focused mostly on the need for economic development to usher in democracy or the need to replace traditional values with modern ones so that political development can occur. An almost linear conception of the effects of economic development on political development dominated the field, even when social scientists recognized the importance of cultural variables. Two seminal works characterized this genre of work: Seymour Martin Lipset's (1959) article titled "Some Social Requisites of Democracy" and Daniel Lerner's (1958) *The Passing of Traditional Society*. Through cross-sectional analysis, Lipset found a positive correlation between economic development and democracy. He raised the distinct possibility that democratization without economic modernization was unlikely, by that suggesting a theoretical starting point for future scholars. Lerner influenced Lipset's work, drawing on the association between sociological changes and "modernity" and its implications for modern democratic political development.

The positive correlation between modernization and development seemed elusive to some geographical regions, including Eastern Europe and East Asia. In the vast majority of Asian societies, democracy remained elusive despite rapid and sustained growth and modernization. By the mid-1980s and into the 1990s, a large and growing East Asian middle class, transformed the political landscape. Sustained demographic change in East Asian societies, including increased urbanization, declining fertility rates, and increased literacy—all strongly associated with the arrival of democracy in the West—did not lead directly to democracy in Asia. For many years, political development and democracy diverged in the East Asian context, because nationalistic elites consolidated political power through economic modernization. Thus in the context of political development, East Asia collectively transformed its political system from one involving a closed system representing a limited spectrum of elites to an expansion of elite recruitment from a much broader spectrum of social and economic groups. Yet, the central thesis of this work proposes that democratization is taking place within the context of the previously defined authoritarian economic and political structures. Therefore, democracy as it emerges in Asia reflects this context.

When democratic transitions finally did take place, mostly after 1985, the same economic and cultural factors that delayed the establishment of democracy continued to affect democratic consolidation in East Asia. Each country's past cultural development affected the emerging shape of democracy. The most common method of liberalization and democratization remains the co-optation of dissidents and opposition leaders into the existing political elite structure. These authoritarian and non-liberal experiences differed significantly from the West's cultural and historical experiences of the past hundred years or so, where political parties occupied a unique and important role for catapulting opponents into leadership.

"Western" notions of democracy could not entirely supplant the pull of Asian culture and history, despite the former's global association with modernity. While all Asian countries operated in a modern economic global structure, they still preserved many traditional values and ideas. Traditionalism remains an integral part of modern Asian political institutions such as parliament, bureaucracies, and political parties. As McCloud (1995: 286) observes, "The nature of the state in Southeast Asia has evolved since independence and now more closely reflects indigenous forms that have been amalgamated from resurgent neotraditional values tempered and shaped by pressures and demands of the late twentieth century."

A closer examination of the economic modernization process in East Asia also reveals a creative tension between traditionalism and modernity. In East Asia, Western economic and political ideas failed to displace the particularism of traditionalism with universal values. For practical reasons of cultural continuity, the entire modernization process itself, in all its accompanying forms—political, social, and economic—became embodied in a traditional and Confucian core. Traditionalism survived modernization by becoming a part of it and interacting with it. Meanwhile, modernization succeeded by adopting traditional elements.

Within the context of these observations, one piece of scholarship remains highly influential because it recognized the power of culture and tradition for modernization. Samuel Huntington's (1968) groundbreaking work on political development, *Political Order in Changing Societies,* provided the theoretical basis for linking traditionalism and modernity. His analysis foretold much about Asian political development today. His book, based on a complex notion of cultural change and maintenance, focused on the development and decay of political institutions. The work's major significance lay in highlighting the need for traditional and modern cultural symbols for effectively governing a transitional society. Furthermore, Huntington stressed the importance of political elites in successfully orchestrating economic and political modernization by using rituals and symbols.

Two major hurdles—not addressed fully in Huntington's work—must be overcome in using culture as a foundation for studying developing societies. First, comparative studies must control, at least partially, the differential effects of culture across nations. One explanation for the lack of progress reflected in the political development literature may rest in past attempts to overgeneralize and undercompare by using large data sets which conceal the differences by not allowing cultural and historical development patterns and contexts to be fully accounted for. Failure to control for cultural and historical variations in the cases studied can contribute to such a problem. Gary King et al. (1994: 37) in *Designing Social Inquiry* argue that if cultural understanding forms the foundation of theoretical questioning, the common historical and cultural experiences of nations require a systems design approach.[2] The second problem for using culture as a foundation for research is inherent in the broad and often contradictory definitions of the term. In the social sciences, the precise meaning of "culture" remains elusive because of parochial disciplinary concerns. Each discipline deals with the issue of culture differently. In spite of these problems, the issue of culture remains a central point of inquiry because it is at the center of human phenomena. This problem will be discussed in extensive detail in the next chapter. Culture drives the framework developed in this work. Adapted from Charles Ragin's work (1994: 83), culture provides the following benefits to this work's theoretical foundation:

1. To give voice and agency by examining Asian political elites within the context of each society's distinct history and culture.

2. To interpret and reinterpret historical and cultural events: to integrate common and different cultural characteristics within historical context to portray political development accurately.
3. To advance theory by decreasing noise and increasing comparability. The primary focus on East Asian nations emphasizes commonalities in culture, developmental patterns, and elite functions.

Given the cultural orientation of this work, the complexity of the central research questions, and the most common systems design, an eclectic research strategy that employs a variety of theories and techniques of analysis is necessary. A carefully constructed framework using theories of culture, the developmental state, and elites are brought to bear on the performance of Asian political systems, using both qualitative and quantitative methods of analysis. The theoretical synthesis is reflected in a derivation of the Asian Political Development model and the quantitative analysis of party systems in Chapter 4. The case studies in Chapters 5 through 8 provide multifaceted analysis that points to an Asian model of political development.

DEMOCRATIZATION, POLITICAL PARTIES, AND THE ASIAN CONTEXT

Political parties and the role they play in democratization illustrate why social scientists should pay close attention to political parties. Political scientists have long recognized the importance of political parties. A long tradition of scholars have explored the contribution of parties to political development (Dahl 1971; Lawson 1980; Lijphart 1984; Vanhanen 1990). For some, political parties play an important role in aggregating and articulating citizens' demands (Lawson 1980), or provide a vehicle for controlling the legislature (Duverger 1954: 82–83) or for political socialization (Westholm and Niemi 1992). In a public policy context (for example, in industrialized Europe), Hans-Dieter Klingemann et al. (1994) show how party responsiveness remains the key to a responsive democratic system. Even in the developing nations, Scott Mainwarring et al. (1995) show how party systems in Latin America evolved. Another example in the Asian context is Gregory Noble's (1998) attempt to show how party politics shape industrial policy in Japan and Taiwan. One underlying commonality in this vast literature, whether a major or minor concern of the respective authors, is that parties impact significantly on the political development trajectory of nations. In other words, all countries have parties, and there is no empirical example of a democracy without competing parties in the context of modern politics.

Since political parties play an integral role in political development, they must be viewed in relation to how power and legitimacy are defined in a cultural and historical context. Power and legitimacy are cultural constructions, embedded in historical contexts, and acted out in parties and party systems. With Asia's experience in political development, the foci for exploration involving political development and parties can be defined as follows: (1) the establishment and institutionalization of political parties and party systems; (2) the role of the developmental state in structuring the democratization process; and (3) the role of culture as a parameter setter (especially about defining legitimacy and democracy) reflects core issues regarding democratization.[3]

During the post–World War II period, many postcolonial nations established democracies, only to experience political decay as institutions failed to consolidate democracy. In many instances, these "democracies" atrophied and became one-party states or outright dictatorships. Then in the 1980s, many of these regimes, who also happened to pursue autarchic economic policies, collapsed and elites experienced an upwelling of opposition and calls for democracy. In Asia, from South Korea to the Philippines, "stable regimes" were swept away by democratic transitions. However, these transitions tell only part of the story. Political development in these countries entered the "consolidation stage."

Many leaders in these new democracies will have to overcome many social, political, and economic difficulties while building institutions capable of promoting societal empowerment. History for these new democracies of the 1990s is not on their side. Throughout history many new democracies deteriorated over time, ended their experiments with democracy, and degenerated into one-party states because of mass and elite dissatisfaction with democracy. What determines the success of these transitions and consolidations? Since not all transitions are ultimately successful, the consolidation process is very important. However, a variety of endogenous and exogenous factors affect democratic consolidation, including economic performance, perceptions of governmental effectiveness, and the ability to survive in a globalized economy. These factors form the basis for evaluation of a regime's performance, and that, combined with culture acceptance, defines a regime's legitimacy.

The term "political legitimacy" consists of many evaluational components. These include economic, political, and cultural components used to gauge the overall acceptance of the regime. These three interrelated components vary in degrees of emphasis depending on roles that specific groups play in shaping expectations of and functions of government. For example, elites may have different views of legitimacy from peasants. In some societies, elites succeed in socializing the masses to accept their views of governance, but in other societies the chasm between the masses and the elites remains wide. Further complicating perceptions of legitimacy are the multitude of schisms within the elite and the masses. The

Asian cases represent all these complex problems and issues. However, significant and rapid modernization and the rapid economic growth in the region provide the social scientist with an interesting and challenging laboratory. In addition, the varying degrees of cultural similarities among East Asian nations facilitate comparison. Rapid economic growth and social changes against the backdrop of historical and cultural continuity shaped institutional formation and democratic consolidation in the entire region. The persistence of traditionalism and the encroachment of modernity present an interesting nexus for political construction and the testing of our assumptions about democracy.

Political Parties and Competition

Samuel Huntington (1968: 89) argues that political parties, as distinctively modern political institutions, make mass participation and organization possible. Mass democracy refers to democratic elections and political parties (Michels 1962). They are institutions that organize mass political activity and representation. Many political scientists (e.g., Lijphart 1984; Sartori 1976; Huntington 1968) point to political parties as an integral part of political development.

The legacy of decolonization presents a challenge for the institutionalization of democracy, and party system in particular. The *Zeitgeist* of postcolonialism, as reflected in the nationalism of a cadre of Western educated elite, conflicted with traditionalism. The clash of traditionalism and modernity epitomizes the politics of a transitional society. Ability to manage this cultural problem ultimately defined the success or failure of political leadership. Its failure resulted in the weakening or disintegration of elite solidarity. However, initially after decolonization, many nations adopted Western-based models of parliamentary systems because these institutions connoted modernity. However, once adopted, these institutions bequeathed by the "mother country" underwent a series of mutations. Indigenous elites modified existing institutions for two primary goals: to maintain power and the political status quo. These two goals reflected a consistency with a higher goal of nation building through modernization. Sometimes parliamentary systems made useful adaptations; other times they decayed whenever adaption did not occur or when it failed. Even rarely where democracy eventually took hold, the essence of parliamentary government was very different from that envisioned from a Western perspective.

Many of these nations experienced quite different manifestations of parliamentary systems from those accustomed to in Western democracies. Often they did not follow representative functions, but allowed one-party domination. At other times, parliaments, despite their constitutional intentions, failed to perform the function of a supreme organ of legislative decision making. In fact, commonly, the political parties represented in parliament reflected age-old political traditions of personalism, regionalism, and tribal rivalries. These political parties were quite different from those in the West or the United States because developing nations were initially preindustrial and characteristically contained primordial cleavages. Political parties perform interest articulation and aggregation functions of elites primarily over the masses, but they may also exacerbate primordial cleavages, especially in a multiparty context. Multiparty systems aim toward representation (articulation) over aggregation. Asian party systems reflect strong aggregative tendencies, particularly in South Korea, Taiwan, Japan, Malaysia, and Singapore, as evidenced by a dominant party system and their successors. Recently established Asian party systems lack the importance that their European counterparts possess. In particular, they are merely functional vehicles of a plethora of elite interests, including the bureaucrats, military officers, and corporate tycoons. Thus, in terms of functionality, the Asian context carves out a specific niche for the political role of parties that is quite different from European and American parties, because Asian parties lack the direct connection to law making.

The framework for party analysis developed over the years remained Eurocentric and focused on Western party systems (e.g., Michels 1962; Lijphart 1984; Rae 1971; Sartori 1976; Taagepera 1989, Ware 1979, 1996). From this school of thought, ideas of competitiveness, party systems, and parties representing cleavages emerged. However, very little systematic analysis of Asian party systems as a region or as individual countries exist, except Alan Ware (1996)—who devotes a short chapter to party systems in non-liberal regimes. This should not come as a surprise; many of these countries adopted democracy only recently, and the term "semi-democracy" appears more apt for describing them. Thus, despite the Western bias inherent in the study of parties, the tradition of studying political parties must draw initially from the literature reflecting that experience and culture.

Beginning with the 1960s, the paradigm of political parties studies among comparativists solidified. For example, Sartori (1976: 58–64) asks a rhetorical question, "What is the difference between political parties and factions?" Ultimately, he arrives at a minimalist definition: "A party is any political group that presents at elections, and is capable of placing through elections, candidates for public office" (Sartori 1996: 64). A party system therefore is the "system of interactions resulting from inter-party competition" (Sartori 1996: 44). As a system, it involves the actors (parties), patterns of interaction among the actors (cooperation and competition), and rules and procedures for competition and cooperation (both written and customary).

Competition constitutes the *raison d'être* of political parties and party systems, both within and between political parties. A definitive characteristic of party systems, competition reflects the salience of social cleavages in the political system (Downs 1957; Sartori 1976; Neuman 1956; Weiner and LaPalombara 1966). We cannot, therefore, speak of party systems in one-party states. As Sigmund Neumann argues, a one-party system is a contradiction in terms (Neumann 1956: 395). Without political parties, democracy, which reflects a plethora of competing and mutually exclusive interests, cannot exist. Party competition is one indicator of democratic consolidation, in that an institutionalized party system will manifest healthy patterns of competition. Competition involves changing the majority party occasionally through elections. The existence of a competitive party system demonstrates the government's toleration of organized political opposition. Nations displaying homogeneity among political parties or a lack of party system competitiveness attest to a democratic consolidation process divergent from the Western experience.

For Asia, the litmus test of party competition seems crucial given the historical experiences with authoritarianism and postcolonial nationalism. Authoritarianism, as referred to by Simone and Feraru (1995: 104), is characterized by an "absence of real competition for political power?" By examining party systems and their competitiveness in Asian cases, we can draw some generalizations and conclusions about democratic consolidation and the decline of traditional authoritarian methods of political control. The breakdown of the "Asian Political Development Model," as discussed in Chapter 4, requires that political parties become independent organizations which break from their past and assume an identity independent from the elite who dominated the ancient regime prior to a democratic transition. In most Asian nations, this has not occured.

Three Literature Sources: An Alternative Approach

Establishing and maintaining political parties and party systems, however, is only one aspect of democratic consolidation, which in turn is part of political development construed broadly. All parties perform political functions but their degree of autonomy from other actors, such as the military, the bureaucracy, and the monarchy vary according to cultural and historical context. A comprehensive examination of political development requires a multifaceted approach. As such, this research rests on a tripod of perspectives: literature on culture, the past work on elite theory, and the more recent research on the developmental state theory and globalization. Three principle reasons explain the rationale for three disparate sources of theory:

- Past works on political development cannot readily explain democratic consolidation in East Asia today because of their ahistorical and non-cultural context.
- Political development theory fails to draw from the divergent forms of economic development that unfolded in East Asia.
- Many theories of political development are ethnocentric and rely extensively on institutional arrangements (through rules and mechanisms) as opposed to sociocultural arrangements which are articulated through institutions and political leaders.

First, past work on political development cannot account for the divergent patterns of democratic consolidation now occurring in East Asia. Empirically, there are two models emerging, one based on a dominant catch-all party (Malaysia, Singapore, Japan, Taiwan) and another model more akin to the European multiparty system (South Korea and to some degree Thailand). This genre of work (Almond and Coleman 1960; Rostow 1960; Lerner 1958) focused primarily on modernization as a universal phenomenon conducive to democracy. Collectively, the modernization literature addresses an important question in comparative politics concerning the relationship between economic modernization and political change, but it fails to two accounts. It fails to recognize the role of traditionalism in shaping an indigenous form of a modern economy as demonstrated through the culture and historical experiences of the country. Also, related to the first deficiency is its failure to recognize how the cultural and historical development of an indigenous economy affected the formation of political systems. Specifically, in the Asian context, the culture of traditional audits links to authoritarian and patron-client systems.

Second, past works on political development fail to explain political development in the politics-culture-economics nexus. Thus, the meteoric rise of East Asia's economy and its effect on political culture, institutions, and state-society relations cannot be readily explained by existing theory. Political development theory can advance when political scientists study these integral linkages and their synergistic effects. The developmental state explanation about East Asia's state-led rapid economic rise provides a useful starting point. The developmental state argument initially emerged as an alternative explanation to the liberal, neo-Keynesian, market-based explanation for regional economic growth (Johnson 1987, 1995; Wade 1990; White and Wade 1990; Amsden 1989; Deyo 1987). Developmental theorists discuss extensively the connection between politics and economy, but much of that literature focuses on political economy instead of political development. In addition, much of the development state literature downplays or even ignores globalization and how it undermines state autonomy. By using the model of state-directed economic development in a context of the global economy and then applying it to political development, interesting possibilities arise. Political development and economic development's linkages provide new ideas about Asian politics. In particular, ideas about economic construction also apply to political construction, including democratic consolidation.

Lastly, political development literature marginalizes the role of political leadership, or more specifically, the role of political elites in the modernization process. Inherent in the ethnocentric biases of comparative politics, the study of rules and institutions marginalizes the contribution of leadership to political development. The paramount importance of rules and institutions in Western societies cannot be universalized to non-Western systems. Unsurprisingly, political science places inordinate effort on studying institutionalization of organizations without first examining the social and cultural parameters of national politics. For example, while studying "form" (party structure and election results) can inform us about essence (ideology and logic) of party systems, studying the essence can first direct a researcher's search for specific elements in party organization and then tie those observations to some democratic form and ultimately to democratic consolidation. By examining elite theory and then applying it to political development through culture, social scientists can draw connections between institutions and individuals. In other words, an explanation about the cultural behavior of elites can tell us how they construct Asian political systems.

DEMOCRATIC CONSOLIDATION IN A CULTURAL AND SOCIAL CONTEXT: MOVING AWAY FROM PRECONCEIVED NOTIONS

A cursory examination of the political development literature shows the paucity of research on political parties as it pertains to East Asia. A large part of the problem stems from the recent establishment of party systems, primarily over the past ten years. Asian democratic transitions permit a study of under-explored and ongoing democratic consolidation issues. These studies help strengthen the theories of political development by integrating culture and historical experiences into political development theory. For example, to what extent do past experiences within the political realm and economic modernization affect the establishment and consolidation of democracy? What is the role of indigenous culture in shaping the transformation process?

At the core of the democratization debate is the extent to which economic modernization contributes to democratization. Seymour Martin Lipset's (1959) seminal research intensified the debate and set the trajectory for future research about the relationship between economic development and democracy. Recently, the collapse of the Eastern bloc reinvigorated the debate on democratization in East Asia. Meanwhile, many Asian nations underwent their own version of democratic revolutions. Sometimes, the pressure for democratization came from below as in the Philippines (1987) and Thailand (1992) or leaders orchestrated their own departure. In South Korea and Taiwan (1987), formerly authoritarian regimes gingerly orchestrated their own transformation. Yet in academic social science, the debate about democratization often assumed a "universalist orientation," that all societies were ultimately becoming democratic, in an undifferentiated and Western mold.

The universalist scholarship is both ethnocentric and ideological. The application of the Western social science paradigm without regard for theoretical anomalies or the misfit between theory and data demonstrates ethnocentricity. Forcing models to fit the Asian cultural and social context requires "data massaging" or reinterpretation of old theories. For example, Downsian rational voter models and principle-agent theory—a derivative of rational choice—assume a utility-maximizing behavior irrespective of cultural context. These kinds of models are based on the European and American political experiences. It is also ideologically driven: universalists link the establishment of liberal democracy with the globalization of capitalism assuming both a monolithic construction of economic systems and their effects on politics throughout the developing world. These scholars, including Friedman, Fukuyama, and Diamond, argue that the institutionalization of democratic procedures (e.g., contested elections, the formation of opposition parties, and universal suffrage) signified a global march toward democracy. Yet the term "democracy" refers to a generic conceptualization of politics, totally devoid of cultural connotations and historical context. In other words, the dramatic political transformation of Eastern Europe, Asia, and Africa evoked a normatively-based response that "democracy is good and it is spreading throughout the world along with capitalism." In this unfolding scenario, the subtle connections between economics and politics become unimportant because Western-style democracy and capitalism shares the same essence. Political development in the Third World becomes a production of economic globalization.

Given the various views of the democratization process, where does this research fit? Two broad schools of thought regarding recent democratization trends in Asia exist.[4] One school, the universalists, see the spread of Western-inspired democratic ideals throughout the world (Fukuyama 1995; Quigley 1995; Friedman 1994; Reed 1993; Diamond et al. 1989). Universalists diminish cultural context and construction's role through faith in the transcendency of generic institutions and rules. At the core of the democratic universality thesis lies the assumption that authoritarian cultural and historical experiences will disappear and a universally common democratic culture will rise from the ashes. These societies will ultimately adopt procedures, institutions, and cultures that embrace democracy. Often, market forces are the catalysts for democratization. For example, Francis Fukuyama's (1992) thesis states that liberal democracy became a powerful global ideology. As if to assume the universality of Western-style democracy, Edward Friedman (1994) says that the lessons of Asian democratic transitions are generalizable to other regions in the world.

What is wrong with this universalist conception of democracy? For one, the universalists underestimate the endurance and effects of traditional cultures in shaping present-day elite and mass political attitudes. In turn these values affect the formation of democratic systems. Specifically, given past authoritarianism as constructed through culture, to what extent can we expect these governing elites to step aside and allow significant mass participation? Additionally, given the history of traditional and non-democratic methods (according to Western standards), particularly patron-client relations, to what extent can we expect a complete attitudinal and procedural transformation of a political system? One essential flaw in the universalist's conception of democratization haunts them; his theory derived from a Western liberal context. That means that the assumptions about the cultural and philosophical underpinnings of Asian democracy and Western democracy are at least similar. Nothing can be further from the truth. Asian democracy today and in the future remains a product of a historical and cultural context different from the West's liberalism. Instead, Asian political systems embody "order" as a core value.

Misunderstanding the role of the state is another problem with the "universalist" view of democracy. The East Asian state possesses a developmental orientation. Governments, even if they are authoritarian, possess underlying constituencies of support because they promote rapid economic growth and provide a growing economic pie for both elites and citizens. Therefore, internal pressures for democratization, especially when they come from above, are evolutionary rather than revolutionary. The significance is that evolutionary change, both political and economic, allows the distribution of power to change gradually, thereby insuring an orderly transition. In such systems the former elite can continue to shape the trajectory of political development. Democratic transitions in most of East Asia occurred after the state achieved high levels of legitimacy unlike those in Eastern Europe where the entire economic and political structure decayed and crumbled. In East Asia, democratic transitions were evolutionary rather than revolutionary and this brings import to the present contours of institutions, political culture, and state-society relations in the period of democratic consolidation.

Evolutionary democratic consolidation allows for the structure of power relations to derive from past authoritarian systems. What changed

with democratic consolidation in East Asia regarding state-society relations is the extent to which the state can use excessive coercive measures
and still maintain its legitimacy. Also increased citizen participation,
both in extraparliamentary protest and electoral impact by voting, define
the new political landscape (Robison and Goodman 1996; Rodan 1996).
However, the political terrain reflects much continuity to the authoritarian past. Access to the levers of government has eluded most citizens
because of the newly transformed elites' adept use of accumulated political capital along traditionally authoritarian means. Meanwhile, the institutions used by elites to control the political system also changed.
Governing elites may no longer use the military as an institution for
governance, but they now must rely on the bureaucracy or even political
parties. From Japan to Thailand this pattern will be explored in the case
studies. In other words, the universalist view fails to consider the tradition of the autonomy state seriously.

Culture-centered explanations of Asian political development question
universalist explanations. "Revisionists," both culturalists and statists,
question the universalist scholarship on democracy (Huntington 1996;
Simone and Feraru 1995; Johnson 1994, 1995; McCloud 1995; van Wolferen 1990, 1993; Kataoka 1992; Mahbubani 1992; Cotton 1991a; Moody
1988; Pye 1985). Culturalists examine how enduring cultural characteristics affect political change in a historical context. Statists examine politics by placing the state at the center of analysis. According to them,
politics organizes around the activities of the state. Statists and culturalists both place significant importance on historical development. Some
culturalists and statists are area study experts, and agree that democracy
is not necessarily a universal phenomenon, especially in a Western form.
James Cotton (1991a: 322), for example, questions whether Asian political
systems will merely replicate Western ones.

Culturalists, such as McCloud (1995) and Mahbubani (1992), suggest
that the contours of democracy conform to cultural norms. The cultural
perspective points out salient traditional cultural values and their implications for democratic authority. Pye (1985), for example, explores the
link between the culturally derived meaning of power and political authority and organization. Karel van Wolferen (1990), from a cultural perspective, and Chalmers Johnson (1994, 1995), from a developmental state
approach, conclude that Japan is not a liberal democracy. At this argument's core rests the notion best summarized by Vera Simone and Anne
Feraru's statement that "all of the [Asia] postcolonial political systems
are to some degree authoritarian" (Simone and Feraru 1995: 104). While
both culturalists and statists regard East Asian politics as varying authoritarian, each camp views the other's approach as problematic. For
statists, cultural analysis shifts attention away from state action toward
non-institutional explanations of political phenomena. Meanwhile, cul-

turalists would believe that the statist explanation does not fully account for the historical and cultural context of those institutions. Overall, both statists and culturalists seem unable to transcend their respective boundaries. Culturalists point to culture as an explanation for the persistence of authoritarianism, while statists focus on the state's past role.

An integration of the culturalist and statist perspectives provides the best approach to explaining East Asian political development. By synthesizing the culturalist and statist explanations, a clear picture of Asian political development can be depicted. In particular, the weakness of the party systems in Asia represents a major impediment that prevents democratic consolidation in a liberal form, and this can be traced to both the statist and culturalist positions. Most comparativists agree that weak party systems in developing nations are endemic (Johnson 1995; Friedman 1994; Diamond et al. 1989; Moody 1988; Pye 1985; Huntington 1968; Welch 1967; Ward 1963). Therefore, when we observe democratic transitions and patterns of consolidations in Asia, it is crucial to understand that weak party systems and their low levels of responsiveness differentiate Asian and Western democracy and are an integral component of that process. Part of this reseaech empirically examines Asian party systems as part of political development. Other parts examine political development from a holistic perspective based on cultural construction. Given the different Asian cultural, historical, and economic experiences compared with the West, the argument that Malaysia today is the United States 150 years ago or that Malaysia 150 years from now will look like the United States needs questioning.

SUMMARY: DIFFERENT FORMS OF DEMOCRACY

This chapter provided a general overview of the sources of literature, the scope of the project, and the theoretical contributions of the project. The following chapter, Chapter 2, discusses the literature on culture, and Asian culture specifically, by exploring some salient characteristics of Asian political culture and how that translates to the phenomenon of "modernization without Westernization" and Asian-syle democracy.

Chapters 2 and 3 expand the framework of the relationship between democracy and Asian political culture. Studying Asian democracy involves a review of developmental state theory and culture and how they together affect democratic consolidation. The use of culture for economic modernization and effect of the modernization process on democratic trends constitutes the central area of exploration.

Empirical analysis and theoretical application in Chapter 4 bring together the prior chapters. It integrates the three sources of literature (developmental state, elite theory, and culture theory) to create an "Asian Political Development Model." Parts of Chapter 4 also examine Asian party systems and provide empirical evidence that Asian political development progresses differently than in Anglo-American and European systems.

Chapters 5, 6, and 7 provide the appropriate details and voices to three Asian nations—Japan, South Korea, and Thailand—which represent particularly interesting cases. It traces political development by exploring the cultural and economic foundations of democracy while simultaneously remaining sensitive to the historical context of each nation. Part of tracking political development in each respective country involves a discussion of the linkages among economic development, culture, and politics.

Chapter 8 provides a research summary, explores the study's practical and theoretical implications, and provides a context to draw one's own conclusion about the future trajectory of Asian political development. It also suggests ways for improving the theoretical framework used. Lastly, it discusses the theoretical implication for other cultural regions. To summarize, the role of culture in the political development process is of central concern to this project. While this project examines broadly the relationship between Asian politics, culture, and economics, it also provides a useful approach for studying the demcratization process elsewhere. The shape of democracy, in all societies, is based on the cultural and economic experiences, and others may find this approach useful. The main contention of this research is that Asian power elites maintain a closed monopoly on policy formulation and implementation. Party systems are not competitive and major sectors of society including labor, environmental groups, women's groups, and leftist groups are unrepresented or underrepresented in these political parties. Public opinion in Asia remains only weakly connected to electoral change (Langford and Brownsey 1988: 14–16). Ironically, the governments responsible for modernization within these Asian nations are also responsible for the stunted quality of democracy. Under conditions of rapid economic growth, the systematic exclusion of the "non-growth" segments of the population becomes common practice. If legitimacy increasingly draws from economic growth, major future economic turbulence will undoubtedly undermine the political elite's ability to maintain political control. Asian leaders must reinvigorate their leadership through a multiplicity of sources, including traditional, charismatic, and legal-rational sources. The era of rapid Asian growth, while facilitated by the state, made it difficult for the state to rely on noneconomic sources of legitimacy. Continued democratic consolidation, perhaps, remains one possible avenue for increasing the elites' legitimacy.

NOTES

1. The terms "East Asia" and "Asia" refer to both Northeast and Southeast Asian nations, geographically encompassing Japan, South Korea, Taiwan, the Philippines, the People's Republic of China (PRC), Malaysia, Indonesia, Singapore, Thailand, Vietnam, Myanmar, Laos, and Cambodia. The primary focus in terms of national case studies is Japan, Thailand, and South Korea.

2. An alternative approach, commonly called the "most different systems design," is advocated by Przeworski and Teune (1970: 34). They argue that using similar cases with many common attributes makes it impossible to explain different outcomes. In other words, constancy across nations cannot account for and explain differences in the dependent variable.

3. Democratic transition and democratic consolidation are two distinct processes decribing the generic term "democratization." The former refers to the rules and procedures for societal governing through democratic ideals, while democratic consolidation refers to the sustained, long-term democratic operation of a political system. Democratic transitions represent only the beginning for democratic consolidation. This research explores transitions and consolidation from a historical and cultural perspective.

4. There are significant variations within the two schools of thought. These two schools are theoretical constructs that allow organization of a diverse quantity of work relating to this subject. However, they are in no way exhaustive of the numerous approaches.

2

The Cultural Origins of Asian Democracy

> The Asian orientation toward the group, rather than stressing the individual, affects not only basic political values but a wide range of ordinary political behavior.
>
> Lucian W. Pye (1985: 27)

BETWEEN REALITY AND MODERNIZATION THEORY

Modernization theorists correctly suggest a positive correlation between modernization and democratization. Initially, however, rapid economic growth in East Asia did not portend immediate democratization. Instead, the military dominated politics for most of the post–World War II period. The primary political characteristic of military-led regimes was political repression and an authoritarian orientation to governance. Coupled with economic growth, Asian elites found political stability. Asian democratization process initially lagged behind expectations, but eventually the socioeconomic modernization in the entire region produced significant movement toward the adoption of political liberalization. Modernization theorists could claim some vindication. On one hand, East Asian nations became more democratic through social phenomena associated with modernization, but real democracy remained elusive until the 1980s for many of these countries. While elections took place regularly in South Korea, Thailand, and Japan, real power remained in the hands of the ruling elite from industry, the military, the bureaucracy, and political stalwarts allied with these interests. For the average citizen, the choice consisted of one general or another, or (in Japan) a false choice between the Liberal Democratic Party (LDP) or the Japan Socialist Party (JSP), when in fact the "opposition" remained disunitied and incapable of displacing the ruling party.

However, rapid modernization introduced increased literacy, urbanization, communications, and an increasingly larger middle class sought political participation. One by one, the authoritarian dominoes fell as Asian societies moved toward establishing parliamentary systems, a distinguishing characteristic of "Western democracies." By 1997, most East Asian nations had instituted some form of parliamentary democracy. For example, in 1986 Chiang Ching-kuo lifted Taiwan's martial law and began preparations for democratic elections. South Korea, in 1987, had its first democratic elections in 25 years, and in 1997 Kim Dae Jung, dubbed Asia's Mandela, defeated the ruling Grand National Party and became president. In the Philippines, the "people-power revolution" swept Ferdinand Marcos from power. Even in Singapore, the semiretirement of Lee Kuan Yew signaled imminent changes. Meanwhile in Japan, the LDP's near-forty-year monopoly on power was broken. The angry electorate drove the disgraced and fractured LDP from power in the 1993 elections. Was a new era of democracy dawning in Asia?

The democratic wave sweeping through Asia in the 1980s and early 1990s represented significant challenges to the study of Asian political development. While democratization studies continue to dominate scholarship on political development, the political reality in many Asian nations has shifted from "democratization" to "democratic consolidation." To describe and understand the emerging patterns of democratic consolidation, there is a need to create culture-centered explanations for two reasons. The need to create culturally relevant explanations derives from the apparent tangential progression of Asian political development. The tangential developments are anomalies which can be explained by an alternative theoretical conceptualization, in part drawn from political culture: (1) The existence of Western-based institutional forms in Asia has not led to Western-style democratic consolidation involving an effective party system. (2) The nature of legitimacy in any given society is at least partially culturally driven, and therefore, any emerging form of democracy must both explicitly and implicitly have a cultural foundation. Coupled with the cultural peculiarities of Asian political systems, the history of economic development and the current empirical manifestation of a politico-economic nexus is seen in "Asian-style capitalism." This state-centered capitalism relied on the close cooperation between state and economic actors, to the extent that economic control and political dominance were cemented by an Asian power elite. It was these elites who through their social, political, and economic clout, defined the nature of these countries' democratic transitions and consolidations.

To what extent can culture explain new patterns of democracy? Can political systems that have no conception of individual-centered rights suddenly embrace civil liberties and human rights? Underlying these questions is a more general debate about the nature of democratic consolidation. Is it a matter of merely constructing institutions, as Friedman et al. (1994) suggest, or is there some other set of dynamics that shapes the process?

BUILDING SOCIETIES WITH CULTURE

Culture cannot readily be disaggregated from the study of political development because it provides the context for political action and political structures. Culture as used in this research is conceptualized as an environmental factor which affects the political realm in a normative way; culture helps to determine what forms of government and governmental activities are just or acceptable. For example, the earliest classical philosophers, beginning with Plato, studied the role of culture in the governing process. While Plato did not have a conception of nationalism, or of a dynamic polity—including mobility and technological change— nonetheless, his idea of a carefully cultivated guardian class is particularly appropriate because of the similarities between Plato's guardian class and that of the modern Asian political elite. Even though Plato's ideas were anchored in the city-state, it was a traditional society based on the *Gemeinschaft* principle wherein citizens born into society assumed specified roles. Each citizen represented a component of the organic whole and traditional Asian societies were also constructed according to this principle.

The guardian concept in Plato's republic finds a functional equivalent in the Confucian *junxi*, or guardian class. Plato, in *The Republic*, sought to create the appropriate environment for cultivating the guardian class. In particular, he wanted to create public servants possessing undivided loyalty to the political community. Certainly underlying his idea of a guardian class were notions of social structure and political culture. Broadly construed, Plato's republic possesses intricately woven cultural foundations which make its continuance possible. The ideas about concepts such as citizenship (including rights and responsibilities that appertain to whom) and governance (the rules, norms, and expectations) are based on cultural formulations. Once created, they must be inculcated into the population so as to interface and become part of an existing political culture. This crafting of political culture, a part of statecraft, is essential for the survival of Plato's republic and all nations since. Without a cultural foundation, any political system, including Plato's republic, would soon die because of a lack of agreement regarding that society's moral purpose.[1] Education plays an important role as a conduit for disseminating cultural norms for social construction as in Plato's republic. Socialization assists in maintaining the viability and operation of political systems.

In modern day social science, cultural explanations about democracy and economic development invoke heated academic debate because culture as a concept is difficult to define. Additionally, cuture is both a contextual and intervening variable, seldom operating alone, but in conjunction with events, actions, and social forces. Therefore, there is a tendency to search for more concrete explanations. For example, Moore (1967) and O'Donnell et al. (1986) examine structural factors (e.g., economic and institutional) to account for democratization. Subsequent data sets, including the Polity Series Data sets, developed during the 1970s through the present and provide non-national and longitudinal data based on the assumption that democracies share more commonalities than differences. At the core of this controversy is the role of "liberal democracy" as a universal norm, and thus the debate is couched by ideological assumptions disguised as theory. The liberal democracy debate is captured by the Francis Fukuyama's (1994) "end of history" thesis and Samuel Huntington's (1993) "clash of civilization" thesis in *Foreign Affairs*. Fukuyama's thesis regarding the spread of liberal democratic ideas and institutions throughout the world is juxtaposed against Huntington's thesis about inevitable cultural conflicts. Together they present very different historical observations and projections of global futures. The former points to the Westernization of political systems in general, including Asia, and the latter points to different developmental patterns for specific regions of the world. This research criticizes the universalist trajectory of political development while pointing out variations in democracies based on cultural context and economic development.

In this chapter, the cultural foundations of politics are examined in general and as they pertain to East Asia. As Huntington (1996) stated, we should not expect liberal democracies to emerge from regions in which liberal philosophy is alien. This raises the question about the extent to which some cultures are conducive to the development of democracy. While culture itself affects democratic consolidation to some extent, it is economic modernization and the way culture is used in that process which can tell us about the shape of evolving political development patterns. It will become clear, in the next two chapters, how economy, culture, and politics are not clearly demarcated domains, but rather they are intricately linked and reflected differently in each country. East Asia is a laboratory or valuable testing ground for the proposition that a convergence of forms between Western and non-Western political systems is taking place.

The primary concern of this chapter is with creating the necessary foundation for understanding the dynamics of state formation and maintenance, which in turn informs us about the consolidation processes in the region. More specifically, exploring cultural theories of the state accomplishes the following: (1) it clarifies the proper use of culture as an explanatory variable for economic growth and political development; (2) it better defines the culture-economy nexus which is at the foundation of Asian politics; and (3) it helps us look at the role of culture in state construction as a process of integrating and balancing traditionalism and modernity. To accomplish these goals, a review of some relevant studies on culture by anthropologists, sociologists, and political scientists is undertaken. The underlying purpose is to give identitiy to these societies' consolidation processes within the cultural, historical, and economic context. Then, the focus shifts to how culture is used to construct a structure of power, both in terms of institutions and political actors. In the second half of this chapter, these theories are applied to East Asia by focusing primarily on Confucianism and traditionalism and some tentative distinctions about "modernization" and "Westernization" are drawn. The last section of this chapter examines how these cultural propensities affect politics and how they lead to "modernization without Westernization."

CULTURAL THEORY IN SOCIAL AND POLITICAL SCIENCE

A wide range of social scientists, including anthropologists, political scientists, and sociologists, concern themselves with culture. Yet, there is no consensus among social scientists, let alone political scientists, about the precise explanatory power of culture. In the 1970s and 1980s culture-based social science research receded from its heyday in the 1950s and 1960s as political studies took on the characteristic of economics.[2] This undoubtedly was partly based on the consummation of the quantitative revolution in many of the social sciences, including political science. Statistical analysis played an integral part in that revolution and the disadvantage of studies in political culture, beyond the survey approach, it is not amenable to quantification (Aronoff 1983).

Further increasing the marginality of political culture analysis was the ascent of rational choice, since it is based on utilitarian, universalistic, and individualistic assumptions. The criticism directed toward rational choice also applies to the social scientist's greater problem of preoccupation with theoretical generalization which negatively affected the ability to accurately explain political development in culturally specific cases. Political culture, because of its highly specific spatial and temporal characteristics, received less and less attention as the discipline sought to work in the realm of generalizable theories. As Pye (1985: 18) states, "In trying to fit into a single picture all that was known about people experiencing profound social change, political scientists achieved a peculiar kind of abstract 'thick description,' one which delineated categories but was not so culturally or situationally specific as to explain the actual state of the political realm in particular cases."

Unlike rational choice, cultural theory can account for altruistic, particularistic, and group-oriented behavior more readily in part because the assumptions and approaches comprising the two are mainly inconsistent with each other. Rational choice aims to predict while cultural theory seeks to explain. The former also proceeds further by displacing culture as an explanatory variable because it lacks the characteristic of precision. However, looking at the development of Asian democracies over the past ten years, it is clearly evident that nation and regionally specific cultural factors affect the preferences and practices of citizens (Johnson 1995; Johnson and Keehn 1995). As Aaron Wildavsky (1987: 4) argues, social preferences vary across countries and are products of endogenous experiences which are cultural. So many political questions, it appears, cannot be adequately studied without a cultural framework.

Interesting and significant questions require the social scientist to consider the power of culture and its pervasive effect on social phenomena. One recent controversy places culture at the center of discourse as evidenced by the "Asian values" controversy (Mahbubani 1995; Bell 1995a, 1995b; Jones 1994; Kim 1994). For example, Samuel Huntington's "clash of civilizations," partially in response to Francis Fukuyama's "end of history" argument, strongly argued that different cultural forces in global politics, which are endogenous in origin, could lead nations to conflict. Fundamental differences in values—including what democracy means and its various ideological constructions—are part of this "clash." In that sense, culture is at the core of the democracy debate; preferences for the form of democracy vary according to the desires of a country's citizenry and elite, which in turn are shaped by the collective past and future expectations, that is, by a set of shared norms and traits commonly called culture.

Another challenge comes from non-quantitative empiricists (e.g., Chalmers Johnson, Larry Diamond, and Edward Friedman) and political essayists or practitioners (i.e., Fareed Zakaria and Kim Dae Jung) who state that culture as an explanatory variable failed to transcend description and take on an explanatory orientation without attempting to explain all or nothing. In the philosophy of logic, many would say that culture is a tautology. Chalmers Johnson (1995: 39–42), for example, argues that Confucianism in East Asia cannot be an explanatory variable for recent regional economic growth. Referring specifically to China, he argues that for many years, Confucianism was used to explain the lack of economic development [a point also made by Marx], but now many culturalists argue that cultural values explain economic growth in China and the region. Obviously, the source of economic growth is not culture, but something extraneous to it.

The tautology problem is also evident in the culture-democratization debate. Friedman (1994) sees culture inhibiting democracy, yet many Asian nations have now become democratic. Zakaria (1994), in his interview with Singapore's Lee Kuan Yew, points out these observations. But he ventures even further by implying: "Is culture merely a tool to justify authoritarianism?" (Zakaria 1994: 25–26). Is Friedman (1994) correct when he says that he foresees the democratization of mainland China because he does not focus on authoritarian culture as an explanation for China's future? What can culture really explain?

This apparent paradox—one in which culture explains all or nothing—derived through the quest for clearly demarcated casual explanations. Culture is not the magic potion; it is an important variable that is often subtle. Instead, culture is like a tool box. To a researcher it is analogous to a framework for analysis. For political elites in everyday life, it affords them choices for constructing a society by emphasizing particular cultural values over others and by de-emphasizing those deemed less desirable.

Political culture works in conjunction with the action of political elites and other contextual factors. In this seminal work, Edelman (1964) explored how rituals and symbols were used by elites to solicit support according to a specific environmental context. Culture, therefore, operates within a specific spatial and temporal arena with distinct actors and institutional structures. As Elkins and Simeon (1979: 140) state, culture is "seldom direct and seldom operates alone" and "culture complements" other variables rather than "competes" against them. Furthermore, Robert Scalapino (1989: 12), for example, favors a multifaceted approach to understanding Asia. He states, "Thus, in dealing with the evolution of modern Asia, one must determine the precise mix of culture, scale, timing, leadership, and policies that shapes the contours of a given society."

The culturalist construction suggests that a complex and simultaneous relationship between politics, economy, society, and culture exists. Culture is both an endogenous and exogenous situational variable that is both direct and indirect. In some ways, it is a foundational variable upon which the social spheres of economy, politics, and society are constructed through the actions and interaction involving the elite and the masses. It is analogous to a complex web, a coherent system greater than the sum of its parts.

Exogenous cultural variables include the penetration of Western values into local cultures as evidenced through the process of globalization. Other exogenous forces that affect the cultural construction of society

Figure 2.1
Endogenous and Exogenous Functions in a Social System

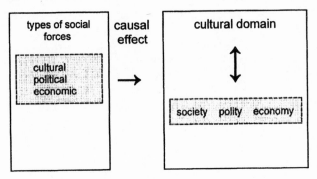

include Western norms of governance (i.e., democratic accountability, institutionalization of rules and procedures, and a system of checks and balances) and Western market-based imperatives (operation of market forces, privatization, and openness of the economy). These exogenous pressures take the form of imperialism in the pre–World War II period and globalization in the post–World War II period. This complex relationship which illustrates how culture can be accommodated in research is depicted in Figure 2.1.

There is also another dimension that is not readily captured, but deserves attention. Time is not visibly apparent in Figure 2.1 but is nonetheless important if the model is to be dynamic. While time in itself does not change that which is exogenous or endogenous to a system, changes in the international and domestic spheres are constantly taking place as symbols and behavior are recreated, reenacted, and adapted to a modern world. Of course the definitions of modernity and traditionalism change with the passage of time. For example, traditional Japan or South Korea in 1930 is different from that in 1830. So culture takes place in a specific time and place. This conceptualization is useful for understanding and shedding light on the problems of culture as a foundation for political studies. The vexing problem of culture consists of its dynamic nature, that is, it cannot be frozen in time or place. Instead it is a relational concept in terms of place and time. Given the amorphous and dynamic nature of culture, how can it be useful in explaining social phenomena such as democratization of economic development?

One solution for the "all or nothing" paradox of cultural explanations for economic development is to think of Confucianism as both sources of economic growth and economic stagnation. However, culture is a catalyst for growth or stagnation only when particular tools are used. Leaders can use cultural elements to mobilize the population for modernization, as in Mao's Great Leap Forward and Park Chung Hee's Industrial Saemaul Movement, or Ikeda Hayato's "Double Your Income" slogan.

Culture affects democratization similarly depending on the particular characteristics that elites emphasize. In terms of the democratization process, combining culture with other variables can explain why Confucianism is originally a source of authoritarianism and later a source for democratic consolidation. In an Edelmanian sense, elites use specific rituals and symbols to create economic growth and to shape the contours of democracy. Based on the "culture as toolbox" analogy, the context and purposes for which the specific rituals and symbols are evoked can make a difference in whether culture promotes democracy, authoritarianism, or economic growth. Thus, for example, the Confucian symbol of community can be used to buttress authoritarian systems or it can be used to create a democratic community. Similarly, the notions of purity in Confucianism can be evoked to divorce the political elite from commerce or to promote order and discipline afforded by traditional and Confucian thought necessary for economic growth in late-capitalism. In late-capitalism, the global rules for becoming industrialized are already determined by a globally hierarchical economic structure which favors dependency outcomes for most nations. However, through the skillful construction of political-economic systems, Asian elites succeeded in promoting growth through the use of culture. Therefore, culture possesses a plastic characteristic which makes it malleable to modern capitalism.

The argument above introduces culture as an alternative approach for understanding social processes, but it is a simplistic and sketchy argument. In order to gain a better understanding of culture, some definitional and conceptual issues need examination. Only then can cultural analysis be applied to Asian societies in a more meaningful and structured manner.

THE REALMS OF CULTURE

Cultural theories can help in the inductive construction of political models that best describe and explain political and economic development in Asia. To do this, however, the initial step is to define culture and determine how it is conceptualized. According to Samuel Barnes (1994: 46), there are three levels of culture:

1. the realm of the observable (artifacts, symbols, and actions)
2. beliefs and values (which can be tapped by surveys)
3. shared assumptions and meanings (which are more elusive)

The first level of culture is mostly seen in archaeology, which frequently involves the uncovering of earthly remains to reconstruct society. Another approach to the first level of culture is field observation. Symbols and actions focus on individuals or group behavior for the purpose of description rather than theory building. Archaeology and historic preservation represent two applications of the first level of culture.

The second level of culture concerns itself with beliefs and values which are not as readily discernable and must be studied through interviews, surveys, and focus groups. It is amenable to quantification and much of the empirical work in political science work on culture fits into this level. The best-known examples are Ronald Inglehart (1977, 1990) and Scott Flanagan's (1987) works on postmaterialism and Gabriel Almond and Sidney Verba's (1963) survey of attitudes in five countries. This level of cultural analysis does not look at culture as a building block of society, but rather as a product or byproduct of social processes.

The third level of cultural analysis, one of primary interest to this research, is at the level of shared assumptions and meanings, and it places culture at the center of research for descriptive purposes. Only after detailed description can useful theory be generated. With regard to political development, culture needs to be linked to the contestation of power. Examples of this approach include Brint (1994), Mazrui (1990), Pye (1985), and Geertz (1973). From these works, two definitions of culture can be extracted and used to clarify its meaning. According to Clifford Geertz in *The Interpretation of Culture* (1973: 250), culture is "symbol systems, man-created, shared, conventional, ordered, and indeed learned, that provides human beings with a meaningful framework for orienting themselves to one another, to the world around them, and to themselves." A similar definition, but one that is oriented to politics is provided by Brint (1994: 3). He defines political culture as "mental pictures that are relevant to the holding and contestation of power in society."

Political culture as used in this research draws on both Geertz's general definition of culture and the element of power in Brint's definition. Culture in general means the environment of shared values and understandings that is created and modified to provide the parameters for social construction. Applied to politics, political culture refers to the environment of shared values and understandings, that is created and modified over time so that meaningful political life can be constructed endogenously by elites and so that the meaning of political action is culturally coherent, ordered, and consistent. This makes it possible to link culture to political and economic construction of society by focusing on elite behavior. In the process of doing so, observations and projects about democratic consolidation in specific cultural contexts, both nationally and regionally, also become linked to a cultural context. Analysis of democratization in this manner preserves the continuity of historical analysis and the contextual framework of cultural analysis.

The sense of nation or community as an organic whole cannot be separated from political development in Asia. Because of colonialism and globalization, nationalism creates a context which contributes to or deflects from political change and continuity based on how a society reacts to external forces. In the Asian countries, nationalism allows elites to consolidate power by bridging a gap between traditional and modern societies, thereby allowing modernization. Society, according to both Cohen and Anderson, is a cultural construct resulting from years of elite and mass activities, meticulously inscribing rules and norms and carefully selecting symbols to buttress them. Anderson (1983: 7) states, "the nation is always conceived as a deep, horizontal comradeship." In any specific geographical region or country, such as Asia or Japan, conceptual terms like legitimacy, democracy, and political power take on cultural meanings which can be observed empirically in institutions such as political parties, bureaucracies, corporations, and the military.

Institutions function not merely by formal rules and constitutionally circumscribed powers, but also by implicit norms and understandings manifested through the values and traditions invoked repeatedly for the purpose of integrating society into a whole that is greater than the sum of its parts, or an organic society. As Edelman (1964: 96) states, political settings are contrived to elicit specific responses and suggest certain "connotations, emotions, and of authority." Cultural analysis, in a constructionist mode, provides the researcher with a useful tool for studying the evolution of power and the practice of leadership, and it is a useful tool for understanding power in social context, over time, and in a variety of countries.

The "culture as social construction" approach, when specifically focused at the regional or national level, can help in creating some useful generalizations and explanations about the democratization process. The meaning of power, which in any given society is culturally derived, has both spatial and temporal characteristics. For example, we can speak of "power" in the context of 19th-century Japan or in contemporary United States, each with its own set of symbols, assumptions, and shared arena for acting out culture.

The cultural context of power consists of a historical context complemented with a spatial environment. In other words, it is one of both the place and the time. The malleable plasticity of cultures suggests the possibility that different forms of political, economic, and social systems would emerge. Over time and space, the greater the common cultural characteristics that two or more societies share, the more it would be expected that the political, social, and economic spheres of society among them would share common development patterns. At the same time, a shared experience with international forces (e.g., colonization pressures or globalization) also works to bring about some similar characteristics among countries.

What does this mean for the Asian cases examined? If one were to apply the ideas of cultural analysis to the democratization process currently unfolding in Asia, there is reason to expect that economic modernization, political democracy, and social changes are not unidimensionally "Western" in form and function, but that institutions in Asia will be a product of the Asian experience, culture, and outside pressure. Kishore Mahbubani (1992) notes that those Asian societies, in general, will maintain Asian characteristics, but would also adopt some Western features, in what he calls "fusion." The existence of traditionalism alongside modernity in East Asia attests to this hybridization. Another scholar, Michael Rozman (1991a: 38), argues that while these differences between the West and Asia are declining, the core differences will persist.

For example, the paradox of modern institution juxtaposed with traditional political behavior reflects the reality of past and present political development. To this day traditional patron-client relations still play a dominant role in Thai politics despite the existence of political parties, which are both modern and Western. Another example is the initial adoption and later adaptation of the British Parliamentary system in Kenya and Zimbabwe, very Western and modern in the sense that these are institutions developed along contemporary notions of British democracy, but the traditional kind of leadership exercised by Daniel arap Moi and Robert Mugabe belies different objective circumstances of a traditional society in contrast to the "mother" country. In addition, governance in these traditional cultures reflects a non-liberal and non-Western orientation. Therefore, Western institutions representing liberal democracy, when adapted to the indigenous conditions of developing nations, manifest many traditional characteristics because of the cultural construction of power as exercised by elites. Clearly the essence of a political system as defined by local culture should not be reduced to the general form of "parliamentary democracy."

On one hand, there are exogenous influences as shown in Figure 2.1, but, at the same time, political elites must construct political, economic, and social spheres that are indigenous or at least culturally acceptable to the specific time and place of the social system. Otherwise, legitimacy of these systems would prove elusive lacking a core. Cohen (1985: 44) states that, "Indeed, the greater the pressure on communities to modify their structural forms to comply more with those elsewhere, the more are they inclined to reassert their boundaries symbolically by imbuing these modified forms with meaning and significance which belies their appearance." Perhaps this explains why nationalism in the PRC today and in prewar Japan became an important modern-traditional foundation for constructing a political order.

A somewhat different conclusion about the relationship between exogenous values and endogenous values in shaping the form of the three spheres was made by Chakarin Komolsiri (1995). Based on field research in Bangkok, Thailand, he concluded that many elites subscribed to the "fusion" option in which the core values of the society would not entirely vanish, but would coexist with imported "Western values." But even in this research, Komolsiri found that traditional values do not vanish from among most members of the elite; instead they are adapted for a modern era. Political institutions as products of cultural construction are modern, traditional and Asian, and not unidimensionally Western and modern. These points are explored in the three case studies in Chapters 5 through 7.

CULTURAL FOUNDATIONS OF ASIA

The cultural foundations of Asian politics derive from traditionalism, Confucianism, and Buddhism. In Asia, Confucianism and Buddhism (in the case of Thailand and to some extent Japan), fit well with the traditional kinship-based political systems revolving around agricultural economic systems and in closed social systems which promoted order through hierarchy. In modern Asia, leaders draw on both tradition and modernity for legitimation. In a Weberian sense, the precise mix of traditional, legal-rational, and charismatic sources of authority varies from one country to another. Furthermore, the specific content of each source of legitimacy varies according to historical context, leadership style, and the level of political development. The specifics of cultural theory help explain this logic.

Cultural theory, in terms of defining its role in political and economic development, has been the focus of this chapter. In particular, the argument was made that cultural analysis is useful for understanding the meaning behind symbols, rules, and norms that underlie the use of power within a specific space and time. In Chapters 3 and 4, the focus shifts to an institutional one, to a look at economic bureaucracies and political parties. However, before developing that focus, a careful explication of Asian cultural foundations will lay the foundation for exploring the specifics of Asian political development.

There are two levels of cultural analysis that are germane to this project. The first is at the national level and the second is at the regional level. The national level of analysis operates in the context of a cultural boundary formed within a specific geographical boundary. More precisely, the process of nation-building requires that some peculiar cultural characteristics are emphasized over others. For example, in Singapore, the concept of the guardian class, is grounded in Confucianism because of the weight that philosophy has in Singaporean tradition. However, in Japan, Confucianism is not the underlying philosophy for the guardian class to the extent it is in Singapore because Japan's tie to the Sinic culture as reflected in Confucianism is weaker. The legitimacy of the Japanese bureaucracy in relation to citizens at large is derived from a more traditional basis of deference to authority in addition to their proven performance. Therefore, certain cultural values are emphasized because they are readily present in a political system.

In both the Japan and Singapore cases, deference to authority is central to the cultural construction of politics (Pye 1985), but the former draws its inspiration from traditional Japanese society, while in Singapore, authority is also tradition-originating but influenced more by Confucianism.[3] In both cases, however, culture is central in explaining the legitimacy of the bureaucratic apparatuses, which have been the dominant actor in the developmental states' persistence. However, despite the general similarities of East Asian culture, there are particularistic differences.

While differences are important, so too are the similarities. Despite differences in the specific cultural attributes that affect politics, there are similarities in the developmental processes of East Asian nations which assist in applying the most similar systems design model. In particular, the relative strength of bureaucracies, in contradistinction to the weakness of political parties, coupled with the economically driven nature of political development is a universal East Asian phenomenon. Even culturally, East Asian nations only recently became modernized and, therefore, traditional values remain largely intact because modernization was indigenized and superimposed over traditional value systems. Traditional societies commonly share a communitarian outlook on life—much of which is still evidenced in the shape of capitalism, economics, and social relations throughout the Asian Pacific.[4]

The task of describing and understanding the democratization process is twofold in that we are concerned about how individual countries are similar or dissimilar from each other and whether some general observations applicable to East Asia can be drawn. The question which calls for an answer is, "To what extent is there a general model of Asian political development and what accounts for the differences among specific countries?"

TRADITIONALISM AND CONFUCIANISM AS ASIAN POLITICAL CULTURE

Traditionalism and Confucianism form the foundation for political culture in Asian nations, especially pertaining to public notions of legitimacy and norms about power. The implications for leadership are vast and the literature on legitimacy does an excellent job in detailing the relationship between culture and authority. For example, Max Weber (trans. 1947) in *The Theory of Social and Economic Organization* stated that there were three sources of political authority: the legal-rational, traditional, and charismatic. Because modern ideas concerning rationalized economic and political organization are incompatible with traditional and non-Western values, the particular mix of authority in Asia still relies necessarily on tradition and charisma (e.g., client-patron ties) to shape the legal-rational source of authority. In other words, the sociocultural imperatives of traditional society are crucial for the structuring of modern legal-rational institutions. As Dankwart A. Rustow (1967: 157) argued, political legitimacy is based on a combination of traditional, rational-legal, and charismatic authority. In developing societies, that mix relies more on traditional sources of authority than in industrialized nations such as the United States.

The precise mix of cultural components of authority varies across countries as determined by elites' perception for self-survival and nation-building success. Different traditional symbols and practices facilitate each transitional society's survival in a modern Western-based, contemporary international system. The elites' selective use of cultural symbols makes it possible to exercise their leadership in such a way that the three spheres of society, the economy, politics, and social, are coherently integrated (Shils 1972: 36–40). Value integration, a component of culture, is essential for social order (Weiner 1967: 158–59); Confucianism and traditionalism are integral parts of a society's value system in East Asia.

The integration of economic, political, and social aspects of a society occurs in a specific contest found by location and time as described by Anthony Giddens (1984: 169–79). As modernization takes place in Asian nations, the particular mix of sources of authority must change to adapt to new constraints imposed by socioeconomic realities (both exogenous and endogenous). Thus the move toward political liberalization and democratization is caused by external and internal changes which prompt leadership to alter the precise mix of authority sources. More concretely, the ability of specific Asian elites to use effectively the three sources of authority varies in two fundamental aspects.

First, socioeconomic change over time would create different constraints and facilitators of elite action. So, the ability of the military to manage and direct, for example, Thailand's political development is fixed by specific sociocultural requirements. In today's Thailand the military cannot be effective leaders because the entire dynamic of society has changed. Not only will citizens refuse to condone a military coup, but the socioeconomic processes of Thailand today could not be effectively or efficiently managed by the limited expertise of the military. The

Thai military elite of the 1990s lacks the legitimating capacity once possessed years ago. Traditionally, the militaries in Thailand, South Korea, and the Philippines are primarily economic and social mobility institutions which were integrated into more modern political institutions, such as political parties and the bureaucracy. Now, however, the militaries are increasingly blockaded into their barracks.

Secondly, different kinds of elites can use a particular mix of authority to offset changing constraints imposed by new realities. Alternately, elites, to some extent, can take advantage of the emergent new and favorable environmental factors. The successes of particular elites at managing these two conditions substantially lengthen their longevity as the dominant or major players in politics. For example, in Thailand, the senior military officials have successfully integrated themselves into the new political order by seeking elected office and by forming new political parties as a ladder to national power. At the political level, the collective elites' ability to successfully take advantage of changing constraints and resources determines the extent to which a "crisis in political development," as mentioned by Pye (1966a: 62–67), is averted.

In East Asia, culture's role in shaping constraints and resources provides a common basis for synchronizing the developmental form and process of political, economic, and social spheres. The use and shape of authority are also conditioned and shaped by culture. For example, the military's dominant role in prewar Japan was legitimized by military professionalism and nurtured by a spirit which originated from *Bushido* (warrior ethic). The latter, in turn, drew heavily from Zen Buddhism and Shinto. Shinto and Zen Buddhism were earlier influenced by Confucianism. Another example was the adoption of the rotating paramount ruler system evidenced in contemporary Malaysia. The paramount leader, *Yang di-Pertuan Agong*, is chosen from among nine hereditary rulers of the Malay states. Not only was it a traditional instrument of governance, it was also adapted for the modern world by circumscribing the ruler's power and confining him to a ceremonial role. In this example, traditional culture in a modernizing society provided the constraints and rationale for establishing such a system. Traditionalism makes modern ideas of democracy in Asia possible. In East Asia, traditionalism and Confucianism provide the constraints and resources (cultural capital) for democratic transition and consolidation.

Confucian Social Construction

What is Confucianism? Confucius (Kong Fu Zi), an ancient Chinese philosopher, wrote on social and political philosophy, which later demonstrated significant implications and applications for governance in China, Korea, Japan, Taiwan, Singapore, and Vietnam. Confucianism is a social and political philosophy about how societies ought to be governed, much like Plato's *The Republic*. The absence of industrialization and the notion of progress, associated with social change, made Confucianism a useful tool for organizing closed agricultural societies because it was a code of ethics developed within a traditional context. Later, the advent of regional integration, in the form of trade, enhanced Confucianism's spread throughout the region (McCloud 1995: 32–33). Ultimately, however, trade during that time centered around specific ports and cities and even then involved a small group of merchants. In sum, these societies remained relatively closed compared to the developmental states of today.

Confucianism today exists in particular areas of East Asia, which broadly construed, represents a Sinic (Chinese influenced) Cultural Region founded through the influence of Confucianism intervening in each locale's traditional politics when Korea, Vietnam, and Cambodia were subject to Chinese political control. Historically, Confucian ideas and the Buddhist religion (Mahayana) spread throughout Northeast Asia (i.e., China, Korea, and Japan), as these kingdoms adopted Confucian-based models of government, excepting Japan. For Japan, Confucian philosophy was imported but adapted to indigenous governing systems to conform with the existing feudal system. As Kumagai (1995: 137) denotes, Confucianism intermixed with Buddhism, Shinto, and Christianity to become the impetus for Japan's modernization. The significance of this, as discussed later, is that the disdain for commerce characterized by traditional Confucianism was not manifested in Japan during the late Tokugawa and Meiji era. Meanwhile, in Southeast Asia, Confucianism did not serve as a significant impediment for commerce as the Chinese diaspora led to the establishment of Chinese business networks, which have presently come to play a major role in the economic development of that region (Hui 1995). In continental Southeast Asia, Buddhism is the predominant religion in many countries, but the form was Theravada Buddhism.[5] Confucianism, through the Chinese diaspora throughout the years leading up to 1500, became diffused into Southeast Asian society in Thailand and Malaysia, and subsumed into indigenous traditionalism. Nevertheless, in Taiwan, Vietnam, and Singapore, Confucian thought demonstrated much greater effect on social construction because of their long-term direct ethnic ties with China. The anomaly is the Philippines, located far off the Chinese coast, and colonized first by the Spanish and then the Americans from 1902 to 1948, except for the Japanese occupation during World War II. Indonesia, being primarily Muslim in population, also is an exception. Nonetheless, even in these countries, the diaspora proved economically beneficial as a burgeoning Chinese merchant class became the business incubators for these countries.

The diffusion of Confucianism is significant, but also is its flexibility in adapting to indigenous traditionalism precisely because it is primarily a moral philosophy rather than a religion. This makes Confucianism adaptable to existing indigenous religions and traditional values without directly confronting them. The central political tenet of Confucianism is its reliance upon the sage emperor and a guardian class for the moral foundation of governance. It places importance on loyalty to the family, trust among friends, and acceptance of hierarchy and obedience (Robinson 1991: 223). These Confucian-based value systems became integrated into the norms and values of leaders and masses over time to form the traditional and charismatic sources of authority. The primary purpose of the state in Confucian thought is the proper development and maintenance of the community. Legal-rational forms of authority in traditional China reflected communitarian values, and even today these community-oriented values are visible in Asian patterns of authority. Elites culturally construct Asian authority to fit a traditional notion of a *Gemeinschaften*, in which individuals are part of an organic whole, analogous to that expressed by Ferdinand Tonnies (1887) in *Gemeinschaft und Gesellschaft*. Over time, however, they have adapted or reconstructed them to fit the modern world. From the perspective of the elites, this cultural continuity is essential; it provides a link to traditional and sometimes charismatic sources of authority while simultaneously allowing accommodation and resistance to outside pressures as modernization takes place.

The community as a symbol, for example, is a common theme expressed in East Asian politics and economy. Both reflect traditional communitarian and Confucian values through the politics of nationalism in South Korea, Japan, and Singapore. Community as a political symbol allows the Singaporean elite to maintain strong control over dissent and allows the Chinese communist elite to replace the waning potency of Leninist-Maoist ideology with Confucian notions. In the economic sphere, the most recent example is the family-style chaebols in South Korea, in which employees make major sacrifices for the corporate community in the name of "community good." In Japan, the symbol of "community" provides the source for political quiescence and clientelistic linkages between citizens and the local LDP and the national LDP to preserve the "communtity."

Examples above can provide some insight about the role of Confucianism in society, but there is no consensus about Confucianism's degree of influence in East Asian political, social, and economic organization today. However, many scholars consider its influence significant. For example, Simone and Feraru (1995: 2) describe it as a "powerful secular ethical tradition" while Park and Cho (1995: 119) state that Confucianism can be equated to a "code of latent ethics and values." Furthermore, Zeigler (1988: 29) states: "Ordinary people in Asian societies are no more likely to read Confucius than ordinary people in the United States are to read Adam Smith." Yet, just as many Americans trace capitalism, at least superficially, to Adam Smith's *Wealth of Nations*, many culturalists point to the Confucian sources of the present-day constitution of East Asian societies.[6] Through years of cultural reproduction through mass and elite interactions (i.e., recreation, re-enactment, mutation), many of these values have diffused themselves into the economic, political, and social realms of society and therefore provide the foundation for political development.

Confucianism is not a religion but a philosophy setting the parameters of social structures and relations, including a society's economic life. Many researchers have pointed to the role that Confucianism played in the rapid economic rise of East Asia (Wong 1988; Hofheinz and Calder 1982; Tai 1989). However, Confucianism and traditionalism are often intricately linked in these explanations. For example, Hofheinz and Calder (1982: 43) point to the common agricultural tradition combined with strong Confucian-based centralized government as a defining feature of Asian political and economic systems. These political systems, they argue, propelled the economic miracle of the region. By viewing economic and political aspects of society as cultural constructs as actions orchestrated by elites, it becomes possible to explain economic and political development from a cultural context.

Confucianism Complements Traditionalism in Asian Politics

Asian societies today experience dramatic socioeconomic change through the modern processes of industrialization and technological transformation. Traditionalism affects Asian politics today because deeply seated traditional social values are replicated continuously by people's actions. Confucianism, in modern day Asia, has become a part of traditional Asia as people relied on both to guide social behavior. However, for countries such as Thailand or Malaysia, Confucianism did not become a part of their tradition. In Thailand, Buddhism has modified traditionalism, while in Malaysia, Islam as a cultural force modified traditionalism. Asian traditionalism contrasts with Western traditionalism as to differences of essence. The former draws from Eastern philosophy while the latter draws from a liberal tradition. Additionally, traditionalism in Asia affects modern day politics more than in the West because modern society as it exists today is a Western creation. In a recently modernized or modernizing Asian nation, traditionalism buffers the discontinuities in society caused by the onslaught of modernization.

Claude Welch (1967: 20) stated that, "In a sense, tradition mediates between the forces of change and the acceptance of change." Tradition,

just like modernity, is part of today's Asian culture. According to Eric
Hobsbawn and Terence Ranger (1983: 1), "Invented tradition is taken to
mean a set of practices, normally governed by overtly or tacitly accepted
rules and of a ritual or symbolic nature, which seek to inculcate certain
values and norms of behavior by repetition, which automatically implies
continuity with the past." Based on Hobsbawn's definition, traditionalism means the systematic adherence to accumulated ideas, values, symbols, and rituals which have formed the foundation for social, economic,
and political construction of society over time. People's actions manifest
traditionalism as they draw on ideas, values, symbols, and rituals representing elements of the past. In Asian societies today, we see this in
notions of group loyalty, deference to authority, and patron-client relations.

Three principal characteristics define traditional Asian societies. They
are: (1) deference to authority; (2) patron-client relations; and (3) group
orientation (Pye 1985). Dissecting clearly the extent to which these cultural characteristics originate from tradition or Confucianism is difficult.
In most East Asian societies the two share a communitarian outlook.
Furthermore, Confucianism was originally based on Chinese traditions
and, once created, it became a part of Chinese culture and spread eventually throughout the Sinic region by mixing with local culture. The existence of traditionalism based on the Eastern philosophies of Buddhism
and Confucianism, in all countries except Malaysia, suggests high levels
of regional cultural comparability based on the notion of a traditional
society.

The communitarian approach to politics is a central commonality that
both traditionalism and Confucianism share. According to Tamney (1991:
401) and Hsu (1975: 87), Confucian political philosophy defines political
roles and functions according to a familial model. Role specialization and
hierarchy within the family are applied to politics. In the traditional mul-
tigenerational family model, the patriarch's decision-making role derives
from his seniority in age. Meanwhile, other members of the family have
precise roles to perform within a hierarchically structured family system.
The whole system, when applied to political and economic organization,
mirrors the basic family organization. In the political and economic
realm, just as in social relations and familial systems, age equates to
experience and wisdom. (Even today, the role of the gerontocracy
throughout Asian politics is legendary.) Overall, the communitarian approach to social organization promotes social harmony by emphasizing
deference to authority, hierarchical patron-client relationships, and
group orientation. Both Confucianism and traditionalism share these
three at a basic level.

Deference to Authority

The Confucian theory of stewardship best describes the relationship between state and society in East Asia (Hsu 1975: 174). The *junzi*, or the Confucian guardian class, is supposed to serve the people and community while the citizens are to respect their government and leaders. Government is responsible for making the best decisions in the interests of the community. Taken to a higher level, the implication is that the government's expertise is preferred to the ignorance of the masses. Bureaucrats acquire this expertise through years of study and experience. Therefore, the common person should not readily dispute the government's expertise. This model, originating in China, eventually was adapted to modern Korean, Japanese, and Singaporean political systems.

When mores are broken at the familial level, punishment is swift and sometimes ostracism results. In modern Asian societies, political dissent becomes difficult because it disturbs social harmony and threatens the tradition of political hierarchy based on deference. Therefore, periodically Singaporean senior public officials and academics comment in mass media on the virtues of obedience and vices of excessive dissent. Their social education campaign seeks to buttress traditional values underlying governance. The Singaporean government appeals to Confucian ideas, while in Malaysia, where Confucian influence is virtually nonexistent, Prime Minister Mahathir appeals to tradition and Islam. In both cases, tradition's purpose is to defend "soft authoritarian" social engineering experiments by reminding challengers that the nature of "power flows from the moral superior" (Pye 1985: 86–87).

The notion of the guardian class is also found in many traditional societies including Asian ones. In traditional Asian societies, power flows from the moral superior at the top of the political hierarchy and empowers many Asian bureaucrats. This source of authority is based on Confucian ideas in Singapore, Taiwan, Korea, and to a lesser extent Japan. In Thailand and Malaysia it is based on religious traditions, Buddhism and Islam respectively (McCloud 1995; Pye 1985). Civil servants are selected by a merit-based criterion (i.e., exams and educational background), which is a key component of Confucianism. As such, they are impartial, in theory, and removed from much of the patron-clientism of traditional politics. This impartiality is very much similar to Plato's guardians and gives them the legitimacy to govern.

Based on the traditional and Confucian value system, the contemptuous disposition of politicians becomes evident. Senior bureaucrats and military leaders could claim the moral superiority to govern based on Confucianism and traditionalism and display it through their general detachment from the trivialities of politics. Through the process, they shroud themselves in the Confucian notion of *junxi* or the traditional notion of impartial rulers who remain above partisan politics and patron-client networks. Politicians are objects of contempt because popularity and connections, instead of merit, led to them securing leadership positions. They rely on popularity to remain in power and politicians must personalize their action by using traditional networks and methods which undermines any perception of neutral competence. This leads to a problem between the formal institutional rules and the personalized nature of patron-client relations. In Asian societies this gap is a more serious problem because formal democratic procedures are not rooted in the cultural notions of governance or of power. As Pye (1985: 23) observes, in Asia, "the nearly universal theme" is that of "charges and countercharges of corruption."

The perceived incorrigibility of politicians in stark juxtaposition to the "cleaner" image of bureaucrats contributes to the lack of trust for electoral politics. Citizens often view politicians, in contrast to bureaucrats, with disdain because of their perceived lack of impartiality. Bureaucrats have a greater level of respectability. This respectability varies from country to country and from one time to another. In Asian countries that have experienced long-term economic growth, the respectability of bureaucrats in the postwar era is much higher than in those countries with slower growth. Recently, however, in response to economic problems and pressures for deregulation, bureaucrats in both Japan and South Korea receive increased criticism.[7]

Respect for bureaucrats can be traced to traditional values of deference to authority and to the Confucian notion of merit that provided the basis for bureaucratic selection. In particular, education, which is at the core of civil service selection, and professional examinations draw from the Confucian notions of a meritocracy. However, meritocratic selection also draws its legitimacy from modern and Weberian notions of government. A meritocracy in contemporary Asian societies is also deeply intertwined with Weber's ideas of a modern legal-rational bureaucracy. The success of bureaucrats in establishing and managing a developmental state contributes to their increased respect. Legal-rational approaches can, for example, be found in the recruitment patterns in the civil service. National universities such as Tokyo University and Kyoto University (Japan), National University of Singapore, Seoul National University (South Korea), and National Taiwan University (ROC) were established to train national bureaucrats. Chalmers Johnson (1982), for example, researched the dominance of Tokyo and Kyoto Universities' graduates in the Japanese guardian class–based economic ministries during the 1950s–1970s and demonstrated how an esprit de corps formed during their university years.

However, merit selection is not the only reason for high levels of bureaucratic legitimation. In East Asian countries with a strong and successful developmental state (that is, a state committed to growth and having a track record of rapid growth) the deference to bureaucrats is stronger than in those countries where the economic bureaucrats have less-accomplished track records. The success of the bureaucrats in promoting national economic growth, then translates into prestige and continued validation of their high social prestige and the meritocratic system as can be seen in Japan, Singapore, and South Korea, in contrast to Thailand and the Philippines, the latter reflecting examples of countries where the developmental state failed to deliver sustained economic growth over long periods of time.

The political implications of deference to authority are that it gives the military, the bureaucracy, and the business elites a greater moral advantage for authority than elected officials. Not only are elected officials partisan, compared with bureaucrats or military officials, but the sole selection criterion consists of popularity. Various factors account for the low levels of expertise by elected officials. Two of the most obvious are that political parties do not play a significant role in governance in modern East Asia and that the role of elected officials is not to make policy, but to provide legitimacy to policies originating from the military or bureaucratic and corporate elites. These factors complement traditional ones in marginalizing elected officials. As Donald G. McCloud (1995: 145) states, "Factors such as popular deference to authority, reinforced by the educational advantage of the bureaucratic elite, further enhanced the position of the bureaucracy in the political system."

Elected politicians historically have had greater difficulty legitimating themselves because of their lack of policy expertise and general lack of higher education (violating the Confucian educational merit criterion). This, however, is beginning to change as parties become more institutionalized.The issue of how political parties and their agents can transcend a poor image, their incongruity with traditional and Confucian culture, however, remains a persistent problem. This explains, in part, why bureaucrats become politicians in Japan or why military officers run for political office in South Korea or Thailand. Bureaucrats and military officers possess the necessary cultural capital to become politicians—to restore order and provide continiuity of succession in an otherwise chaotic party system.

Patron-Client Relations

Another salient characteristic of Asian politics is patron-client relationships. The patron-client relationship is defined as a mutually dependent hierarchical relationship in which the superior and inferior are bound together through mutual loyalty. At the societal level, patron-client relations are manifested in "the politics of entourages and cliques, of personal networks and associations, [which] are critical for the building of coherent national power structures" (Pye 1985: 27). Patron-client systems within political systems represent an informal and hierarchical form of traditional politics. Many scholars recognized the importance of patron-client relations in the political development of nations (Martz 1997; Hagopian 1996; Keyes et al. 1994; Thak 1979; Scott 1968). Patron-client relationships are relevant in political development because some scholars suggest that they typify a political system based on personalism (Pye 1985 and Riggs 1966). For example, patron-client relationships in Japan contribute to the highly personalized nature of politics, as factions within the LDP and the personalism between rural politicians and residents. These two factors work to weaken political parties as institutions (Curtis 1971). In Thailand, patron-client relations contribute to the high levels of rural vote buying, as orchestrated by the Thai Nation and New Aspiration parties. Each party consists of a coalition of highly personalistic party machines with regionalized networks of patron-client relations.

Patron-client relations undermine the legal-rational approach to political and economic organization and assist in maintaining specifically localized sociocultural imperatives by keeping them traditional and Confucian. While some suggest that patron-client relations are harmful, others view patron-client relations as ameliorative by making modern and Western economic and political models more adaptable to a transitional society.

Patron-client relationships assist in defining a role for elected officials by forming the basis for citizens to extract concessions from the bureaucracy. Local residents, by using their elected representatives as intermediaries, can obtain specific easements to general policy or solve disputes involving bureaucrats. The strength of local patron-client ties between politicians and members in the bureaucracy or with other senior politicians makes reelection more likely. The overriding concern of an average voter is, "To what extent can the candidate running enhance the condition of the village or town through his connections?" For example, the recent Prime Minister Banharn Silpa-archa of Thailand built extensive patron-client relations by providing residents of Suphan Buri with new schools, roads, bridges, and community centers. (Some joked that they should call the entire province Banharn-buri.)

In Japan, the web of patron-client relationships of former prime minister Tanaka Kakuei is also legendary for its strength and pervasiveness. Despite being jailed for bribery and fraud, Tanaka continued to maintain significant power in the LDP until his death in 1985. Again, his ability to bring back "bacon" to his rural district perpetuated his continued reelection. Incidentally, not surprisingly his daughter has now replaced the deceased Tanaka as an LDP member of the Diet.[8] In Asian politics, well-established family names have significant meaning because patron-client relations personalized politics.

While on the surface, patron-client relations and other traditional bases of politics appear antithetical to Confucian notions of a meritocracy, the two coexist in harmony. To illustrate, Japanese patron-client relationships play a significant role in the day-to-day bureaucratic operations with junior bureaucrats being clients of older senior bureaucrats. Yet, all bureaucrats in this example were hired originally through competitive national civil service entrance exams. Also, patron-client relations can support other Confucian precepts including the maintenance of a clearly defined social hierarchy and the notion of communitarian governance. Appearance of impropriety is mitigated if patron-client relationships produce some tangible or psychological benefit for the community as the Tanaka and Banharn examples demonstrate.

Furthermore, traditional patron-client relationships make Confucian notions of elitism and the paternalistic authoritarianism of patron-client relations coexistent. Patron-client relations complement Confucian notions of community and personalize politics but maintain the meritocracy of the bureaucracy. Because politicians take the blame for corruption, bureaucrats can maintain their isolated demeanor without suffering the public ire.

Given the pervasiveness of patron-client relations, cultural analysis becomes necessary for the study of East Asian democratization process. The existence of personal politics shifts the democratic consolidation process away from the formal rules and institutions and more toward the culturally based meanings about democracy, political parties, and power. The gap between the formal rules of democracy (e.g., institutional arrangements) and the realm of traditional politics must be reconciled, otherwise a legitimacy crisis results. Chapters 6 through 8 explore the relative success of reconciliation on a country by country basis.

Group Orientation

The last component of political culture worthy of attention is the group orientation of politics. In traditional Asian politics, groups or clans played important general governance and individual socialization roles, but political development studies failed to capitalize on this. As Pye (1985: 26) states, little of that knowledge is applied to political development in Asia. Sometimes, this group orientation may manifest itself as regionalism (e.g., South Korea), where each geographic group fights for its own privileges. Politics consists of competing "in" and "out" groups that fiercely vie for political power and the fruits of victory. However, in Japan, this group orientation provides the foundation for national harmony and is manipulated to elicit political quiescence.

Collectivism originates from both traditional political culture and Confucian ideas. Group orientation and a sense of belonging is an important part of societies which have localized social, economic, and political orientations. For years, traditional societies engaged in agricultural processes and required a collective approach to managing economic and social life. Political elites, upon embarking on economic modernization, found this collectivist orientation useful and perhaps even necessary for constructing nationalism and for mobilizing the masses for labor intensive production in factories. Collectivism lays the foundation for a culturally constructed economic system that is a characteristic of labor discipline, a sense of a comradery among workers, and stability in the political realm. Most important, however, is that the socialization process continues to reinvent collectivism for a modern era. Political leaders, when they evoke symbols based on collectivism, can legitimate themselves traditionally by appealing to the strong desire of citizens to belong to a larger *Gemeinschaft*. At the local level, such as factories and in villages and towns, group orientation promotes social harmony. At the national level, it helps legitimize political leaders who seek to establish an organic national essence. In the PRC's case, it led to nationalism constructed around Mao's "cult of personality."

As in most cultures, the Asian family fosters the transferal of cultural values from one generation to the next. Recent research into families in Asian countries, for example, shows significantly different kinds of socialization goals in contrast to the West. For example, Rohlen (1989) and Park and Cho (1995) found that education, formally at school and informally at home, would reflect the prevailing culture, to promote social harmony. Kumagai (1995) found that Japanese children, for example, learned early the importance of conformity to group norms rather than individual assertiveness, even at the individual's short-term detriment. It is not surprising then, that adult behavior emphasizing a hierarchical and collective corporate culture reflects early childhood socialization. Political institutions display these core values because cultural socialization determines significantly the behavior of individuals within institutional contexts.

MODERNIZATION WITHOUT WESTERNIZATION

Business leaders believe that cultural values affect a nation's orientation toward production and consumption. Cultural values also contribute to the matrix of societal goals and expectations about macroeconomic and microeconomic performance and Asian businessmen believe that they are integral to the "economic miracle" throughout Asia. For example, a recent poll of Asian executives found that 80.6 percent of them thought that Asians possessed a different set of values compared to the West. Two-thirds of the Western expatriate executives in that survey agreed. Also, 80.6 percent of the Asian executives polled said that these values, in some way, either substantially or significantly, contributed to economic development.[9] If cultural values produce marked effect on economic development, is it plausible that they influence political development?

This chapter reviewed the literature on culture and established a foundation for economic and political research through a broad approach to cultural theory in an Asian context. By drawing from a variety of disciplines including anthropology and sociology, it provided a cultural framework based on social construction of political and economic reality. In addition to cultural construction, the changing nature of Asian culture, as impacted by modernization and Westernization, illustrates the need for a dynamic political model that accounts for cultural and economic change. Cultural reinvention functions to update traditionalism for a modern era. Therefore, culture never stagnates because the meaning of "traditional" is collectively still referred to as "traditional."

This chapter also addressed the inadequacies of cultural analysis in political development literature. Frequently, culture is either an intervening or an independent variable. Instead, political scientists should view culture as a situational variable that is simultaneously intervening, independent, and dependent. The symbolic and interpretive traditions of cultural analysis embarked on such an approach, but they were overlooked in the political development literature. This chapter argues that cultural analysis of this type can provide explanatory value about the congruence between political, social, and economic development in modernity. The next two chapters explore a general cultural model and Chapters 6 through 8 apply that model to three countries.

In the empirical area, the primary discussion focused on traditionalism and Confucianism and how they affect political meanings in these respective countries. In particular, the focus was on three salient characteristics of East Asian traditional political culture: deference to authority, patron-client relations, and group orientation. Also, Confucianism and traditionalism, within the three primary cultural characteristics, represent complementary rather than exclusive influences. These salient characteristics provide a cultural lens for defining democracy, political parties, and power within a specific cultural environment. Particularly in Asia, cultural analysis proves useful because the saliency of traditional and charismatic sources of authority, rather than the legal-rational sources, dominates the political landscape. Even within the exercise of the legal-rational source of authority, significant elements associated with traditional and charismatic sources continue to show their effects.

At the conclusion of this chapter, one ponders the following questions: To what extent can we say Asian economies and polities are modernized? To what extent does culture affect political and economic organization in East Asia and does culture play a correspondingly similar role in each? Lastly, if culture affects economic organization and society's views on governance, how is that reflected in the democratization process? Then, is East Asia converging toward a Western liberal form of democracy or something significantly different?

This chapter raises more questions than it answers. For example, while both Singapore and New York, *prima facie*, appear modern and "Western" from an airplane, a lengthy exploration will reveal a complex milieu of differences that combine tradition and modernity. Sometimes, traditional ways coexist with modern ways, but other times the two merely synthesize to create something entirely new. Then on occasion, traditional ways are cast aside or, sometimes, modern ways are rejected. The meaning of "modern" in the eyes of many Asians is often synonymous with Western. Thus, the adoption of Japanese parliamentary government in 1890, for example, was seen as both "modern" and "Western." Edwin O. Reischauer (1983: 374), the late professor at Harvard and U.S. Ambassador to Japan, wrote the following to describe this cultural mosaic:

First, is Japan becoming essentially like the countries of the West or will she remain Eastern at heart? As I said, the answer cannot be a simple choice between the two but something more complex. Among the great shaping forces of Japan as she now exists are characteristics deriving from the past, some shared with the rest of East Asia but some uniquely Japanese. Among those are the strong work ethic, a pervasive esthetic sense, an intense feeling for decorum and orderly processes, and above all a strong orientation toward group identification and group activity, albeit with a matching sense of individual endeavor, achievement, willpower, and personal improvement. These are a few examples of strong survival from the past which, when manifested in modern institutions, make Japan different from the countries of the West and the rest of the world as well. They are hardly to be identified as Eastern traits in general, though some could be called East Asian. But basically they are Japanese. Japan is and will remain very Japanese.

While the quotation above pertains to Japan, social scientists can induce similar observations about other transitional societies. Therefore, Japan is not alone, but shares similar experiences with other rapidly industrializing nations.

NOTES

1. See E. Durkheim (1964) [1902], *The Division of Labor in Society* (New York: The Free Press). He notes that symbols and actions define community and provide members with affirmation.
2. The debate concerning area studies and quantitative cross-national research reflects an ongoing schism in political science. Recently in *PS: Political Science and*

Politics (1997) 30 (2), a symposium titled "Controversy in the Discipline: Area Studies and Comparative Politics," explored some of these issues. The decline of cultural studies is best articulated in "Perception vs. Observation, or The Contributions of Rational Choice Theory and Area Studies to Contemporary Political Science," by Johnson (1997: 170–74) in that symposium.

3. This is especially the case with Singapore. The nation of Singapore, as a cultural construct, is not a product of history, but rather a modern creation by Lee Kuan Yew and his associates.

4. For more on this argument, see Scott C. Flanagan (1982), "Changing Values in Advanced Industrial Societies: Inglehart's Silent Revolution from the Perspective of Japanese Findings," *Comparative Political Studies* 14 (4): 403–44.

5. Two major branches of Buddhism exist. One branch, known as Mahayana or "Greater Vehicle," made its way from India into China, and eventually to Japan, via Korea. It focused on the possibility for all mortals to reach enlightenment. Therevada Buddhism or the "Lesser Vehicle" spread throughout Southeast Asia and emphasized a more ascetic life for enlightenment.

6. Just as there are misrepresentations and selective interpretation of Smith's work—which incidentally was often critical of industrialists—so it is to the average Asian citizen's understanding and exposure to Confucianism.

7. Recent developments in South Korea and Japan, in the 1990s, suggest that much of the respect that bureaucrats possess is being eroded. In South Korea and Japan the incidence of scandals involving bureaucrats is on the rise. On one hand, this phenomenon may be a result of the temptations of increased affluence in these societies as a whole. However, it is also possible that the Confucian and traditional culture that promoted the "guardian class" notion is breaking down from internal policy failures, such as increased economic difficulties in Japan and South Korea, and also from externally imposed homogenization of economic and political systems (e.g., the General Agreement on Tariffs and Trade [GATT], the International Monetary Fund [IMF], and the human rights regime) which is undermining the traditional anchors of authority.

8. See Ishibashi and Reed (1992: 366–79), about the role of connections in creating dynastic succession among LDP Diet members.

9. For details of this poll, see "Asian Executives Poll," *Far Eastern Economic Review* 159 (11) (March 14, 1996): 30.

3

The Developmental State, Political Elites, and Asian Democracy

But there is a need to be fair and not to demonize those [governing officials] in less than ideal circumstances who do not want gridlock democracy, weak and cowardly democracy and democratic practices and forms that over-emphasize the individual and neglect the community, that glorify combat, that foster unbridled conflict, that guarantee against harmony, consensus and cohesion, that threaten to destroy order and democracy itself, and that engender the prospect of total chaos.

Excerpted from Prime Minister Datuk Seri
Dr. Mahathir Mohamad's speech at the Senate
House, Cambridge University, as quoted
from the *Straits Times*, March 16, 1995, p. 11

DEVELOPMENT AND DEMOCRACY

The linkage between economic development and democracy in Asia is a strong and vital one. As the complexity of the societies increase, leaders are increasingly realizing that aspirations for political empowerment by the middle create a challenge to old and traditional forms of governance. This chapter explores the connection between democracy (a cultural construction of politics) and economic development (an economic manifestation of culture) in East Asian societies. The chapter explains how the existence and operation of the developmental state affect the form of democracy emerging in Asia. The drive for modernization, as undertaken by the developmental state, affected democracy in two ways. First, it empowered specific political actors, such as the bureaucracy, corporations, and the military, over other groups, especially labor unions. These elites, through the coercive capabilities of the state, sought to control, subvert, or coopt political opposition because they potentially challenged the established political and economic order created by elites. Specific interest groups frequently excluded from the policy-making process include ideologically unacceptable groups, consumer groups, peace groups, laborers, environmentalists, students, and some intellectuals and artists. Exclusion is not accidental, but specifically by design (Compton 1996; Deyo 1989). The decision criterion for excluding specific groups involves the question of whether these groups represent a threat to the economic growth paradigm. The government coopts or suppresses those groups who question rapid growth or dispute the establishment's monopoly over the process. East Asian historic examples attest to how the state used culturally adapted notions of "national unity" and "modernization" to elicit supportive responses which supported rapid growth and political quiescence. Two examples include the Miike coal mine strikes in Japan in 1960, and the 1996 forced passage of labor reform laws orchestrated by the ruling South Korean New Korea Party (NKP) in response to militant strikers.

The process of modernization, as it unfolded in East Asia, demonstrates how culture, economics, and politics reflect an exercise of elite power. The following question considers these linkages: How has the meaning of power and who wields it changed over time in response to socioeconomic change? In many developing countries, the pressures of modernization often led to political fragmentation or conflict between elites and elites and masses. However, for a sustained period since East Asian modernization commenced, many of these states avoided political paralysis that characterized governments plagued by a participation crisis as noted by Joseph LaPalombara (1971: 46). He explains:

Political parties emerge, creating a vast range of problems for national elites. Disaffection may occur when, rightly or wrongly, politically mobilized masses come to view forms of participation as essentially ineffective. The very existence of mass electorates invites the escalation of highly charged ideological politics, on one hand, and elite attempts at controlled manipulation and mobilization of these mass publics on the other.

In East Asia, political elite–orchestrated economic development succeeded in mobilizing economic endeavors and in relegating political affairs to established elites. The elites accomplished this by using a cultural construction-of-society approach. The elite's use of symbols, both traditional and modern, and political coercion are tools of the trade for both economic and political modernization. The principal task of the elites consists of relieving the emerging divergence of the modern economy's logic and traditional orientation of its political infrastructure. Elites must use tradition to bridge the gap between modern and traditional institutions that are necessary in a modern international system.

By examining the role of culture in economic organization and the latter's effect on the unfolding democratic consolidation patterns, a coherent pattern of linkage between the two emerge. First it examines the meaning of democracy, and then it links culture and economics to democracy by exploring their effects of traditionalism and Confucianism on economic development. Then, developmental state theories show an alternative Asian economic modernization path and how that affects the shape of the democratization process and the consolidation now taking place. Last, a discussion of empowered and marginalized actors and how they affect democracy emanates from the syntheses of cultural theory and developmental state theory. The synthesis reflects sensitivity to culture and thereby lays the foundation for the Asian political development model in Chapter 4. First, however, we must ask a critical question about the meaning of democracy.

THE MEANING OF DEMOCRACY

Form (i.e., institutions and processes) and essence (i.e., including normative conceptions of democracy and government) based on culturally derived meanings and practices complicate the study of democratic institutions. Of course, many argue that the level of democracy, rather than its presence or absence is a central concern of research. Others may examine the distinction between "rule by the people" and "consent of the governed." Both orientations help define democracy. More precisely, democracy consists of a two-step conceptualization based on Guillermo O'Donnell et al. (1986). One step refers to procedural democracy. This dimension of democracy pertains to the established rules and procedures of governance and involves such things as universal suffrage, regular elections, establishment of alternative political parties, and executive accountability. Another refers to substantive democracy that emanates from procedural democracy over time. Substantive democracy possesses two significant characteristics. First, substantive democracy allows for political fluidity in that no fixed and ossified majority dominates the policy-making process. Second, resulting from this political fluidity is a fair distribution of social and economic benefits to all social groups.

On a theoretical note, one can only speak of how much democracy, rather than strictly the presence or absence of it, for the vast majority of societies. What may seem like a democracy to one person may not appear so to another. For example, even countries that many people consider as archetypes of modern democracies are not without their critics (Parenti 1974, 1978, 1993; Barber 1984; Crozier et al. 1975; Dye 1972; Lowi

1969; Schattschneider 1960; Mills 1956).[1] Criticism of American democracy emanates from many different ideological persuasions, but all have in common their frustration with the democratic process. Dissatisfaction with democracy originates, in part, from the problem of perceptions and normative beliefs. What is not enough democracy? What is the proper form of democracy? Is democracy an intrinsic political goal (as in the West) or is it possibly something instrumental to some particular normative end, such as a stable society?

The shortcomings of American and Western European systems, typically considered democratic, are duly noted in the literature. From at least a minimalist definition, however, most consider these countries democratic because public input is allowed, contestation for political power takes place, and generally peaceful transition of power is institutionalized. The West and its tradition of democracy, especially the Anglo-American variant, is a rough model of democracy. In the West, parties and democracies have become synonymous with each other. Political parties, as institutions that link people to policy, assume important articulative and aggregative roles in these democracies. Evaluating parties and party systems, as to their evolutionary history and functions in society, informs us about a particular system's democratic characteristics. The general study of parties and party systems provides a basic framework for analysis and most political scientists recognize the importance of political parties in political modernization.

The same can be said for parties in developing nations. In the political development literature, parties are considered an important component of political modernization. Weiner and LaPalombara (1966: 399) state that political parties (1) Promote national integration; (2) Promote political participation; (3) Increase the legitimacy of the state; and (4) Help manage conflict. Pye (1966b: 396–97) argues that they also promote a forum for the "mutual competition of ideas" and Putnam (1976: 144–46) notes that they are important entities for breaking the power of the oligarchy and for getting elites to respond to the masses. Party system representativeness or competitiveness tells us about the structure of power in political systems, that is, the form of democracy. However, it does not tell us about the essence of a particular nation's political system in terms of its mass or elite political values, including the normative functions and meaning of parties. Therefore, cultural and economic constructionist approach provides a context-based analysis. Analysis of party systems represents an important aspect of comparative research into political development based on institutional analysis. However, coupled with a cultural analysis, a much clearer picture of a political system's attributes and processes emerges.

Institutional analyses of democracies have been around the field of political science for some time. The standard approach for examining democracies (Dahl 1956, 1971; Pateman 1970; Schumpeter 1950) consists of scrutinizing the procedures or "institutional arrangements" that allow social interests to coalesce into policy. For Dahl (1971: 1), the government's responsiveness to citizens is a central component of democracy. Most political scientists would argue that the important defining characteristic in most Western liberal democracies is political competition involving political parties and interest groups.[2] Building on the accountability notion, Simone and Feraru (1995: 104) state that the distinguishing feature of a pluralist democracy is the ability of opposition political parties to displace the ruling party at the polls while the lack of it signifies some level of authoritarianism. In summary, accountability of government to the public and the degree of citizen's contribution to policy represent important characteristics for evaluating the quality of democracy. Asian new democracies exhibit significant levels of authoritarianism. The success of democratic consolidation rests on the ability to create a viable party system.

Political parties and governance are intertwined with democratic processes. Without political parties, modern democracies cannot effectively organize many people. Political parties, however, make governing complex, as it exacerbates diverse, rapid changing mass attitudes and promotes social instability by accentuating social divisions. Particularly in developing systems, where the distinction between the public and private becomes blurred as "the political" assumes a center stage, parties perform aggregative and articulative functions. The functions of political parties in the developing nations differ from their counterparts in the West. While political development literature points to the importance of parties, many Asian area specialists point to the problem of institutional development (Rozman 1991a: 15; Diamond et al. 1989; Langford and Brownsey 1988; Pye 1985, 1966b: 369). In developing societies, the absence of a party system leads to the deinstitutionalization of participatory channels. Participation occurs through long-established patron-client systems founded on the politics of personalism rather than based on party ideologies. Gary Rodan (1996), for example recognizes this problem. He focuses on extraparliamentary activism as symptomatic of political decay among Asian nations. That approach informs us about citizen demands outside the political mainstream, but exclusive focus on the extraparliamentary fails to provide insights about the shape of party systems in the future. Furthermore, such an approach minimizes the importance of political parties as a tool of the power elite. By focusing on individual behavior, the focus on political parties and their role in political development becomes marginalized.

As an alternative form of political expression, extraparliamentary opposition may signify some level of political openness or the elites' inability to repress such movements (Rodan 1996: 17–20). However, it does not represent a substitute for competition among political parties. Without institutionalized party opposition, the political elites resort to co-optation or repression as the primary tools for controlling dissent as evidenced by the Tiananmen Square and Kwangjen massacres. Most extraparliamentary activity acts as a "safety valve" to release pent-up political pressures but does not lead to systemic change except when the equilibrium is punctuated by violent and cataclysmic change occurring in a system that can no longer contain dissent. The lack of an institutionalized political opposition capable of taking over the reins of power accounts for the intense and periodic conflagration involving activists and the state. If an effective party system existed, such violent change would occur less. Systemically weak party opposition tells us a lot about the nature of Asian democracy and future political changes in these countries and the whole region.

The permanent minority status of opposition creates the problem of co-optation—the opposition must work through the existing dominant party if it seeks to affect policy. Without an effective party system, there is serious potential for delegitimation of the ruling elite. The preferred outcome, for elites, is co-optation of opposition needs and demands. This outcome allows the elites to address political issues on their terms. The result is the continuance of the elites' monopolization of political power; Japan fits this example. The second suboptimal outcome consists of the failure of co-optation. In this scenario, political discontent festers over long periods of time, radicalizes opponents, and undermines any legitimacy the state earned through economic growth; South Korea fits this scenario. If a legitimate party system existed, the political elite could become democratic and address salient opposition issues more readily without fearing retribution (in some cases death) from opponents.

MODERNIZATION AND ASIAN DEVELOPMENT THROUGH A CULTURAL LENS

The singular quest for rapid modernization underlies the context of East Asian political drama since independence. Domestic considerations and external pressure forced political elites to adopt plans for national survival. Nation-building, with socioeconomic modernization at the forefront, represents a complex intersection of a variety of endogenous social forces including nationalism, xenophobia, elitism, paternalism, traditionalism, and authoritarianism. It is within this social context that elites use political culture to remain in power and to develop the nation. Asian political development differs from that in the Western, Latin American, or African context because the former involves a political culture involving a nexus of traditionalism and Confucianism which form the basis for rapid growth and political order. Because of the rapidity of industrialization and the linkage between culture and economic development, Asian societies experienced the superimposition of modernity over traditionalism.[3] Traditionalism played an integral role in constructing nationalism and economic development during the early nation-building stage. Later it affected democratic transitions and consolidations by casting a traditional shadow from the past over designing modern institutions, such as party systems and electoral procedures. For example, while societies exhibited years of authoritarianism at one level, a communitarian element of benevolence also ameliorated the harshness of authoritarianism. This communitarian society or mutual aid society originates from the traditional or *Gemeinschaft* orientation of village life. Its principles are incorporated into the nation-building process by politically savvy elites. Additionally, patron-client relations fused political hierarchy and group harmony with nation-building. The importance of harmony allowed the elites to exercise power from a socially authoritarian base.

Traditional values supplemented Confucian notions of community by creating a horizontal comradery among those who occupied the same background, such as clan membership, caste, or geographic locale. This horizontal comradery provided a social control device and was useful for soliciting compliance and conformity for fear of ostracism. These values also promoted nationalism, both economic and modern national identity. Under the modern *Gemeinschaft*, national construction required protecting those who were part of the community by providing a stable environment for social relations and by promoting full employment. The difficulty of laying off workers in Japan and South Korea, even during the current Asian crisis, attest to the strength of the feeling of community. National construction based on nationalism, creates xenophobia by excluding outsiders. Long-term foreign residents in Japan become aware of a polite form of ostracism. For Korean residents in Japan, however, exclusion is visceral and systematic. Pye's (1985: 169) comments follow:

Because the Japanese have such a vivid feeling of the boundaries of their group identification, they tend to treat in-group and out-group people in completely different ways. They can be exquisitely refined in handling the slightest differences in status with exactly the correct etiquette, but then can be extremely rude to those whom they have no obligations—a fact that Benedict [the late anthropologist and author of *Chrysanthemum and the Sword*] used to explain the brutal behavior of Japanese troops in China, and which is now used to explain the subway behavior of the Japanese and their conduct as tourists.

Traditional values promote ethnic exclusion of foreigners who are excluded from employment opportunities. As one example of how traditional values transcend the past and appear in modernity, it illustrates how traditional values link past behavior to present actions. These cultural characteristics are not economic imperatives, but social-cultural ones. Stated differently, East Asian societies do not exist to embrace capitalism but, instead, embrace capitalism to sustain a way of life. When international economic pressures drove postcolonial Asia to "modernize" and "Westernize," the indigenous political elites inherited a paradoxical environment. On one hand, they had to build their nations economically. This involved the adaptation of Western industrial techniques. On the other hand, the sociocultural imperatives of society prevented the wholesale adoption of "Western" values and forms of government. The economic system that consolidated in the post–World War II period maintained traditional social-cultural imperatives that Westerners view as rigid or even authoritarian, but for political elites, the developmental state served the dual purpose of fostering modernization and creating a political system molded by traditional values. Traditional values make it possible, in East Asia, to construct a political system that is congruent with its economic system. Modernization theory failed to understand the persistence and diffuseness of traditional values in constructing modern political and economic systems. What emerged in East Asia is an alternative form of capitalism, built on a foundation of traditional values. East Asian capitalism strengthened these values and weakened a whole host of divergent social interests which would have otherwise shaped the democratization process.

Traditional social constructions involving sociocultural imperatives, such as the mutual aid society or the clan-based "us versus them" distinction, do not vanish but are repackaged in the modernization effort. As Cohen (1985: 75) argues, "Cultures, ways of thinking, attachments to community, are much more resilient than many scholars of society have supposed" because the elites adapt tradition to fit a modern era. The developmental state represents a modern economic manifestation of this retrofitting while Asian-style democracy is the political manifestation.

Political culture, as expressed in traditionalism and Confucianism, provide the building blocks for constructing economic and political institutions. As societies modernize, economic and political institutions must adapt to a variety of internally generated and externally imposed stimuli. Elites construct a society's economic and political institutions, and they are also responsible for maintaining and adapting them to the changing domestic and international environment. While political culture is the foundation for political and economic construction, the elites are the primary actors who build these systems. Furthermore, the elites have significant economic and political stakes in the successful development of a society's economy and political system. As Tsurutani (1974: 96) states, "effective modernizing" requires elites to possess commitment, the appropriate skills, sociocultural intelligence, and dominance.

ELITES AND THE DEVELOPMENTAL PROCESS

Political elites played a major role in East Asian industrialization by providing the necessary economic and political leadership. If these same elites maintain a monopoly over a nation's political life, the development of substantive democracy remains elusive. If on the other hand, serious economic dislocations occur, then the political legitimacy of these elites will become questionable.

National development in Asia is synonymous with elite leadership based on the cultural traditions embodied in the *Gemeinschaft* orientation of traditional societies. This resulted in a strong *esprit de corps* or a cadre of interlocking elites, akin to that described by C. Wright Mills (1956) in *The Power Elite*. Mills (1956: 288) states:

The inner core of the power elite consists, first, of those who interchange commanding roles at the top of the dominant institutional order with those in another: the admiral who is also a banker and a lawyer and who heads up an important federal commission, the corporate executive whose company was one of the two or three leading war materiel producers who is now the Secretary of Defense, the wartime general who dons civilian clothes to sit on the political directorate and then become a member of the board of directors of a leading economic corporation.

The case studies in Chapters 5 through 7 explore the specific structure of elite relations in greater detail. Generally, the intensity of cohesion among the interlocking elites in East Asia would be stronger than in Western societies. In East Asia, the social status of a position assumed an important role in the recruitment and selection of members of the elite. These elites share a particularly rigorous educational process geared for a bureaucratic elite course, or fast track, as in Japan. Elites, in Korea until 1980, may define themselves as part of a graduating military class, such as the class of 1960.

Education plays a central role in the selection of bureaucrats according to Putnam (1976: 108), because it socializes the elite into a homogenized view of society. In Asia, elite socialization and the resulting dynamics of the interlocking directorate intensified the shared traditional and Confucian culture and the common experiences of confronting modernization. While tradition in this instance may appear to conflict with Confucian notions of a meritocracy, the two are, in fact, mutually enhancing. For example in South Korea, the military academy fused merit principles and group orientation in training officers. Rigorous training protected Confucian notions of merit but by virtue of enrollment, enduring ties, in a *Gemeinschaft* sense, resulted in a collective membership in an elite circle. The University of Tokyo and the University of Kyoto play the same role in creating Japanese bureaucratic and political elites. The close and enduring friendship represent the traditional elements reflecting a *Gemeinschaft* orientation, while the merit principle remains protected because these schools are the "*crème de la crème*" of academic institutions.

The common experiences of the elites (i.e., education, military service, common regional or clan background) provided a shared foundation for arriving at a consensus about modernization. Putnam (1976: 112) notes these common socialization experiences strengthen elite cohesion. In some Asian countries, these common experiences were more enduring and more central, and this affected the cohesion of the elite. The countries that experienced a strong cohesion among the elites include Japan, Taiwan, and Singapore. On the other hand, South Korea, Malaysia, Thailand, and the Philippines experienced weaker elite cohesion due to regional and ethnic differences or greater ethnic heterogeneity. In these cases, the common experiences were drawn along these lines of demarcation and therefore intensified these cliques. Overall, however, the homogenization of elites through a specific kind of socialization is responsible for the creation of a more amenable "guardian class" in East Asia. The consensus-oriented behavior thus established the foundation for the developmental state and enabled it to prosper, although sometimes conflict over resources or methods to achieve goals were not present.

On the contrary, intraelite conflict, especially at the bureaucratic level, flared along ministerial and functional lines of jurisdiction. The South Korean economic bureaucracy feuded with the military for budgetary allocations. Even in recent Japanese history, the ongoing and often antagonistic intragovernmental bureaucratic turf battles are well known and described by Chalmers Johnson (1982) in *MITI and the Japanese Miracle*. Japanese intraelite turf battles between bureaucrats and politicians was also the theme in J.A.A. Stockwin's (1988) *Dynamic and Immobilist Politics in Japan*. This said, however, a general sentiment among the elites emerged—the need to modernize and maintain a steady course of sustained economic growth. Political maneuvering involved the techniques to employ, and who in particular benefits, rather than the need for economic modernization.

THE DEVELOPMENTAL STATE

Lee Kuan Yew, the longtime prime minister and now senior minister of Singapore, once remarked that if 300 key officials died in a plane crash, Singapore as a nation would collapse (*The Mirror*, May 10, 1971: 4). While such statements appear exaggerated, elite theory suggests that the scenario is not altogether implausible. The developmental state, as it evolved in East Asian nations fused the Asian power elite together through a powerful ideology of economic growth as the penultimate national good. This ideological component of culture remains imbedded in the traditional notion of *Gemeinschaft* around which Asian societies are constructed. Given the weakness of political institutions in rural areas after independence, Asian leaders needed to embrace the mutual aid idea, even if it were a myth. For without it, legitimacy would be construed as principally modern and that would not be acceptable to the culturally conservative masses. Preserving traditions reflected the need to disown the vestiges of colonialism, too. The elite bureaucrats wrapped themselves in the right mix of tradition and modernity and represented an enlightened "Confucian or traditional guardian class" working for the interests of the commonwealth.

The developmental state consists of individuals acting within an organized bureaucratic and political structure for economic modernization. Their zealous and focused efforts are built on the faith that economic growth would increase their legitimacy and put the nation on a trajectory of modernization without Westernization. The economic elites use the government for economic modernization by crafting a "plan-rational" approach (Amsden 1989) or what White and Wade (1985) call a "guided market economy." This plan-rational approach fuses economic approaches and social-cultural imperatives. Skeptics view these controls as systematic annihilation of competition to cement the bond between political and economic elites through bureaucratic intervention.

Understanding the developmental state, as to its origin, functions, and its perpetuation, provides insight into political development in Asia. One problem, the failure to incorporate the implications of the developmental state, resulted from American political scientists' desire to delink democratic politics and capitalist economics. In a developmental state, however, politics and economics overlap. Chalmers Johnson (1987) first pointed out the political effects of a developmental state by mentioning that elites actively work to limit pluralism. Pluralism, representing the proliferation of political interests, is anathema to a developmental elite which seeks to channel government and society's resources into rapid modernization.

Western economic theory, when juxtaposed against the historical evolution of East Asian political economies, cannot explain the anomalies resulting from the developmental state, especially in the political arena. Some scholars assume that market forces alone propelled the growth of the East Asian economies, but nothing is further from the truth. In contrast to the invisible hand, Asian nations experienced a highly visible and interventionist hand. However, Western economists are disinclined to accept state intervention as a source of economic growth in Asia. According to Chalmers Johnson (1995: 56–57), during the Cold War, U.S.

policymakers and academicians failed to recognize the fundamental differences between the American-based market system and the East Asian mode of economic organization because of our preoccupation with the perceived dichotomous nature of economies. Either they were "free-markets" or "command economies" and economists ignored a third, Asian paradigm of economic organization (54–55).

In "state-guided economies," a term used synonymously with the developmental state, businesses and other interest groups operate under a structure based on a "tacit agreement initiated by the state" (Haggard and Chen 1987: 102). However, unlike present Western capitalist systems, developmental states exhibit corporatist propensities, absent strong independent and institutionalized labor unions. Western corporatist theory (Schmitter 1979) cannot adequately describe East Asian political economies because they resemble corporatism without labor and bureaucrats do not play the primary leadership role in mediating interests. The primary leadership role, at the mature stage of the developmental state, emanates from the economic bureaucracy. Members of that economic bureaucracy, dubbed the "economic elite" (Johnson 1987: 142), have clearly specified policy goals: (1) political stabilization; (2) creating an economic environment that promotes the relative egalitarian distribution of income; (3) setting national economic goals and standards; (4) shielding bureaucratic elites from political accountability, thus creating and using an insulated state which can carry out policy without political intrusion; (5) investment in education to produce qualified technocrats and skilled laborers and managers to fuel growth.

It is one thing for the elite to formulate the kinds of national goals mentioned above, but it is another matter to implement them. Huntington (1971) argued that modernization and tradition need not be mutually exclusive. In some Asian countries (e.g., Japan and Singapore)—in which the elites successfully reconciled conflicts between and within tradition and modernity—economic and social modernization succeeded. A country without a national indigenous culture that also reflects high levels of social disunity and status segregation (e.g., the Philippines) experienced greater difficulty in modernization. While one can only speculate why this is the case, the success stories of East Asia, compared to the failures in Latin America, Africa, and even in Asia itself, point to some clues. Interestingly, Alice Amsden (1989) and others argue that Asian countries that adopted the correct policies succeeded and those who did not fail to modernize rapidly. A cultural case, based on the ideology of modernization, consisting of modern and traditional elements, around which peoples can unite, remains peripheral to their debate.

Most successful East Asia states adapted Western economic ideas and combined them with indigenous social-cultural imperatives. Some states, such as the Philippines and Papua New Guinea failed to reconcile traditional culture with modernity. Subsequently, both modernity and tradition failed as a catalyst for rapid growth because Western colonialism penetrated the culture and fragmented it. The problem reflects a fragmentation of a potential developmental elite, in that they do not possess a shared traditional political culture. Alternately, the elites do not have at their disposal the appropriate symbols and tools to mobilize the masses. In such a case social confusion becomes the basis for economic stagnation and political decay. The resulting lack of economic growth and the deinstitutionalization of transplanted parliamentary systems and other "Western" conventions make it impossible for these regimes to attain high levels of political legitimacy. Economic policy, as a tool of statecraft, must do three things to be deemed successful. One, it must lead to increased confidence and cohesion among the elites. Two, it must transform the illegitimate nature of a regime into an accepted one. This occurs through the concentration of political and economic power within the elites and is, therefore, not conducive to the onset of democracy. Three, it must preserve *Gemeinschaft* with either mutual benefit or shared deferred economic gratification.

MODERNITY AND TRADITIONAL CULTURE: IDEOLOGY AND TOOLS

While developmental state theory does not consider culture an important consideration in the modernization process, the arguments above clearly point to the salient role of culture in the development process. Regarding the construction and operation of a developmental state, culture plays a dual role, one that is both ideological and technical. First, let us focus on the ideological dimension. It gives the political elites an anchor to construct policy and helps create a sense of *esprit de corps* among them. Furthermore, by using traditional and modern symbols, it makes nationalism possible. According to Benedict Anderson (1983: 7), nationalism allows for horizontal comradeship based on a *Gemeinschaft*, despite the reality of exploitation and inequality.

What symbols and rituals do the elites use to create a sense of progress (a modern phenomenon) and yet preserve the social-cultural imperatives of society (a traditional sense of community)? While specific symbols vary across countries and temporal dimensions, a general observation is possible. Not surprisingly, these symbols and rituals combine both modern and traditional elements. Masses and elites receive cultural inoculation and continuous booster doses, by participating in a society, so that tradition is maintained and recreated over time.

Ideology

Under the rubric of modernity, elites emphasize the lure of modernity and progress as embodied in consumerism and nationalism for the masses and international and national prestige for the elites. While developmental states seek to limit consumption to maximize the personal savings rate, the lure of deferred material wealth and increased income is one fundamental value that elites instill in the masses. (Specific examples that come to mind are the "Double Your Income" national slogan in Japan, beginning in 1960, or forced savings in Singapore.) This includes the widespread availability of Western popular culture and other trappings of modern civilization, especially the idea of convenience and a "good life." Consumer appliances, such as televisions and vacuum cleaners, and even American fast food, symbolize a modern society.

Despite the ubiquity of Western products embodying a different set of values, the government intervenes occasionally to curtail the availability. If the government deems that a product threatens traditional social underpinnings, the state acts as a gatekeeper. In Singapore, for example, political elites ban Western pornography, while in Japan and South Korea it remains controlled. While protecting local markets may be the sui generis of these policies, many banned items such as Western pornography or the Western print media, in Singapore and Malaysia, reflect political and cultural concerns. These concerns, in Singapore and Malaysia, involve issues of social control. In particular, elites view Western values and media as a political threat to the elite's cultural construction of power. Artifacts of Western popular culture such as pornography convey individualism and ego-centrism, both of which undermine *Gemeinschaft*-based societies. By associating American values to Western decadence and by pointing out the virtue of Confucianism or Islam in resisting these threats, the state asserts its presence by appealing to a traditional "sense of community."

Political elites not only enjoy the modern amenities that economic growth makes possible, they also derive some significant levels of social prestige and international recognition when developmental policies succeed. Most important, it perpetuates those in power by inducing political stability as valued in traditional and Confucian political cultures. Meanwhile, non-governmental elites, primarily business elites, prosper economically in an oligopolistic system. However, in stark contrast to the bustling cities across East Asia, especially in Japan, South Korea, and Thailand, the traditional village life remains nostalgic even if it is a Potemkin-like political and social construct. Idyllic village life remains a potent symbol because the post–World War II migration to the cities is still a fresh memory and many urban migrants have sought to recreate an urban setting that resembles their rural village. What urban migrants desperately seek is a sense of belonging that characterized the traditional village life.[4] Nationalism serves as a functional equivalent. The emphases on the uniqueness of each nation and the sense that members of society partake in a national community reflects a logical extension of the traditional community mentality.[5] This idea plays an important role in nation-building along modern and traditional lines. Other social-cultural imperatives, such as consensus orientation, egalitarianism, and a system in which everyone has a role to play, are all symbols that harken back to an idealistic traditional life. The use of traditionalism makes it possible for society's members to place themselves in a specific time and place. Thereby a sense of identity, initially constructed locally, is resurrected as national identity. National identity keeps intact the connections to the past. This connection to the past is vital for avoiding the social crisis manifested in many countries that experience the rapid social change wrought by industrialization. For capitalism to become firmly planted in East Asia and then to thrive requires this kind of balancing of tradition and modernity.

Another function of culture lays the traditional and modern foundational bases for crafting policies or techniques necessary to cause economic legitimation. Specific instruments—including policy loans, forced savings, deferred consumer gratification, and government regulation of industry—are policy tools that contain cultural components. In liberal democracies, citizens would not tolerate such intervention. However, in traditionally based Asian societies, cultural beliefs about deference to high bureaucratic authority, the need for economic security, ideas about the national good, and the need for a collective modernization approach strengthened the elite's authority. The case studies in Chapter 5 discuss, in greater detail, the degree to which cultural tools affect developmental state policies.

Tools and Techniques of Administration

The developmental state literature does an excellent job in describing and analyzing the tools for implementing a policy of rapid growth. This section briefly covers some of these, considering the sociocultural rationale for employing these tools and techniques. The focus is on the following:[6]

• Five Year Plans
• policy loans and forced savings
• regulations and nurturing of infant industry
• promoting family-style corporations

These techniques are successful because elites link their formulation and implementation to culture. As for economic construction of society, the elites used skillfully specific and general cultural values containing both traditional and modern elements. These four policy tools or techniques, then, are as modern as they are traditional. One can empathize with Western trade negotiators when they complain that these economies do not behave like "mature" or "modern economies." These economies are cultural constructs and, as such, they comprise an important element for the legitimation of the elites. Naturally considerable resistance exists, for political and economic reasons, to altering significantly the cultural configuration of the developmental state. Economic liberalism undermines the sociocultural imperatives which allow for domestic political stability and for these societies' participation in the Western and modern world system. A paramount need for political and economic coherence in social organization cannot be maintained by the application of "Western economic models." Without the appropriate type of economic organization, no political system, no matter how it is structured can survive as the established norms and institutions lose their culturally accepted meanings. In that sense, while these tools appear merely as economic instruments, they also contain sociocultural elements as discussed in the case studies.

Five Year Plans, as an example of one tool with cultural elements, have a long history in the annals of central planning. In Asia, however, Five Year Plans, promote economic growth through export-led growth instead of import substitution industrialization. Unlike many Five Year Plans in Latin America or in African countries, Asian Five Year Plans had a built-in accountability system; unprofitable firms at least initially lose governmental support. Amsden (1989), writing on South Korea, and Johnson (1982), analyzing the Japanese economic system, explain the evolution of an accountability system between firms receiving corporate welfare and bureaucrats who must account for the general success of the economy. Simultaneously, the failure of these accountability mechanisms can explain the Asian economic crisis in 1997–1998. Interestingly traditional values underlie the rationale for determining which specific firms receive aid over others. While both Amsden and Johnson discount the role of culture in central planning, it is well known, for example, how Park Chung-hee developed close personal ties and would even review work sites in person before deciding who would receive government contracts with *chaebol* elites. The decision-making process was undergirded by a cultural sense of comradeship and patron-client systems.

Asian Five Year plans differed from their counterparts in the communist bloc countries because they contain a capitalist premise. Economic development occurs when a nation competes successfully within the global economy while simultaneously helping domestic corporations through the erection of trade barriers, both formal and informal. In Japan and South Korea, strong coercive measures forced compliance of corporate elites, however, the power of the state weakened over time. To that extent, in Japan, Five Year Plans reflect primarily macroeconomic orientations rather than microeconomic in practice.

The success of the Five Year Plans forces bureaucrats and elected officials to take them seriously because these instruments develop some level of legal-rational legitimacy. From a mass perspective, these plans create an image that the power elite is not only in touch with their concerns, but also that the country is moving in a particularly desirable direction because these plans succeed in improving the material standards of the masses. The powerful effect of such macroeconomic successes is that it creates an imagined community based on the twin pillars of economic nationalism and social stability based on a traditional and Confucian sense of community.

Policy loans and forced savings represent another set of macroeconomic tools frequently used by all developmental states. Policy loans, according to Chalmers Johnson (1982), are low interest loans with favorable repayment plans which provided funds to specific firms in targeted industrial sectors. At the earlier and intermediate stages of economic development, policy loans place the state in a powerful position. Lacking capital, cash-hungry firms cultivated close ties with the economic bureaucracy. By regulating and controlling access to capital, the developmental state successfully solicits general support for its economic and political policies. Furthermore, this leads to a modern byproduct of patron-client relations in the political economy, in which corporations represent the client and the government bureaucracy is the patron. The direction of the patron-client relationship changes as the economy becomes more complex and the relationship reverses to a considerable extent. Then, the government becomes dependent on the actions of corporations and therein the developmental state loses some of its autonomy. The case studies in Chapters 5 through 7 examine this matter in greater detail.

Forced savings makes it possible for the developmental state to offer policy loans. Instead of relying extensively on foreign capital, the economic bureaucracies can rely on the savings from the income of an increasing middle class. The greater the savings rate, the more aggregate capital available for policy loans, and the lower the interest rate on that capital. Savings have been a major reason for the economic success of many East Asian nations but Japan and Singapore in particular. Economic elites realize the importance of high savings rates. For example, Amnuay Viravan, the Finance Minister of the Chavalit Yongchaiyudh government in Thailand, announced in January 1997 the intent to encourage a greater level of savings and decrease consumption to combat the deteriorating economic growth there (*Bangkok Post*, February 8, 1997). Even then, the government laments that growth is only 6 percent. This propensity to save and defer consumption reflects the elite's use of traditional values. Furthermore, the lack of comprehensive welfare forces people to save and become self-reliant, by that making increased capital available for policy loans. The absence of extensive state-sponsored welfare conforms to traditional culture that relies on community intervention to relieve personal tragedies.

Policy makers also avail themselves of a third instrument—regulation. Two types of regulations, administrative guidance and formal policy, help bureaucrats in controlling the corporate elite. Administrative guidance consists of verbal, written, or implied directives and fits the traditional hierarchical context with the corporate elite subordinate to the state. Regulations supplemented administrative guidance and forced compliance from the corporate elite. Together, administrative guidance and regulations gave the developmental state an organizational scheme for the economy. The state dominated the corporate elite and the bureaucracy directed overall macroeconomic policy and specific microeconomic policies. Together, state and corporate actions provided a check-and-balance system which controlled the excesses of the capitalist system and the backwardness of traditionalism. Maintenance of social order and legitimacy for the state flowed from economic success. Strong state scrutiny made it difficult for corporations to thwart administrative regulations, especially at the early stages of economic modernization. However, most important, regulations promoted sociocultural imperatives and allowed the harmonization of politics and economy. Clearly, the East Asian economic model, developed in Japan and emulated throughout East Asia, provided a distinct form of economic organization in contrast to the Western liberal capitalist model. This economic model also affected social organization.

The promotion of traditionally oriented corporate behavior is another important tool used by policy makers. Promoting traditional values requires the use of administrative guidance, policy loans, and regulations. It is also embedded in the *raison d'être* of the Five Year Plans. By using administrative guidance and policy loans, the government can modify corporate behavior away from a strictly capitalist orientation toward a communitarian essence. In particular, worker promotion, lifetime employment practices, and conditions of employment characterize the core of "family-style corporations." This approach to worker-management relations makes it possible for a less adversarial relationship to exist between the two as corporate-sanctioned enterprise unions. Enterprise unions work within the context of a management controlled environment to negotiate wages, benefits, and hours. The major strength of this system is that not only is it possible to stabilize wage increases, but it also prevents the organization of workers in independent unions that might lead to the strengthening of labor-oriented parties. In that sense, it is sound policy for the economic and political elites to encourage the formation of enterprise unions.

STATECRAFT AND THE ECONOMIC COMPONENTS OF ASIAN POLITICAL DEVELOPMENT

Johnson (1995 and 1987) and Deyo (1987) were among the first to systematically point out the nexus between the developmental state and the problem of democracy in Asia. Their main argument was that the successes of the developmental state undermined the democratic processes in Asian societies by strengthening authoritarian tendencies. Meanwhile, Rozman (1991a: 15) and Bruce Cummings (1987: 44-83) point out the bureaucratic-authoritarian tendencies of developmental states: power remains in the exclusive domain of a *de facto* one-party system. Johnson (1987: 143) states,

Continuity of the government may be achieved by explicit or by a rigged system that nonetheless achieves a monopolization of power. Such quasi-authoritarian political monopolies are disappointing to liberals, but it should be understood that they are ultimately legitimated not by their ideological pretensions, as in Leninist systems, but by their results.

Economic legitimation detracts from political liberalization and adherence to it makes democratization difficult. For years, the Asian populace paid a price when economic interests worked to undermine political democracy. Many Asians thought that elite control reflected the costs of economic growth. Johnson suggests that Asian developmental state–based political systems exhibit economic legitimation which rests on the ability of the state to deliver on their ideology of modernization. Democracy does not represent the primary concern of the political elites and even the citizens-at-large, but additionally democracy is a political victim of modernization. This argument is significant because modernization theorists often point to economic modernization as a source of democracy. In Asia, this is simply not so, for in developmental states, pluralism remains muted so that elites extract, concentrate, and disperse resources to maximize social control and economic growth. Elites staff the administrative organs of the state to administer resources. This pattern persists as long as the political system can promote growth; thus the changes resulting from the Asian crisis of the late 1990s are likely to have heretofore unanticipated consequences for the developmental state. The specific composition of the elites and their relative strength across functional lines varies according to many factors, the most important being the complexity of the economy. The elite in Asia consists of senior military leaders, high-level bureaucrats from the economic ministries, corporate executives from large firms, and the cooperating politicians discussed in greater detail in the following chapter.

The idea that Asian elites limit democracy in Asia by making the political system less competitive is theoretically plausible given the cultural and economic foundations of the Asian polity. However, Asia is not necessarily undemocratic, but, instead, the degree and level of democracy there should alarm and discomfort those who believe that Asia is "substantively" democratic. For democratic theorists, new questions arise from the assumption that modernization and political democracy go together. James Cotton (1991a: 321) so astutely observed that in Japan, we have Weber's "plebiscite democracy." Is semi-democracy (as plebiscitary democracy may become) the most prevalent form of democracy possible given its cultural, economic, and social foundations in these societies?

NOTES

1. A powerful criticism of American democracy can be found in Rustow (1967: 9), which notes that Southern states have effectively one party systems and that "alternation of parties" occurs less frequently even in countries we consider "democratic."

2. The idea of a political system based on competition, akin to market-place adversarial relationships, is not new. Joseph Schumpeter's *Capitalism, Socialism and Democracy* (1950) and Anthony Downs' *Economic Theory of Democracy* (1957) are two seminal pieces in which the political realm and the economic sphere share similar liberal characteristics. A more current work is *Japan's Political Marketplace* (1993) by J. Mark Ranseyer and Frances Rosenbluth. This rational choice–based research shows how parties in Japan play an important role in the policy arena, much more than traditional Japanologists believe.

3. Scott Flanagan (1987) and Ronald Inglehart (1990) argue that value change in Japan and other rapidly developing societies often represents an amalgamation of values, where society reflects both traditional and modern values, which Inglehart refers to as "post-materialist" while Flanagan conceptualizes Japanese value change along two dimensions: the libertarian-authoritarian and materialist–non-materialist.

4. For examples see White (1970) or Dator (1969). The need for a sense of belonging and its absence in large cities drove many Japanese to this new religion which provided a surrogate "village community." Also, McCloud (1995: 42) observes that the corporate village may represent a traditional village replicated in a modern setting in Southeast Asia.

5. Black (1966: 86) states that how to integrate individuals into the modern urban society represents a major political problem of nation-building.

6. For more information on tools, techniques, and compliance, see Johnson (1982), especially chapters 5–6, and Amsden (1989).

4

Asian Political Development Model and Empirical Evidence

[A]n ideology based on the notion that "the market can do no wrong, is sacrosanct, is your benefactor, savior and ticket to prosperity, is now as extreme as was the Communism and socialism of yesteryear."

Richard W. Stevenson (1997: 12)

The class structure of many developing countries implies a cruel choice between faster economic development and well-defended civil and political rights. . . . Often the rise of this "growth coalition" is attended by conflict as it tries to displace groups with real coercive power, capable of taking the law into their own hands. It may try to harness a popular political movement using nationalism or revolt against exploitative class relations as a rallying cry. Once it can influence state power, it has to use that influence to shape a social structure which is conducive to wealth accumulation through productive investment. Most likely this will require some curtailment of the political and civil rights of those who oppose the changes, and the powers of democratically elected legislatures.

Excerpted from Robert Wade (1990: 372–73)

CULTURALLY CONSTRUCTED ASIAN DEVELOPMENT MODEL

This chapter explains and analyzes the Asian Development Model and presents some empirical analysis about Asian democracy based on the model. The Asian Development Model incorporates the cultural and economic experiences while remaining sensitive to the influences exerted by the exogenous environment, especially the impact of the late–Cold War period and globalization. The underlying assumption posits that Asia's quest for modernization and national security affected the distribution of political power in these societies.

The applicability of the general Asian model to specific countries represents an important consideration in its creation. This model must reflect the cultural and economic sources of political construction and maintain historical sensitivity for many reasons addressed in Chapter 1. Simultaneously, the model must be accurate enough to generate general propositions about the direction of East Asian democratization while simultaneously remaining adaptable to specific cases. Summarized, the model links together the culturalist and developmental state perspectives through the actions of the political elite. The utility of the model derives from its ability to explain the historical development of political systems. The model explains the cases, and simultaneously each case critiques its accuracy.

This chapter also examines the specific role of elite actors in the Asian context. The case studies in Chapters 5 through 7 build on the model by accounting for specific variations and anomalies. Nevertheless, the focus of this chapter is at the regional level. Each prominent actor in the Asian development model is part of a general power elite within that country. However, elites, while united on some fronts, remain divided on many others. They all possess common interests as elites, but they also possess their own vocational, ideological, and sometimes regional allegiances. The categories of elites discussed in this chapter are the military officers, senior career bureaucrats, the corporate Chief Executive Officers (CEOs), and elected politicians. These elites partake in decision making as individuals and powerful interest groups, influencing the composition of public policy. The political rise and decline of each elite group's power are functions of the internal changes caused by modernization and the division of elite functions in the modernization process against the backdrop of a global context.

The specific elite actor's political function in the Asian Development Model changes according to the level of modernization and the role of culture in sustaining them. First, as discussed in Chapter 2, culture underlies the foundation for the social, political, and economic construction of society. In the East Asian case, integration between the political and economic spheres makes political power contingent upon the success or failure of the modernization effort. As East Asian societies modernize, economic modernization affects which elite group dominates. In other words, each stage of development requires a particular elite mix to achieve advancement into the next stage. For example, at the earlier stages of modernization, the military's role is greater than in the later stages in all of the countries studied.

Second, elites use culture catalytically for propelling the modernization process forward. As discussed earlier, leadership can make modernization possible by promoting nation-building by using both modern and traditional symbols in specific contexts. The elites' use of modern and traditional symbols, furthermore, must be balanced. While it must bring a traditional society into a modern global system, use of modern symbols must refrain from destroying the traditional cultural foundation. Otherwise, these nations would face an internal identity crisis, one without a foundational connection with its history and identity. Common history and identity form the basis for nation-building and for political legitimation. This fact requires the political elite to weave a society together using both modern and traditional sources of authority.

At the core of the Asian Development Model is "developmental elitism," a product of both traditional and modernizing Asian cultures. A peculiar and idiosyncratic hybrid between traditionalism and modernity, developmental elitism draws on both for social and economic modernization. Developmental elitism's defining characteristic consists of nationalism and a modern outlook for economic modernization but traditional orientation for legitimacy. Furthermore, it encourages paternalism for social control purposes while simultaneously promoting modern thinking toward an industrial mode of production. As McCloud (1995: 139) states, "From the very beginning, the political leadership that emerged in these systems—even when democratic institutions functioned—was not representative in a popular sense but was paternalistic." Developmental elitism draws its cultural sources of legitimacy from many traditional values and characteristics but especially from deference to authority, patron-client relations, group loyalty or collectivism, and the successes of modernization. These four characteristics allow the Asian power elite to pursue modernization nationalistically while simultaneously their successes further entrench the developmental elite's political control. In this way, developmental elitism is a product of traditional culture and the environment of modernization. It evolves into an ideology that fuses the traditional sociocultural imperatives with the modern notion of progress to shape economic and political structures and institutions.

Culture contributes to the elite's political monopoly as power remains with the "experts." Thus, political liberalization occurs only as a response to the failure of the political system to manage emerging issues within the context of developmental elitism rather than emanating from the successes of existing regimes. Two such examples are gross environmental degradation, a common feature of all Asian societies (Compton 1996), and consumer protection, particularly in Japan and South Korea. With both issues, developmental elitism cannot provide a satisfactory resolution because it does not recognize the problem forthrightly. Sometimes, this can take the form of inability to regulate special interests, such as in the South Korean economic crisis of 1997. Uncontrolled lending practices of Korean banks, often with tacit government approval, exacerbated the economic crisis sweeping the entire region. Then, pressures for change came from abroad, in the form of global economic harmonization.

As the Asian economic crisis (1997) worsened, Kim Dae Jung became the first genuine opposition candidate to become president. Clearly, political change or adjustments become necessary for elites to remain in power and the new government and the *chaebols* began to seek out a middle ground. The norm, however, is for elites to orchestrate political liberalization to remain in power. A plebiscitary form of democracy, with a limited menu of parties to choose from, thus represents the norm.[1]

For example, did anyone think that the bureaucrats and their conservative legislative agents would lose their monopoly over the Japanese system? Election results unfavorable to the ruling party in Japan, one could say, served as a safety valve for relieving discontent and for warning the ruling party of its decreasing popularity. In no way was the party under the 1955 system supposed to lose its power to an opposition party coalition.[2] Was the JSP just part of a perpetually loyal opposition? Can the Kuomingtang (KMT) in Taiwan realistically lose power at the national level if the Democratic Progressive Party (DPP) remains less pro-development, absent a major legitimacy crisis? The dominant East Asian parties collectively display their amoeba-like characteristics by doing whatever is necessary to remain in power because they are based on personalism. When parties devalue ideology, it can bring former opposition members into the fold without ideological inconsistencies. Lacking modern ideological baggage, such as class issues, these parties can expand to hegemonic proportions.

In Asian societies, political liberalization and democratic transitions are top down; the power elite manufactures them to remain in power collectively and indefinitely. Individual leaders come and go. Nonetheless, that should not be confused with the essence of Asian political continuity, and that is the continuance of a political and economic system founded by a power elite.

The continuity of elite leadership draws heavily from the perceived pejorative character of the opposition. Dissent in Asian societies still faces a severe cultural pejorative. Elites, therefore, can delegitimize the political opposition in the name of deference to authority, community benefit, or stability. The Cold War compounded the perceived illegitimacy of the opposition because authoritarian leaders labeled dissenters as "communist." Thus elites have culturally delegitimized labor unions and political dissent because they represent a challenge to authority. Labor unions concern themselves with interests of specific segments of the population, rather than the elite-determined community good embodied in rapid economic growth. As such, they are purposely underrepresented in the political process. Under such a system, the emerging democracy's parameters remain limited. In particular, the controlled opposition, when juxtaposed against the ruling elite, possesses significantly fewer resources for obtaining the levers of power. Only when significant decline in the economy exists, will the legitimacy of the developmental state come under question. Meanwhile, elites use the dominant political party for their aims and the party resembles an "umbrella" or catch all coalition party. It functions to insulate the power center from citizen-inspired instability by creating a veneer of democratic accountability.

Furthermore, in many political systems, "the national assembly" remains a weak institution that routinely fails to function according to constitutional design. In theory, the national assembly preserves the popular notion of democratic government, but in reality, the national assembly consolidates the existing power relationships within the elite. Who participates and the extent of that participation in Asian nations is a product of a development state. The case studies in the next chapters will develop this theme further. In addition, this chapter addresses the weakness of Asian party systems by comparing levels of competitiveness within the region and with established Western systems. All Asian countries in this study display a general cohesiveness of the elites and their monopoly over power. The purpose of the analysis is to show how party systems reflect that monopoly. Furthermore, among all seven nations in the study, broadly speaking, the legitimate transfer of power rarely occurs, such that power shifts to another collective elite. These conditions reflect systematic processes instead of anomalies. Chapters 2 and 3 highlighted some cultural, ideological, and economic factors that point to an Asian form of democratic consolidation. This chapter builds on these themes by introducing quantitative indicators to support the argument about the undemocratic quality of democratic consolidation in Asia.

THE ASIAN DEVELOPMENT MODEL PRESENTED

How can Asian political development processes be described systematically? It requires sensitivity to cultural, historical, and ideological factors. To review, the major cultural commonality is the influence of Eastern philosophy which has spread throughout East Asia. Historically, Mahayana Buddhism spread throughout China, Korea, and Japan while the Therevada branch spread southward into Thailand and Malaysia. Furthermore, Chinese civilization was the focal point of Asian civilization and Buddhist, Taoist, and Confucian ideas about social organization spread throughout Asia by assimilating into indigenous beliefs. The term

"Sinic region" describes the present-day regions influenced historically by the enduring dominance of Chinese civilization.

From the early 20th century, Japan became the major focal point of Asian civilization through its imperialistic expansion. Historically speaking, the modern developmental state originated in Japan, which became the first non-Western nation to industrialize. While Japan suffered a major setback during World War II, its subsequent economic resurgence provided newly independent and modernizing Asian aspirants with an economic and political model. In part, Japanese colonialism and ideological imperialism left a significant mark on the political economy of Asia. For example, many postwar leaders collaborated with the Japanese during World War II and underwent socialization during the era of Japanese colonial rule.[3] Imperial Japan served as an economic model for the rest of Asia, and its political system provided a blueprint for constructing political culture in these nations.

Keeping in mind how the Japanese political and economic system influenced a variety of Asian elites' approach to modernization, the next few pages describe the Asian Political Development Model's stages and actors. The three stages and four actors comprise the model. Each stage has its own political and economic dynamics, although in historical development, some actors have greater power than others at various stages. The dynamics reflect each actor's inherent advantages within each developmental stage's political division of labor. For example, during the bureaucratic-authoritarian stage, the military possesses an inordinate amount of contextual political power. The military derives its political power from maintaining order and stability during the initial period of the first stage. However, over time, the military is no longer perceived indispensable for administering law and order; its utility to the political system declines and the military elites' power reflects a similar decline. The utility principle also applies to the rise and decline of other elite actors as the political system moves from one stage to another. The three stages of the Asian Political Development Model are:

- bureaucratic-authoritarian
- bureaucratic-corporate
- corporate-bureaucratic

The first, the bureaucratic-authoritarian stage, occurs in the early stages of modernization. The primary purpose of government, in transitional societies, is the establishment of a functional and stable political order. At this stage, the embryonic nature of the economic and political order requires a cadre of well-integrated elites. Levels of elite legitimacy remain low after the initial euphoria surrounding independence, and cultural construction of society represents a major concern. Prone to periodic threats, the elites rely on the military's coercive nature as insurance. Clearly, the positive boost from economic and social stability must wait for some time. Thus, at this stage, the military's role makes them an important actor, if not the dominant one. Other elites depend on the military to maintain a monopoly of power because the non-military elites do not have access to these coercive instruments. In the embryonic stage and whenever a regime experiences dramatic loss of legitimacy, other elites depend on the military. As the Tiananmen Square incident shows, dependence on the military led to their political empowerment.

The military's professional management strengthens the weak bureaucracy as military officers join the ranks of the bureaucracy and apply their management skills to economic and social policies. Many military officers quickly don civilian garb and join the bureaucracy, with the military acting as a feeder institution for the bureaucracy.[4] Ties between the military and the bureaucracy are close, but at times they may also be contentious on jurisdictional issues. However, as societal stability increases, the military's utility progressively declines as other institutions such as the cabinet-level ministries, national assemblies, and judicial courts institutionalize themselves within the political system. Furthermore, a carefully constructed bureaucratic and ideological environment can prevent a J-curve of disorder if government economic intervention addresses the income distribution problem. A good example of this is the subsidized housing programs in Singapore which maintain a communitarian welfare perspective. Singaporean elites used an ideology of paternalism and communitarianism to provide the moral basis of this social policy.

Toward the end of the Asian bureaucratic-authoritarian stage, economic growth becomes firmly entrenched. Society is undergoing rapid socioeconomic changes and the administration systems adopt more legal-rational bases of decision making. During the second and third stages, the military is no longer the preferred entry point to power, but instead the civil service becomes a vehicle for career mobility. The military, at the end of this stage, no longer possesses the capability to intervene directly in politics and instead must seek to join the bureaucrats by becoming part of them. Also, at the end of the first stage, corporate leaders are beginning to hamper the bureaucracy's effectiveness by seeking economic rationalization at the cost of bureaucratic sociocultural rationality. This trend accelerates in the second stage. (Thailand after 1992 is best placed in this stage.) However, at this stage, modernization is still at its infancy and entrepreneurial military officers start many corporations. (People's Republic of China displays this characteristic, for example.) As socioeconomic modernization progresses and the political effects of a middle class become evident, the military's influence declines.

Political liberalization and the eventual establishment of political parties and party systems characterize the second stage. Developmental elitism fully institutionalizes during this stage with the elite's cultural construction of society firmly established. With the economic and political trajectory more predictable, the bureaucracy plays its role of creating economic and social policy with the assistance of corporate leaders. Bureaucratic power, at the latter part of this stage, reaches a pinnacle when administrative tools have greater potency and effectiveness (e.g., South Korea and Taiwan in the 1980s and Japan in the period 1960–1975). Elite manipulation of myths, that ties society together and integrates it, peak during the transitional stage, as society is now neither traditional nor modern and industrialized. During this transitional period, rapid and unsettling change tear at the loyalty of the masses' psyches, leaving them in a purgatory-like state. The problem, magnified to one of nation-building, juxtaposes traditional values against modern organizational precepts. Without its resolution, political development would atrophy, but elites in the developmental state successfully convert the fears and aspirations of modernity into positive mobilizational energy. They recast successfully traditional values and institutions in modern settings, particularly at this stage. Democracy, then, being a modern phenomenon, cannot exist in a largely traditional and Asian culture without modification. It must exist in a specific cultural context with appropriate meaning derived from that culture.

Close relations between government and corporations also characterize the second stage. Corporate elites receive significant benefits from governmental policy because the success of the developmental state depends heavily on economic performance. However, by the end of this stage, power begins to tilt toward the corporate elites, and bureaucratic administrative tools (both cultural and technical) become less effective. Effectiveness declines as power within the political system becomes more diffuse with increased material wealth, decreasing the masses' susceptibility to mobilizational symbols. For example, corporations become less dependent on policy loans as their profits increase, as Japan experienced beginning in the late 1970s. Bureaucrats and the corporate leaders became equal partners, with the former no longer able to dictate economic plans to the corporate sector. Eventually, at more advanced points in this stage, the bureaucrats find themselves at increased odds with corporate leaders. Corporate leaders become less dedicated to the preservation of the sociocultural foundation because they must compete in an increasingly globalized economy. Corporate elites come to view administrative regulation as onerous. Also, bureaucratic insulation, long a trademark of effective policy making, begins to decrease as politicians become involved in policy making and corporate leaders begin to hamper national planning efforts.

A mature economy and an increased role for elected politicians characterize the third stage of political development. In theory, this reflects the most advanced point of Asian political liberalization and represents democratic consolidation. In this stage, corporations wield the most significant political power while the bureaucracy and elected officials become junior partners. The success of the developmental state policies has empowered the corporate elite to the point that they no longer are dependent on bureaucrats for technical assistance and cultural legitimacy. In fact, the goals of the economic bureaucrats and the corporations have often become mutually exclusive and a new disjunction between the bureaucrats and the corporations emerges. For example, in South Korea and Japan now, corporations which rely on labor-intensive operations ship production abroad, something that raises the concern of bureaucrats who value cultural and social impacts of such a trend. Despite these bureaucratic concerns, increased global competition increasingly forces corporations to abandon some sociocultural imperatives, including lifetime employment and bonuses. As bureaucratic elites make concessions to multilateral entities such as GATT and the World Trade Organization (WTO), corporate elites realize the need to function in a world without borders. The transplantation of labor-intensive functions leads to increased unemployment and decreased economic security by shattering the "corporation-as-family" symbol (Reischauer and Jansen 1995; Durlabhji and Marks 1993). The shattering of this belief, in turn, undermines the traditional bases of the developmental state's legitimacy. The twin process of cultural deconstruction and political delegitimation through globalization and its effect on political development is a subject discussed in detail in the case studies. Meanwhile, a presentation of the Asian Political Development Model and a discussion of the individual actors is shown in Figure 4.1. The behavior of elites and the relationship of the model to three political and economic phenomena, as depicted at the bottom of the figure, represent the foci of analysis. The following propositions underlie the logic of the model:

Proposition 1: As the composition of the governing elite moves away from one that is dominated by the military and the bureaucracy, political liberalization takes place.

Proposition 2: As the economy becomes increasingly complex, the composition of the elites must adjust to maintain the legitimacy of the developmental state.

Proposition 3: The political system becomes more mature and complex as power deconcentrates from the charismatic leader or group of leaders to a more diffuse collection of elites.

Proposition 4: The demise of the developmental state represents the most significant indicator of future party competition.

Figure 4.1
Asian Political Development Model

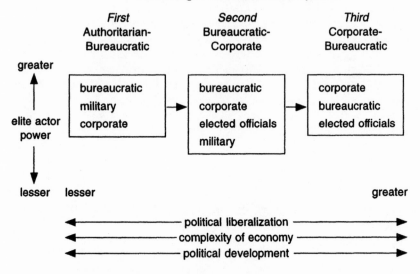

These four propositions suggest an intricate link between political and economic development. Political system change consists of evolutionary rather than revolutionary processes which rely on cultural continuity with the past. Cultural continuity and the elites' ability to perpetuate culture are requisites of democratic consolidation. Political liberalization may occur without democratization, although the two go together in many instances. The former signifies the relaxation of governmental control on political participation while democratization involves allowing increased and meaningful participation in political affairs and contestation for political office. The latter also contains a moral and philosophical imperative because it deals with culture and values. Democracy involves the freedom to form political parties and to challenge authority through elections in a fair and open environment. However, in Asia, past authoritarianism and its agents provide evolutionary change and ultimately affect the contours of democratic consolidation itself, even if fair elections consistently occur.

Liberalization, as Cotton (1991) notes, differs from democratization, although the two share common characteristics. Liberalization can exist without a substantive commitment to political democracy; that is, elites recognize contending groups or interests, but elites retain the ultimate levers of power. (Singapore fits this case well.) In other words, Asian democracy bears the stamp of authoritarianism while the processes of liberalization embody the prevailing traditional and conservative value system. The product, democratic consolidation, then, reflects the evolutionary nature of political change and contains context specific attributes. It is false to impute that Asian democratic consolidation would produce highly competitive party systems complete with many social cleavages reminiscent of Western European or America history. The term "democracy" requires a cultural and moral context relating to the history of governance. Yet democracy and liberalization, as described by Friedman (1994: 5) below, connote a Western distinction between democracy and liberalization which fails to account for the historical development of Asian societies:

Democratization is then understood as the building of institutions, common interests, and new forms of legitimation. Consolidating democracy requires building political parties and alliances capable of establishing credible national agendas and control of the military, making security forces accountable to electoral representatives, and crafting a constitutional arrangement (voting rules, distribution of powers, checks on arbitrary action) that will seem fair, open, and in the interests of all major social sectors, including old and new elites.

The above statements fail to view democracy in a cultural and normative context. Friedman defines democracy in institutional terms, instead of one deriving a moral, cultural, or philosophically oriented definition. Even an empirical analysis suggests that Asian democracies do not fit the definition above, so far. However, before going on to analyze Asian democracy quantitatively, a discussion of specific elite actors and their roles, below, concludes the discussion of the Asian Political Development Model.

The Role of the Military

Historically, the military played a significant role in the political development of Asia, as in other parts of the developing world. For example, in Japan, South Korea, the Philippines, Thailand, and Taiwan, military leaders assumed the top position of leadership in the past, but over time, the military's propensity to assume these roles diminished. In Thailand and South Korea, the military has historically played a larger role in the cabinet than in the other countries, and to this day, the satisfaction of the military is considered important for civilian governments. Sometimes the military does not rule directly, but instead is one of many influential actors whose support is crucial to those in power, as in the Philippines. For example, Marcos lost Fidel Ramos' allegiance just before his departure and that guaranteed Corozon Aquino's position of leadership for some time. When senior military officers refused to support military coups, democratic consolidation started on a firm ground with military support. In postwar Japan, the military plays a minor role in governance, but before that, the military's role affected every facet of government. During the Japanese fascist period, from 1930 to the end of World War II, the military actively cooperated with the corporate elite in producing armaments, helped craft colonial economic policies, and promoted cultural engineering domestically by promoting xenophobic nationalism. As Hall (1968: 318) states concerning Japan, "Although the period 1918 to 1932 is called the era of party government, in actual fact only 6 out of 11 premiers were party men; the other five were career bureaucrats or military officers."

The political strength of the military derives from its formal organizational structure and from the political elites' needs for social order. The military's role in political development is at its zenith in the initial period of the bureaucratic-authoritarian stage because the primary political concern is order. S.E. Finer (1988) argues that the military's organizational and institutional strengths account for its initial success. American military aid during the Cold War buttressed these characteristics by providing financial resources and advanced officer training. Except in Malaysia, the United States played an active role in training personnel and in providing the necessary equipment. Furthermore, except Malaysia, all seven nations have had varying levels of American troop presence over the years. Finer (1988: 5–6) identifies the following as effective institutional characteristics: organization, coherence of the group, and a monopoly of arms. Society's demand for law and order remains the single most prominent excuse used to justify military intervention. All three characteristics enhance the military's "law and order" image.

Historically, the military played a major stabilizing role in the governments of Asia, but as nations experience political development, its role has uniformly declined. In the 1920s and 1930s, for example, the military played a major role in establishing Japanese fascism. After the assassination of Prime Minister Tsuyoshi Inukai on May 15, 1932, the military comprised most of the Japanese "national unity" government (Hall 1968: 332–33). Another example is post–Korean War South Korea, where General Park Chung-hee embarked on modernization through authoritarian control of the economy and political process. In the example, the military, security police, and the Korean Central Intelligence Agency (KCIA) represented the foundation of the bureaucratic-authoritarian state (Im 1987). Also in Singapore, Lee Kuan Yew, since 1959, has used the military and security forces to maintain order in society.

At times the military plays a stabilizing role in Asian societies, but often it experiences institutional decay and contributes to political instability (e.g., Philippines). Two factors account for these two different outcomes. Change in the political environment caused by a changing political culture and the military's declining efficacy provide possible explanations for this. Political culture changes over time as societies modernize and people refuse to acquiesce to direct military rule. Then at other times, the military mirrors increasingly many of society's social problems within its organizational structure, and it becomes acutely politicized by participating in governance (DeCalo 1990). These two characteristics are probably synergistic and not mutually exclusive.

Historical examples, with South Korea, the Philippines, and Thailand, show how military involvement provides either stability or political turmoil. Repressive measures by the military require it to take a political stand; sometimes its choices contribute to instability. For example, in the Philippines, the military supported Marcos' regime and contributed to short-term stability but long-term decay. However, during the Corozon Aquino years, renegade elements engaged in mutiny against the regime, but the vast majority of senior officers and the rank-and-file troops supported the government and contributed to medium-term stability. Also in Thailand, the military played a particularly active role in politics after the 1932 coup, peaking with the authoritarian rule of Field Marshals Sarit Thanarat (1959–1963) and Thanom Kittikachorn (1963–1971). The military formed the backbone of Thailand's political continuity and stability over a long period. Military intervention and participation under that system reflect normalcy in Thai political culture. Then over time, something changed. General Suchinda's abrupt resignation as prime minister in 1992 raised the prospect for a military coup, creating political system instability. Strong and continuous support for the Thai military's direct rule dissipated over time as the country's political culture changed and other elites realized the shortcomings of the military's abilities. In this example, democratization pressure from interest groups, including students, monks, and business elites, found the unelected Suchinda unacceptable. The military's insistence for direct participation, via a military dominated government, would surely have produced significant instability.

Overall, direct military involvement in government at the cabinet level is quite limited in East Asian nations in the post–Cold War era, excepting Thailand. Even in Thailand, the unelected General Suchinda Kraprayoon's failure to maintain the prime ministership signaled a diminished future role for the military.[5] The discrediting of future military involvement, by citizens and elites, suggests that future coup attempts receive much less support from citizens. These events suggest Thailand's departure from the military-led government phase of political development. The form of democratic consolidation occurring there suggests a pluralistic elite system, as characterized by the model's second stage.

Another possible indicator of the military's strength is its ability to

Table 4.1

Asian Military Spending (Percent of Central Government Expenditures)

Country	1970	1975	1980	1985	1990	1994
Japan	7.2%(72)	n/a	5.0%	5.6%	6.0%	4.2%(93)
South Korea	25.7%(71)	n/a	27.8%(81)	26.6%	22.3%	17.4%
Taiwan	n/a	n/a	46.8%(82)	50.0%	30.3%(89)	32.4%(93)
Malaysia	n/a	15.9%(74)	13.7%(81)	10.7%	8.7%	12.0%
Singapore	n/a	n/a	17.6%(81)	17.0%	19.9%	23.4%
Thailand	n/a	17.9%	19.4%(79)	19.7%	17.1%	15.7%
Philippines	n/a	n/a	11.5%(81)	9.5%	10.7%	10.6%

Sources: For years prior to 1980, *Asian Development Bank Annual Reports* (1972, 1973, 1975, 1976); for years after 1980, U.S. Arms Controls and Disarmament Agency (1995).

maintain its resources, especially after the end of the Cold War. Defense expenditures suggest an overall decline in some countries and stabilized or increased spending in others. Except Singapore, however, military spending as a percentage of central government expenditures decreased slightly from the peak years. While the evidence points to no conclusive pattern, but a mixed one, slight movement toward less military expenditures (ME) as a percentage of central government expenditures (CGE) exists (see Table 4.1).

Over time, as economic preoccupation displaced concerns about political order, large military expenditures become difficult to justify. In addition, pressure from other elite groups, including bureaucrats, corporate leaders, and even elected politicians, resulted in a decreased monopoly of the military over national appropriations and policy making. At the mass level, as social values moved away from acceptance of authoritarian structures toward a greater embrace of pluralism, Asians came to scrutinize military intervention and expenditures more carefully. Because of these changes, a significant change occurred in the criterion for governmental effectiveness. The military's ability to maintain order—as the sole criterion for legitimacy—became an ineffective symbol. As in A.F.K. Organski's (1965: 7–16) stages of political development, a nation-state moves from the first stage to the second stage of political development when the primary focus of politics shifts from national integration and order to industrialization. Elites needed a new tool for legitimation—protracted and sustained economic growth. The military, to survive as an important power elite, had to adjust to a new stage in the political development model and accept a diminished role.[6] The symbols of law and order were no longer enough; economic growth became a modern symbol for legitimation and the bureaucrats. Possessing the technical and administrative ability, bureaucrats gradually became the dominant power elite.

The Role of the Bureaucracy

The bureaucracy derives legitimacy through its technical and managerial expertise and cultural acceptance. Historically, the bureaucracy conforms to traditional and Confucian expectations of governance and the guardian class. Yet, the effectiveness of the economic bureaucracy varies across the seven countries, as the performance criterion is an important indicator of long-term legitimacy. The successful use of bureaucratic tools and techniques translated into strong economic growth for many Asian countries. Strong growth increases the legitimacy of economic bureaucrats as leading elites. In contrast to the high prestige of Japanese and Taiwanese bureaucrats, social acceptance and regard for the Filipino and Thai bureaucrats remains lower for cultural and economic performance reasons. The Filipino bureaucrats cannot draw from a Confucian culture or point to economic policy successes. Similarly, the Thai bureaucrats remain weak because of the sustained role of military elites and the rise of the corporate elite. Yet in the developmental state, bureaucrats hold the key to its success.

In particular, two political leaders best illustrate the role of powerful bureaucrats and their linkages to political parties: Japan's Hayato Ikeda in the 1960s and Taiwan's Lee Teng-hui. Both leaders originated from the economic bureaucracy and came to assume their respective country's top political post. The economic bureaucracy's significant political role stems from the interaction between traditional sources of authority, both patron-clientism and Confucian-based legal-rational principles, and its natural Weberian characteristics which make it suitable for modern social organization. Therefore, economic bureaucrats also obtain legitimacy by using modern symbols, including a cultural appeal to economic nationalism. Unlike traditional nationalism, however, modern East Asian nationalism relies on the notion of "a progressing modern civilization" and the allure of consumerism.

Legitimacy and performance account for the bureaucracy's political power in many East Asian developmental states. Besides the cultural myths about competence, it has a variety of tools at its disposal. One, the bureaucracy drafts the legislation (although a national assembly rubber stamps it) and, therefore, it is at the nexus of power. All other elites are dependent upon the economic planning agencies to secure their share of the national budget. Second, and related to the above, economic agencies recruit the most capable employees when the bureaucracy's political power is at its zenith. Graduation from the major national university correlates highly with bureaucratic employment in East Asia. Third, industrial policy originates in the ministries of industry, trade, and planning. These ministries quickly take the credit for the economic boom in Asia.[7]

Despite these advantages, the political power of the bureaucracy is limited in the latter part of the third stage of political development as other actors begin to challenge bureaucratic dominance. In particular, the corporate elites and elected officials' ascendency reduced the power of the bureaucratic elite in the last stage of the model (see Figure 2.1). In the later years of the bureaucratic-corporate stage, cooperation undergirds relations between the corporations and the bureaucrats. The symbiotic relationship between the two requires corporations to work with the bureaucracy for regulatory enforcement, import controls, research and development subsidies, and legislative influence. Simultaneously, the bureaucrats need the corporate elites to organize the production of goods and services for propelling growth. In the early stages of the bureaucratic-corporate stage, the bureaucracy was in a stronger position of power because it controlled access to capital. Bureaucratic action may have immobilized a corporation in the early bureaucratic-corporate stage but may no longer have that effect in the later stages because of corporate success. The success of the developmental state means that corporate success must also follow; ultimately, corporate success through export-led corporate growth translates into capital sources independent of government.

Table 4.2 shows changes in economic-related expenditures as a percentage of central government expenditure (CGE) and CGE as a share of the gross domestic product (GDP). The data reflect the general decline of bureaucratic control over the economy. In particular, the cases of Japan and Singapore show precipitous declines, suggesting that the corporations have exerted greater control over the economy. However, in Malaysia, South Korea, Thailand, and the Philippines, the government's role in the economy increased over the years, suggesting that bureaucratic consolidation continues to progress. Quite likely, the developmental state remains embryonic and the economic bureaucrats have yet to reach their pinnacle of power.

The overall CGE in proportion to the GDP also suggests a similar story (see Table 4.2). In Japan and Singapore, the government's role in the economy, including entitlements (measured as CGE/GDP) suggests a fundamental change in the economy characteristics. Economic change subsequently redistributed the balance of power among elites and forced corporate elites to become more powerful. Thus, power's changing distribution among various elites resulted from structural changes in the economy. These changes are discussed in the case studies in Chapters 5 through 7.

Table 4.2
Bureaucratic Influence in the Economy

Country/Year	Economic Expenditure/CGE	CGE/GDP
	(Declining Role of Government in Economy)	
Japan (1952)	n/a	19.0%
Japan (1958)	n/a	14.3%
Japan (1969)	n/a	8.6%
Japan (1972)	18.4%	10.2%
Japan (1980)	8.6%	10.0%
Japan (1990)	10.0%	9.3%
Singapore (1984)	21.1%	17.6%
Singapore (1991)	n/a	10.4%
Taiwan (1986)	17.6%	13.8%
Taiwan (1992)	12.8%	20.5%
South Korea (1973)	5.8%	5.2%
South Korea (1981)	24.7%	21.5%
South Korea (1992)	18.7%	18.7%
	(Increasing Role of Government in Economy)	
Malaysia (1974)	28.0%	27.1%
Malaysia (1982)	27.2%	45.0%
Malaysia (1990)	24.2%	36.8%
Philippines (1987)	16.1%	22.8%
Philippines (1992)	22.6%	24.3%
Thailand (1975)	5.3%	10.7%
Thailand (1983)	16.7%	18.3%
Thailand (1992)	19.0%	16.1%

Sources: For years prior to 1981, *Asian Development Bank Annual Reports* (1972, 1973, 1975, 1976) and *Japan Statistical Yearbook* (1989–1992); for years after 1981, U.S. Arms Controls and Disarmament Agency (1995).

Table 4.2 suggests that both Singapore and Japan experienced a decline in the government's developmental state-related activities. This suggests that governments increased their social welfare expenditures and that corporate elites were no longer dependent on government subsidies and loans. Therefore, the corporate elites are now more independent of the bureaucracy, as the reinvention of the developmental state takes place.

From the perspective of the developmental elites, the rise of the corporate elite in a globalized economy is an ironic product of the developmental state's success. As corporations prospered, the bureaucratic elite's power declined, because the corporate elites depended less on bureaucratic largesse. For one, corporations obtained their own capital through exporting, and the tools and techniques of administration no longer produced the expected outcome. Bureaucrats, at the latter part of the corporate-bureaucratic stage, can only use persuasion to seek corporate compliance with their goals. In other words, the bureaucrats unleashed their own Frankenstein.

The Role of Corporate Elites

In the age of globalized commerce, the political power of corporate elites continues to increase. With the 1997 economic crash in East Asia, curtailment of the sociocultural imperatives of economic organization becomes a necessary part of economic rationalization pressures. The economic elites' prestige became tarnished and their power diminished as an exposed economy weathered the turbulence of international dictates. Simultaneously, bureaucrats' reliance on the corporate elite presents a paradox. Global corporate power continuously erodes state autonomy and alters the political power configuration. Asian economic problems of late tilt political power toward corporate elites. The extent to which corporate elites can deflect their own legitimacy problems remains a point of contention. However, clearly in many Asian countries, enhanced corporate power results from the need for independence. Increasingly, the bureaucracy cannot ensure corporate survival. Despite the corporate elites' increased disutility for bureaucratic elites, the latter require the former. Corporations remain indispensable by employing the masses and providing the ultimate justification for the modernization ideology. In that sense, the corporate elites' unique position allows them to extract concessions from other elites. Herein lies the possible explanation for the recent crash in Asia.[8]

During the initial stages of the developmental state, the corporate elites are often retired bureaucrats or military officers who developed commercial interests. In the latter periods of the Asian Development Model, many corporate elites become politically involved by organizing political parties and through seeking elected office. In addition, many organize powerful interest groups that advocate the views of industry and lobby government. For example the *chaebol* and *zaibatsu*, in Korea and Japan respectively, represent concentrated economic power that represents political capital in Asian political systems.[9] Increase in corporate involvement in politics reflects a fundamental change in the balance of power among the elites. It is inevitable that the successes of the developmental state would be reflected in the strengthening of the financial and political reputation of corporations. As export-led growth has taken off in Asia, corporate growth has become intertwined with the legitimacy of the state. A recent survey helps to discern increased corporate power. In a 1992 *Business Week* (July 13, 1992) survey, 296 of the more than 1000 largest global corporations are of Asian origin.[10] Multinational corporations increasingly demand regulation or deregulation in their favor and by that undermine the sociocultural imperatives of Asian economies and politics. Given the cozy relationship between large Asian firms and government, these requests for regulatory easements become difficult to resist (Katz 1998: 29–43).

The Role of Elected Officials

Chapters 2 and 3 discussed some reasons for the elected officials' greater potential for corruptibility and disdain by the electorate. The average citizen's low level of affinity toward politicians stems from cultural reasons and from the positive experiences with the developmental state. However, greater political liberalization led to an increased intermediary role for elected officials. These elected officials served as liaison between the populace and other elites. However, the effective decision-making role of Asian political parties and elected officials pales in comparison to their counterparts in Europe and the United States. Traditionally, elected officials operate as junior partners in Asian political systems. For example, in Japan, Johnson (1995: 124) quotes a vice-minister of the Ministry of International Trade and Industry (MITI), who says, "the bureaucracy drafts all laws."

Political liberalization in East Asia occurred after the developmental elites institutionalized themselves. Thus, a lifelong career politician rarely ascended to national leadership under the old system. Political parties in a developmental state frequently consist of former military officials, retired bureaucrats, and former CEOs who brought their personal ties to their elected positions. In fact, many are elected precisely for that reason. The profound implication for political parties is reflected in their lack of sovereignty and institutionalization in their own right. Instead, parties existed as appendages of the developmental state, much like a hollow shell for elites to fill with party patrons, devoid of ideological attachments. Political parties' primary function, then, was to bring together the military, bureaucracy, and corporate members of the elite in the developmental state context. Left-oriented political parties, possessing no base constituency within the developmental states, atrophied and became marginalized. Consequently, they remained weak and contributed to the collective weakness of the left and the overall low levels of competitiveness in Asian political systems. Party systems thus remained weak because political development took root without their participation. With political roles divvied up, the political parties became ancillary to the system, and the entire party system built up around a dominant conservative party. Rarely, in post–World War II Asia, except with the brief interludes of Tetsu Katayama (1946) and Tomiichi Murayama (1994–1995) in Japan and the 1997 election of Korea's Kim Dae Jung, have left-of-center governments held power.

The role of the national legislature in Asia is also significantly different from that in the West. In the West, national assemblies represent the highest organ of state power. Budgets emanate from Asian national assemblies, but the bureaucrats, military, and corporations exert significant levels of control over the political process, in particular budgetary and foreign affairs matters. Frequently, the party's affiliation to the military, the economic bureaucracy, or corporations determines its policy positions and its legitimacy as a political actor. Elites and citizens expect elected officials to maintain, strengthen, and use these connections to bring development projects back home. The major difference between Asian politicians and Western ones is that the former lack ideological attachments. Rather, they operate in a political environment dominated by webs of patron-client relations. Therefore, outside of political stability, a commitment to economic growth, and an abhorrence of "communism," ideology is largely absent in the conservative parties.

Despite these problems, the power of elected officials increased after democratic transitions occurred. The new political culture emerging throughout East Asia provides greater acceptance of elected officials. Slowly, the respect for the military and bureaucracy continues to erode. Globalization of democracy affects a very real phenomenon which elites must address as their societies modernize. Also, the fact that other elites now rely on elected officials for their legitimacy increases politicians' power. Both factors point to greater institutionalization of political parties. However, the form of institutionalization points toward a weak party system with dominance exerted by a single conservative party or a coalition of conservative parties.

Summary of Asian Development Model Dynamics and Elite Actors

Economic modernization drives the dynamics of the model with elites' response to economic modernization fueling political development. Developmental state ideology requires commitment to modernization and that ideology affects the relative distribution of power. As economic complexity increases and the required administrative expertise changes, the system requires a change in leadership.

Elite actions within the legitimation process play an important role in the cultural construction of politics. As discussed in Chapter 3, traditionalism and Confucianism intertwine in constructing the moral basis of the economy. State actors use culture to justify the accumulation of economic power, as capital and access, to accumulate in the hands of the bureaucracy and the corporations. The result is a potentially explosive combination: the synthesis of political and economic power, when state-craft fails to remain focused on the public good of economic growth and political stability. Economic power, translated into political capital, subverts democracy by encouraging a symbiotic relationship between state and corporations at the exclusion of the public. It also increases cynicism in the democratic process by corrupting the linkage between citizens and government.

Corporations use their financial means to fund selected political parties and the bureaucracy can use financial resources to elicit political compliance from the public and from other elite groups. Examples of this in East Asia are too numerous to discuss in detail here, but very briefly, three instances illustrate the pervasiveness of monied interests in politics. In Japan, the role of corporations in financing the electoral efforts of the LDP is legendary. One scandal, the Lockheed Scandal, led to the resignation and eventual imprisonment of Prime Minister Kakuei Tanaka on tax evasion charges. The 1989 Recruit Scandal, involving the provision of pre-public company stock to selected politicians, implicated virtually every major figure within the LDP and even some opposition party members. In South Korea, former Presidents Roh Tae Woo and Chun Doo Hwan received stiff prison sentences in 1996 for corruption, including operating a secret slush fund. Then in Thailand, especially over the past ten years, the ignominious phrase "unusually rich" tarnished the public reputation of numerous legislative and prime ministerial candidates. In all these cases, cash poured in from corporations seeking access and favorable legislation, contracts, and subsidies.

Improper use of political capital for financial enrichment undermines the legitimacy of the state. One, it mocks the guardian-class concept and shatters public trust in elites. Two, it undermines their own credibility by trivializing politics. These two factors and politicians' newcomer status to the power elite combined to exacerbate their low levels of acceptance. Many political elites, to participate in the Asian model of democracy then, must attach themselves to the existing elite structure. This attachment, however, accounts for corruption. Corruption, attachment, and the triviality of politics, in turn, account for low levels of party competition on the cultural note, while the politics of the developmental state provides economic explanations.

In East Asia, politicians benefit when they cooperate with the existing elite rather than oppose them because they are latecomers. Conservative political parties, realizing this, often draw on the bureaucratic, military, and corporate elite for members. The left-of-center parties attempt to take advantage of indiscretions, but their lack of a strong base constituency and financial capital to wage campaign battles contribute to their uniform weakness. The political ideology of developmental elitism excludes any major role for opposition parties.

AN EMPIRICAL EXAMINATION OF THE ASIAN DEVELOPMENT MODEL

This section provides comparative quantitative analysis of party systems between seven East Asian nations and Western democracies. It tests the Asian Development Model by providing evidence regarding the weaknesses of Asian party systems. Also, it provides analysis about variations in competition within Asia. Both exercises shed light on the democratic consolidation patterns in seven East Asian nations, all selected because they embarked on multiparty competition. Multiparty competition refers to the official recognition of opposition parties to compete against the dominant party that existed before the transition.

The Asian Political Development Model outlined is an alternative model of political development endemic to East Asia. Protecting individual rights against the capricious exercise of governmental authority partly comprises the liberal theory of democracy. Therefore, constitutions and institutions exist to simultaneously control and empower government through an electoral system involving party politics. Competition as institutional checks also exists in Western party systems as evidenced by the existence of a gamut of left and conservative-oriented parties. Oddly, these principles do not operate in East Asian political traditions. Political opposition remains weakly institutionalized. As discussed earlier, structural and historical causes of weak opposition also exist. One, the rapidity of economic development in East Asia precludes the organization of labor-oriented parties because political elites actively work to discredit them. Two, the developmental state provides economic incentives to citizens for working within the existing system, whether it is the political or economic system, instead of exercising radicalism. Third, the interlocking directorate among the political elites prevents the left from obtaining policy expertise and governmental power. Therefore, without governmental experience, citizens are unwilling to trust the untested left, or any alternative party, with political power. The political weakness of the left is explored in the following empirical analysis.

Two propositions are examined in the remainder of this chapter:

1. As Asian societies modernize, their elections become more competitive and reflect the new reality of social complexity, but the party system remains controlled by a political party or a coalition of political parties favoring the power elite. The result is an across-the-board low level of party-system competitiveness.

2. The general link between socioeconomic modernization and political democracy is not evident in Asia because economic growth contributes to the political status quo which favors the developmental state elites. In contrast to modernization theory's assumptions, socioeconomic changes in East Asia are not strongly correlated with a Western-style parliamentary democracy.

Measuring Party-System Competitiveness

In comparative politics, three basic approaches to study political parties and party systems are the sociological approach, the institutional approach, and the analysis of competition approach (Ware 1996: 8–9). The sociological approach focuses on social changes that affect cleavages and their manifestations, such as the effect of economic modernization on the modern-traditional cleavage. This approach also examines the relationship between electoral politics and cleavages. Thus, the extent to which parties reflect cleavages reveals the extent and shape of party institutionalization. Ware (1996: 8) identifies Lipset and Rokkan and Almond as those who follow a sociological approach. The institutional approach focuses on rules and procedures for shaping party systems. Scholars identified are Panebianco, Michels, von Beyme, Mair, and Duverger (party systems). The last approach, the analysis of competition, focuses on coalition building and "the beliefs, values, and attitudes of the actors involved which are taken as given within a particular institutional context" (Ware 1996: 9). This research, while focused primarily with the competition approach, is also concerned with sociological factors.

The cultural construction of politics as outlined in Chapter 2 fits within the analysis of competition approach and the Asian Political Development Model fits primarily within the sociological approach. However, the primary concern of this section is the competition approach. Empirical analysis strengthens the analysis of competition approach when used with case studies.

A common approach to the competition approach is to create a competitiveness index, the most common known as the fractionalization index. The fractionalization index (Sartori 1976; Rae 1971) captures how much competition exists within the overall party system. It considers the number of political parties and the extent to which each of them possesses seats in the national assembly. In other words, it simultaneously incorporates the quantity of parties and the dispersion of seats into a single measure. The formula for the fractionalization index is as follows:

$$F = 1 - \sum_{i=1}^{N} p_i^2$$

N is the number of parties in a political system and p is the proportion of seats held by the ith party (Sartori 1976: 307). This measure accounts for the dispersion of seats given the number of political parties for each election in a given year.[11]

The fractionalization index, however, is not without serious limitations. One limitation is that it fails to account for the qualitative characteristics of these parties. Also, the index cannot distinguish differences in the culturally based contextual "meaning" of political parties. The assumption is that all party systems perform identical functions in each nation's political system. Furthermore, there is no way to capture the base constituency of these political parties through the fractionalization measure. The fractionalization fails to account for the cleavage dimensions in society, that is, the type of social and economic interests these parties represent. A party system may consist only of parties that represent a particular segment of the society (e.g., the military, business, or bureaucratic interests). What value is "high fractionalization" if all political parties in a respective party system owe their allegiance to the military or the bureaucracy? What about religious or labor interests? In these cases, the fractionalization index reveals little, at best, or a biased depiction of reality at worst. Therefore, to capture alliances between various political parties of the same party family and to distinguish their respective core constituents, a measure of party variety is needed.

Competition, as measured empirically, in this research has two dimensions: the quantitative aspect of party competition (involving the number of parties and their respective shares of the national assembly) and a qualitative aspect reflecting the support bases of parties. The party variety index number solves the problem of overlapping constituencies by taking into consideration the support bases of these parties. It is the percent of the seats captured, in a particular election, by those parties representing the Asian power elite (businesses, bureaucratic interests, and military) minus the percent of seats captured by the non-power elite parties. The designation of power elite and non-power elite parties is determined according to the sociological approach, taking into account the salient social cleavages. The parties were coded according to six basic orientations or party families.[12] The classification of the parties is as follows:

- *Military/Bureaucratic/Business*. These political parties draw their support primarily from the power-elite composed of the military, bureaucracy, and/or corporations.
- *Farm/Labor*. These political parties have labor unions and peasants as a primary source of electoral support.
- *Ethnic*. Ethnic parties appeal to specific cultural and racial groups.

- *Religious.* Religious parties are based in traditional Asian religions, Islam, Christianity, or new derivatives of them.

- *Regional.* Regional parties primarily emphasize the differences among various regions of a nation and seek to improve their region over others. Electoral support is regionally based.

- *Other.* Includes all other parties that do not belong to any of the above categories.

The fractionalization measure captures how much competition there is among parties while the party variety index shows the extent to which many interests are represented in the party system.

Competitiveness of party-systems measure takes into account fractionalization and the sociological bases of parties. The competitiveness measure consists of the average of the fractionalization measure and the party variety score:[13]

Competitiveness = [(Fractionalization score + party variety score)/2]

Measuring Socioeconomic Modernization

Seymour Martin Lipset (1994), in his presidential address to the American Sociological Association, spoke in detail about the conditions necessary for the fostering of democracy throughout the world. Three of the factors that he mentioned were culture, leadership, and socioeconomic factors. However, he stated that "Clearly, socioeconomic correlations are merely associational, and do not necessarily indicate cause" (16). Past research in political science and sociology, however, has pointed to the connection between modern societies and the development of democracy (Moore 1967; Almond 1974; Lipset 1959; Lipset et al. 1993). Daniel Lerner's (1958) thesis, too, was about the transformation of traditional societies into modern ones, and how that transformation would lead to democratic forms of government.

The modernization argument implicitly states that non-Western societies will resemble Western ones on economic and political dimensions. Francis Fukuyama (1992), for example, refers to the global reach of the market. Free-market economic activity and democracy are inseparable twins according to him. Whether free-market activity, which induces economic growth, and liberal democracy is an intertwined process is open to debate. By taking the standard modernization data and examining political change in East Asia, modernization in itself does not directly lead to liberal Western-style democratic systems.

Modernization historically involved industrialization and economic activities, and universally it has at least the following in common:

1. urbanization

2. industrialization

3. economic growth

According to Gillis et al. (1983: 7) economic development involves a rising share of industry in the national product and a decline in agriculture, increase in urbanization, and a deceleration of population growth. Economic development, while not synonymous with modernization, is part of the modernization process, since it implies the modernization of economic organization within a society.

Socioeconomic modernization data are obtained from the World Bank, the Asian Development Bank, and individual country statistical yearbooks. The World Bank, in particular, publishes annually *Social Indicators of Development*. From that publication an index, composed of the fertility rate, urbanization, GNP per capita, and the percent of the labor force engaged in agriculture, is created by using factor analysis for each election year.[14] In political research too, these are common variables used for measuring modernization (Lipset 1959; Banks 1971; Tsurutani 1974; Lipset et al. 1993).[15]

We know that socioeconomic modernization is a complex phenomenon that is multifaceted. Often, social scientists ask, "What does it mean to be a modernized society?" Does a high GNP per capita necessarily represent the attribute of a modern society? If it did, then Saudi Arabia would be considered a modernized society. However, we know that a variety of factors together account for the phenomenon of modernization, so Saudi Arabia is still largely traditional. The purpose of factor analysis in this research is to build a reliable index of modernization. After compiling the factor scores, they will be plotted against the party system competitiveness scores (for both Asia and the West) to show the relationship between modernization and competitiveness. This in turn will inform us about the shape of East Asian democracy in contrast to Western liberal democracies by comparing different levels of modernization.

METHODS, FINDINGS, AND DISCUSSION

The method used to explore the propositions about the differences between Asian and Western party systems and the relationship between modernization and party system is correlational analysis. The dependent variable is party-system competitiveness, one indicator of democratic consolidation. The independent variables consist of modernization and a variable differentiating between Asia and the West (i.e., a dummy variable). Descriptive statistical analysis as Pearson's R shows correlation and the T-test shows statistical significance. To find correlations and perform T-tests, however, the methodological problem of discontinuous elections is addressed below.

The discontinuous nature of elections in parliamentary systems represents a slight methodological problem in that pooled cross-sectional comparisons by the year would result in an uneven number of cases in each year. In parliamentary systems, elections must be held at least in a specified period of years, but they can occur earlier unlike presidential systems such as in the United States. Two approaches can help resolve this issue. One is to use election results of one year and to carry those forward over the years until the next elections are held. Another approach is to aggregate and pool the elections for specific time periods of ten- or fifteen-year intervals. The problem with the first approach is that elections did not occur in those years for which the competitiveness measure was carried over. It assumes continuity where none exists. The second approach introduces problems resulting from aggregating data—the loss of specificity. This is a cumbersome, but a manageable problem if either method is applied. The method used consists of the aggregative approach that relies on competitiveness scores and corresponding modernization factor scores. This approach readily allows for the comparison of specific time periods. The three time periods are 1945–1960, 1961–1975, and 1976 to present.

Table 4.3 provides an individual country's competitiveness measure and the corresponding modernization factor score for each time period. For example, Japan's data in "Period One" represents House of Representatives elections up to 1960. The competitive measure noted reflects the average of the fractionalization index and the party variety index. Then, all party competitiveness indices are averaged by country for each time period. The corresponding modernization score for Japan in each time period represents the mean modernization factor scores for all election years in that time period. In other words, average modernization scores for each country and each time period can be compared to those of other countries and plotted. These are found in Figures 4.1 and 4.2. The rows "Asia Average" and "West Average" in Table 4.3 represent averages over these time periods.

Analysis of Competitiveness Scores and Modernization Indices

Table 4.3 shows that, across the board, most developing countries are experiencing modernization caused by the Green Revolution and the industrial revolution. Presently, only Japan and Singapore can be considered to be fully modernized, but South Korea and Taiwan, over the past ten years, have begun to rapidly close rank. Even in Thailand, Malaysia,

Table 4.3
Modernization and Party-System Competitiveness

Country	Period One*		Period Two		Period Three	
	Comp	Mod	Comp	Mod	Comp	Mod
Japan	0.52	–1.08	0.48	–0.04	0.50	1.17
Malaysia	*	*	*	*	0.23	–1.69
Singapore	*	*	*	*	0.04	1.61
Taiwan	*	*	*	*	0.35	0.31
Korea	*	*	0.42	–2.09	0.52	–0.14
Philippines	*	*	*	*	0.37	–1.67
Thailand	*	*	*	*	0.47	–2.71
Asia Average	*	*	*	*	0.35	–0.44
Norway	0.69	–0.63	0.72	–0.20	0.70	1.33
United Kingdom	0.48	0.44	0.52	0.61	0.46	1.45
Canada	0.52	–0.47	0.62	0.17	0.54	1.35
Iceland	0.67	–0.90	0.66	–0.02	0.70	1.45
Germany	*	*	0.49	0.35	0.52	1.63
Australia	*	*	0.60	0.25	0.61	1.36
New Zealand	*	*	0.48	–0.21	0.49	0.98
Austria	0.55	–0.80	0.53	–0.26	0.60	0.93
Denmark	0.62	0.17	0.66	0.43	0.73	1.73
Finland	0.80	–1.07	0.80	–0.21	0.78	1.07
France	0.74	–0.55	0.56	–0.03	0.71	1.13
Netherlands	0.84	–0.04	0.83	0.38	0.74	1.62
Italy	0.84	–0.68	0.83	–0.27	0.79	0.72
Belgium	0.78	0.44	0.75	0.69	0.80	1.69
United States	0.53	–0.26	0.54	0.38	0.54	1.16
West Average	0.67	–0.39	0.64	0.14	0.65	1.31

*The three periods are 1945–1960, 1961–1975, and 1976 to present.

and the Philippines, modernization is progressing but at variable speeds. In the West, the factor scores indicate overall high levels of modernization.

In terms of competitiveness, one qualification about electoral systems needs mentioning. Some countries, including the United States, United Kingdom, Canada, and New Zealand (until recently), adopted a majoritarian procedure of democracy through single-member districts. According to Sartori (1976) and Duverger's theorem, proportional representation (PR) leads to increased parties within party systems compared with the majoritarian principle used in single-member district (SMD) systems. Party systems based on proportional representation systems sacrifice majoritarian principles in favor of representation. Institutional structure affects competitiveness by enhancing or decreasing party-system competitiveness (Ware 1996: 193–95). In part, the relative low levels of competitiveness in the United Kingdom, the United States, Australia, and New Zealand stem from an institutional arrangement that hinders smaller parties.

SMDs characterize many Asian party systems, except Japan, which used PR until the electoral reforms of 1994. The present Japanese system uses both PR and SMD and contributed to the demise of many smaller parties. Singapore and Philippines operate along SMD rules, but make allowances for specific minorities. Singapore, as of 1988, requires minority representation in the national assembly with one-third of the candidates to be non-Chinese. In Korea, 1988 electoral reforms restored SMD, but further reforms for the 1996 elections led to 253 SMD seats and 46 PR seats distributed to the parties based on each party's popular vote. From the Asian ruling elites' perspective, SMDs are preferred to PR. Historically and culturally, this makes intuitive sense, given Asian elites' concern with political order and nation building. PR fragments attempt to create a political consensus. In Table 4.3, SMD systems have lower levels of party-system competitiveness. Overall, however, a difference between Asian and Western party systems exists—SMD systems of the West exhibit greater competitiveness than the East Asian SMD systems. Competitiveness by region is shown in Figure 4.2.

Figure 4.2 shows the competitiveness scores of Western and Asian nations. The graphical representation shows that Asian party systems' competitiveness lags behind their Western counterparts. Correlation between region and competitiveness is -0.64 (Pearson's R) and the T-test for significance is -5.86 and statistically significant at the 0.05 confidence level. Differences between Western and Asian party systems' competitiveness exist for many reasons, including procedural, cultural, and sociological.

Among the Asian nations, Japan is among the most modernized, and it possesses one of the most competitive party systems in Asia.[16] However, given its proportional representation system, its competitiveness is low. Singapore is an extreme case, as its extremely low competitiveness indicates. In that sense, Singapore has no effective institutionalized party system despite high levels of modernization. Both South Korea and Thailand exhibit encouraging signs of competitiveness. Thailand in particular exhibits high levels of fractionalization but low levels of political-party pluralism, verifying that nearly all parties represent the genre of the military, bureaucracy, and corporation type. These three cases, Thailand,

Figure 4.2
Comparison of Party-System Competitiveness

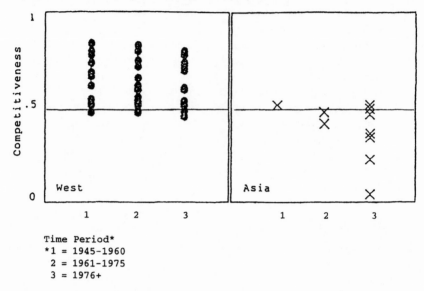

Time Period*
*1 = 1945-1960
2 = 1961-1975
3 = 1976+

Japan, and South Korea, form the basis of the case studies discussed later because they represent a large gamut of competitiveness and varying levels of political development on the Asian Development Model's continuum.

Modernization and Party-System Competitiveness

What is the relationship between socioeconomic modernization and party-system competitiveness in the West and Asia? The following points highlight the analysis between modernization and competitiveness:

- Modernization and competitiveness among Asian countries, both within and among the three periods
- Modernization and competitiveness among Western countries, both within and among the three periods
- Modernization and competitiveness between Asian and Western countries, both within and among the three periods

According to Figure 4.2, many Asian countries, excepting Japan and Singapore, do not rank with Western nations in the modernization dimension. By the 1990s, however, many Asian countries were rapidly catching up. Agriculture dominated the occupational division of labor in only Malaysia (28.6%), Thailand (41.6%), and the Philippines (44.7%), according to

The Europa World Yearbook 1996. In contrast, the data for four other Asian countries show Japan (5.3%), Taiwan (10.9%), Singapore (0.8%), and South Korea (12.5%). The Asian industrial revolution drives movement away from agriculture and directly leads to socioeconomic modernization. However, the connection between modernization and democratization appears tenuous. Virtually no cross-national aggregate level relationship exists between levels of modernization and competitiveness. Thailand, one of the least modernized, has one of the highest levels of competition in Asia, but Singapore, the most modernized, has very little competition. Overall, however, some specific cases, including modernized Japan and Korea, show more competition than Malaysia, a less modernized polity. In Korea and Japan, the negligible variation in competitiveness from one period to another suggests that increased modernization does not affect the competitiveness of party systems within each country.

Western nations have significantly consolidated their modernization over the three periods. Except for a few outliers—New Zealand, Austria, and Italy—the modernization scores are similar, whereas in Asian societies, the scores are more variable. Over time, modernization has increased in all Western nations and in Asia. Interestingly, the temporal stability of competitiveness scores over time exists in the West too, suggesting the accuracy of Lipset and Rokkan's (1967) "frozen cleavage" hypothesis. Beyond a certain threshold, socioeconomic maturation does not translate into noticeably greater party-system competitiveness.[17]

The last issue that needs addressing—the relationship between modernization and competitiveness in an Asia vs. the West comparative perspective—sheds light on differences in political development. Figure 4.3 plots the various competitiveness scores by region against modernization scores.

The correlational analysis concerning the overall cross-national relationship between competitiveness and modernization is weak. The Pearson's R is 0.14 and the T-value is 1.04, which is insignificant. Interpretation of the data and the correlational analysis suggests two things. First, as discussed earlier, modernization beyond a certain point does not lead to increased competitiveness. In the West, modernization and competitiveness are not correlated, suggesting the existence of a left-right cleavage that is immune from incremental changes in modernization beyond a certain threshold. Second, because Asian party systems remain weakly institutionalized, it is uncertain whether the social effects of modernization will translate into increased competition throughout the consolidation process. However, cultural and developmental state factors would preclude this possibility from happening to the extent that party pluralism exists in "Western liberal democracies." Total economic collapse could contribute to a political and ideological crisis which results in redefining the political institutions' boundaries of power. While

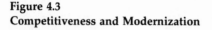

Figure 4.3
Competitiveness and Modernization

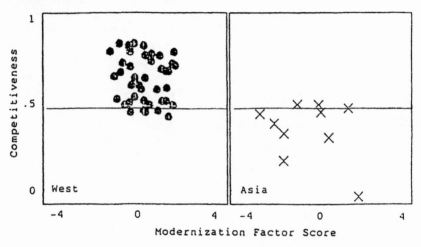

Modernization Factor Score

the data is inconclusive, exception Japan (which had years of elections even before the postwar period), the following case studies make a compelling argument for a non-liberal form of East Asian democracy. Japan's one-party dominant system and its moderate levels of competition appear a plausible model for the rest of East Asia.

ASIA VS. LIBERAL DEMOCRACY: DIFFERENT ESSENCE AND FORM?

This chapter synthesized the previous chapters on the cultural construction of politics and economy through the Asian Political Development Model. The cultural and economic construction of politics approach paints an exclusionary picture of Asian political development with elites orchestrating and maintaining their political system by excluding interests peripheral to the developmental states' survival. The driving mechanism of the model is socioeconomic change, brought forth by the successes of the developmental state. As developmental state policies led to a more complex economic system, the elites applied their newly acquired modern economic management ideology and traditional symbols to create state legitimacy. Internally, the relative power of the various actors changed from stage to stage depending on the role that they played in strengthening the developmental state. The strengthening of the developmental state, however, had a serious impact on the form of democracy in these countries. Given the essence of concentrated political power in Asian societies, generally one would expect a different institutional role for Asian political parties in contrast to Western counterparts. The context of the Asian Political Development Model provided the theoretical framework for analysis. In addition, the empowerment of the developmental elites meant that the political left in Asian societies is weak.

The descriptive statistical tests concerning the development of democracy in Asia confirmed several theoretical expectations. First, evidence from the statistical analysis suggests that a marked difference between Asian and Western nations' party-system competitiveness exists. Asian party systems were less competitive than their Western counterparts. Second, modernization overall did not lead to more political competition at the party-system level. For Western nations, the conclusion stated that beyond a certain threshold, incremental changes in modernization did not greatly affect competitiveness. While Asian societies currently experience rapid modernization, many still strive to reach the threshold. Also, the newness of many Asian transitions requires a qualification that the conclusions reached are tentative. However, the Japanese case, which experienced decades of sustained modernization and multiparty democracy, agrees with the Asian Political Development Model. In that political system, weakly institutionalized political opposition and a supporting role for elected officials indicate possibilities for other Asian nations. The Asian Development Model suggests such an outcome. In Chapters 5 through 7, the level of analysis changes from general and regional to case studies.

NOTES

1. The recent December 1997 election of Kim Dae Jung in South Korea represents a major anomaly to this argument. It remains to be seen, however, how effective he will be in reigning in the economic bureaucracy and dismantling the collusive culture between *chaebol* and bureaucracy. If Kim succeeds, his election represents a significant change in the direction of Korean democracy away from the Asian Political Development Model.

2. In the case of Japan's 1989 HR elections, the opposition had an opportunity to dismantle the LDP's (Liberal Democratic Party) political hegemony in response to the LDP-supported 3 percent consumption tax, which was greatly despised by the public. However, for structural reasons, namely the political weakness of the JSP (Japan Socialist Party) and the labor unions, which provided the JSP with financial support and even candidates, the JSP was unable to mount the kind of offensive necessary. The LDP, on the other hand, could expect large financial support from Keidanren (Organization of Economic Federation).

3. While many Asian leaders refrain from publicizing their past relations with Japanese imperialism for obvious nationalistic reasons, virtually all significant Asian leaders responsible for either developing or maintaining the developmental state, have a connection to Japan. Park Chung Hee, the founder of Korea's

developmental state worked with the Japanese occupation army in Manchukuo, and Marcos of the Phillippines was a known Japanese collaborator while Marshall Sarit of Thailand openly admired the prewar Japanese economy. Lee Kuan Yew was also a Japanese collaborator, and the present leader of Taiwan, Lee Teng-hui was trained at Kyoto Imperial University during World War II. Furthermore, both Park and Lee became fluent in Japanese, demonstrating the socialization effects of colonialism. The significance of these details is that Japan's economic and political system served as a model for many Asian states after World War II.

4. McCloud (1995: 282–83) notes that in many Southeast Asian nations, the legacy of struggles against colonialism legitimated the large role that the military plays in Asian politics. He also notes that there is little difference between the views of the military and civilian bureaucrats regarding economic modernization.

5. The military composition of the cabinet for Thailand, derived from various years of the *Political Handbook of the World* (Binghamton NY: CSA Publications) shows the following percentages of the cabinet held by military or former military officers: 1970, 46.1%; 1975, 14.3%; 1980, 44.4%; 1980, 28%; 1985, 19.7%; 1990, 17.1%; and 1995, 14.3%.

6. In the PRC, the military became an active participant in state-run enterprises, reflecting mission change in mission to survive. This new economic mission, however, recently led to increased personal aggrandizement among military personnel. President Jiang Zemin issued an internal directive concerning increased crime within the military according to the *Far Eastern Economic Review* 160 (31) (July 31, 1997): 13.

7. All developmental state–oriented authors place some, if not most, of the responsibility for high economic growth rates on the economic ministries.

8. For example, see *Asia Falling* (1998) by Callum Henderson, especially pp. 1–14.

9. The *chaebol* are Korean corporations, primarily privately owned within a network of family lineages that controls a vast percentage of domestic market share. The *zaibatsu* were similar entities which exist in Japan. During the U.S. occupation, many were dismantled but were restored during the Reverse Course of the occupation and subsequent years when policies for economic growth favored large horizontal firms. The *keiretsu* system in Japan now involves exclusive supplier contracting relations. Both *zaibatsu* and *keiretsu* share the common characteristic of concentrated economic power.

10. Japan topped the list with 245, followed by South Korea 33, Taiwan 10, Singapore 5, and Malaysia 3. The Philippines and Thailand did not have any corporations in the top 1,000.

11. For example, if two political parties compete in an election and there are one hundred seats to be filled and both parties capture fifty seats, then the fractionalization index for that election is: $F = [1 - ((0.5 \times 0.5) + (0.5 \times 0.5))]$ or $F = 0.50$. The greater the number of parties and the greater the dispersion of seats won by each party, the higher the fractionalization index.

12. For coding purposes, the *Political Handbook of the World*, ed. Arthur Banks, and *Political Parties of Asia and the Pacific* (1985), ed. Haruhiro Fukui, were used.

13. Differentiating the relative importance of either measure is impossible, so this approach was selected. It was consistently applied to all country-year elections, the basic unit of analysis. The result allows for the comparison of Asian competitiveness scores with Western systems. Furthermore, the competitiveness scores are correlated with modernization scores to see the differential effects of social processes on party-system development.

14. While many methods exist to measure socioeconomic modernization (such as averaging, boolean methods, or the use of single factors as proxies), factor analysis prevails over other approaches for two reasons. First, factor analysis standardizes the data in a Z-statistic. This means that each factor score is calculated based on the other data points. In other words, each factor score is relational to others. If the researcher employed only one indicator of modernization, the multifaceted processes escape measurement. Second, each component of modernization (i.e., urbanization, fertility rate, GNP per capita, and the percent of the labor force engaged in agriculture) receives a loading based on the relative contribution of that component to the modernization index. For more information about loadings and factor analysis in general see Rummel (1967) or Kim and Mueller (1978).

15. The data used to calculate modernization were obtained from the *World Tables*, published by the World Bank and *Asian Development Bank Annual Yearbook*, various issues.

16. It should be noted that the asterisks for Asian nations in the table are a result of lack of multiparty elections which were conducted in a reasonably fair environment. In most of these cases, there was no party competing against the governing party. The asterisks for the Western nations in Period One is not a statement about the presence or absence of democratic competition, but rather that modernization data was unobtainable for Germany, New Zealand, and Australia for those years.

17. Recent research by numerous scholars, including Ronald Inglehart (1977, 1990) suggests that this relative stability is breaking down with the introduction of a new cleavage of politics centering around postmaterialist values.

5

Japan and the Tale of Three Asian Societies

A Confucianist cultural heritage shared by the East Asian NICs bolsters managerial and state authority and thus undercuts oppositional labor movements through its emphasis on hierarchy, cooperation, industriousness, paternalism, and the subordination of the individual to the state.

Frederic C. Deyo (1987: 5)

Voters and their proclivities for pork barrel politics remained unchanged [for the 1996 elections]. They continued to think of politicians as lobbyists to whom businessmen and interest groups must turn to win favors from the bureaucracy. Policy debates that had been expected failed to materialize. Personality contests remained as strong as ever. Organizing and mobilizing votes turned out to be the key to success, as always. And rather than opening a path toward a two-party system, in which regular changes in government would be possible, voters once again "bought the stocks" of the so-called *seiken tanto kabushiki kaisha* (the company incorporated to run the government)—namely, the Liberal Democratic Party.

Sam Jameson (1997: 1)

WEAVING THE CASE STUDIES TOGETHER

The three cases examine political development in three countries—Japan, South Korea, and Thailand—with two objectives. The case studies show the applicability of the Asian Political Development Model to each country. In examining political development, two things will be done. First, the case studies explore the effects of Western penetration on political development. Collectively, the model more closely fits Japan and Korea than Thailand, showing the effect of globalization by compressing the model's three stages. As the latest modernizer, Thailand displays a greater degree of simultaneity of the model's three stages, since international market influences compress political development (as to time and space). Second, globalization pressures and their effects on the model's future and the configuration of legitimacy needs are addressed.

The chapter's second purpose is to show the cultural construction of economics and politics within nations. This exercise helps in providing details to the general model. It addresses how each nation's elites use political culture to construct political and economic systems. By situating each case within the context of its culture, the historical context disputes Western assumptions about political development. This chapter compares all three countries' trajectory of political development and ties them back to the general model developed in the preceding chapter.

The logic in choosing Japan, South Korea, and Thailand as case studies is twofold. First, these cases represent an ideal test for the Asian Political Development Model because of the development's differential timing. In each country, the stages of the model took place at different historical time periods. Thus, Japan experienced the first stage in the late 1800s and early 1900s, while Korea's experience with the first stage took place in the 1950s to 1970s. Meanwhile, Thailand experienced that stage during the 1950s to 1980s. Second, each nation experienced a set of unique historical influences and endogenous conditions (including leadership) that led to differences in political development. These endogenous conditions and historical events are listed in Table 5.1.

JAPAN: SETTING THE STAGE

Japan provides an interesting testing ground for the Asian Development Model because it was the first country outside the Western world to become fully industrialized. Throughout the history of modern Japan, the main theme is the simultaneous desire to modernize and indigenize and the resulting political conflict. The two appear mutually exclusive because modernization is thought to equate with Westernization. Indigenization is associated with the conservation of Japanese traditionalism.

Yet, in Japan's long history, constant tension between the pull of traditional culture and the push for modernization is a dynamic around which political development revolves. The Japanese elite's construction of society embodies this dynamic. The pull of traditionalism and the push of modernization led to a hybridized outcome. What emerged in Japan is a blend of modernity and tradition—a carefully constructed so-

Table 5.1
Salient Endogenous Events Affecting Political Development Trajectory

---

Japan

Promulgation of the Meiji Emperor (1868)

The Emergence of *Zaibatsu* (1868–1945)

The Rise of Fascism (1920–1945)

U.S. Occupational Reforms and MacArthur Constitution (1945–1952)

The Rule of Prime Ministers Yoshida Shigeru (1946–1947 and 1948–1953) and Ikeda Hayato (1960–1964)

The Disintegration of the LDP (1992–1993)

South Korea

The Japanese Occupation (1895–1905)

The Korean War and Its Aftermath (1949–1952)

The Ascendancy of Park Chung Hee (1962)

The Promulgation of the Yushin Constitution (1972)

The Rise of the Chaebol (1950–1985)

The Election of Kim Dae Jung (1997)

Thailand

The Young Turk Military Intervention (1932)

Collaboration with Japanese Imperialism (1940–1945)

Marshal Sarit Thanarat (1957–1963) and Thanom Kittikachorn (1963–1973)

Thailand's Arrival in the Global Economy (1980–present)

---

cial, economic, and political system that relied on both modern and traditional cultural symbols. The Japanese versus Western dichotomy reflects a significant problem of identity in political development. While addressed by Japanese leaders in the past, it continues as a concern for modern Japanese historians who study political development (Reischauer 1983). For contemporary students of Japanese politics, the modern-tradition context encompasses the political and economic system. In many ways, the Japanese economic and political systems resemble the West's modernity but in many ways remain traditional (Johnson 1995, van Wolferen 1989; Reischauer 1983). This case study focuses on this dynamic and how it affected the democratic consolidation process. The other two case studies, South Korea and Thailand, will also illustrate the fallacy that discarded traditions were replaced by modern Weberian legal-rational systems.

CREATING THE DEVELOPMENTAL STATE: TOKUGAWA AND EARLY MEIJI PERIOD

Japanese feudalism became entrenched in the 1600s after a period of consolidation during the fifteenth and sixteenth centuries. During the two centuries prior to 1863, military men with administrative skill rose to the top of the power structure in feudal Japan. In 1603, the military leader Tokugawa Ieyasu became the *shogun* or de facto military ruler of Japan and founded the Tokugawa house. While the shogun, the supreme military ruler, was nominally responsible to the emperor who resided in Kyoto, he exercised significant national political and administrative control from Edo (later known as Tokyo). Beneath the shogun's authority were regional warlords, known as *daimyo*, who were responsible to the central authority (*bakufu*) in Edo. Some daimyo—the *fudai*—were Tokugawa vassals by virtue of *sui jolis* who participated in the governance of the nation. However, the *tozama*, as semiautonomous lords, did not participate in national affairs but controlled local affairs.[1]

During the Tokugawa Period, a slow progression from customs-based authority to one of abstract legal codes was taking place independent of the West's influence (Hall 1968: 32–33, 35). Political life during this period reflected highly localized characteristic, with the samurai—assigned to respective daimyo—keeping a watchful eye over social order. As social order became entrenched and violent conflict among the daimyo ceased to exist, the samurai lost their swords—in form but not in spirit—and they integrated into the existing political system (Beasley 1995: 6). The samurai began to participate in matters such as administering districts, providing a system of communication by being messengers and serving as garrison guards. Many samurai formed the core of an emergent bureaucracy and came to assume a position of hierarchical superiority over the masses. However, high unemployment levels contradicted their greater-than-commoners' social status and created an income-to-status discrepancy. The samurai as a warrior class ceased to exist, but the spirit of the warrior lived on in the post-Tokugawa Period. From Confucianism came the ethics of public behavior. Loyalty and honor, as seen in the reformulated *Bushido* (samurai warrior) code, and the spiritual concern for the next life came from Shinto and Buddhism (Beasley 1995: 16–17).

Nationally, Confucian and Buddhist principles of loyalty and piety reinforced symbolic appeals to the emperor as a unifying political force. Loyalty to the emperor became part of a moral code and allowed religion to play an important role in the construction of early Japanese society by inspiring the idea that the emperor's realm consisted only of the spiritual realm during the Tokugawa Period. Hall (1968: 31) states, "Granted that historically the Tokugawa house first grasped power and then set to work to exalt the prestige of the emperor, the fact remains that the shogun subordinated himself to the emperor." Educational institutions, of the early 18th century to 1867, emphasized the teachings of Confucius (Yoshida 1931: 27) to re-enforce a moral yet secular Confucian code. For example, beginning in the 18th century, the highly literate members of the samurai class applied Confucian principles to their administrative capacities. Intellectuals reified the primacy of Buddhism, Shinto, and Confucianism. They laid the seeds for Japanese nationalism by pointing to its unique embodiment of a unified moral code created from these three philosophies. Later, this unique moral code proved a valuable source for social, economic, and political construction by the elites.

Suddenly, the insular political life in Japan ended. Commodore Matthew Perry's visit to Edo in 1853 marked a major turning point in the political fortunes of the Tokugawa shogunate (see Reischauer 1995: 79–80 and Simone and Feraru 1995: 43–47 for brief summaries). That ended Japanese isolation and alerted the Japanese political elites to the perilous effects of isolation. Before Perry's arrival, news about the industrial revolution, Russian advancement into the Kurils, and the fate of China had all filtered in through the Dutch trading post at Nagasaki. Through Nagasaki, Japan maintained its Western connection during the *Sakoku-rei* era (closed country policy) which began in 1639. In 1854, the United States gained access to landing rights. The Treaty of Kanagawa (1854) gave Americans landing rights at Shimoda and Hakodate. From the period before the *sakoku* era, the Japanese simultaneously revered and reviled Western influence, including Christianity and technology. During isolation, the Japanese elite perceived Western ideas as a threat to social order, but they realized the prudence of maintaining a flow of information about Western developments. The elites monitored European developments through Nagasaki, where a cadre of specialists in "Dutch learning" kept the shogunate abreast of major political, economic, and technological changes.

The appearance of Perry's "black ships" sent shock waves throughout the political establishment. Already experiencing political unrest beginning in the 1830s, the shogunate confronted a series of socioeconomic problems. In particular, the shogunate faced acute budgetary dislocations, continued restlessness of the samurai class, and political battles over scarce resources. With the leadership of the Tokugawa shogunate in chaos, in 1865 the Choshu and Satsuma *hans* (clans) succeeded in modernizing their military through direct dealings with the West. These *hans*, previously enemies, entered into a secret compact to overthrow the shogunate in March 1866. The stage was set for new political leadership that would ultimately lead to the consolidation of political authority, marking the beginning of modern Japan. By 1868, Japan entered the first stage of the Asian Development Model.

Under the slogan *sonno joi* ("Revere the Emperor, Repel the Barbarians"), the Satsuma *han* contingent seized power through a coup on January 3, 1868. Shortly afterwards, the new leaders restored the political authority of the Meiji Emperor. While the new elites' original plan sought to restore the political authority of the Japanese emperor, soon external pressures for the need to modernize Japan's antiquated administrative and economic systems dominated elite political discourse. The multifaceted modernization program of Japan drew from the entirety of European civilization (including the arts, customs, educational systems, scientific systems, and its political systems). In the 1870s and 1880s, the Japanese government initiated a period of rapid social, political, and economic transformation from feudalism to an industrial state based on a directive linkage model. Through Dutch learning missions, such as the Iwakura Mission, Japanese intellectuals and statesmen observed, first hand, European societies. Japanese intellectual circles, such as the Meirokusha (Meiji Six Group), acquired important social, political, and economic information and debated their usefulness and applicability for Japan. Particularly influential were the writings on science, philosophy, and modernization of Yukichi Fukuzawa (a Japanese counterpart to Alexis de Tocqueville) who later visited Europe and founded Japan's most prestigious private university—Keio University).

The initial period of modernization involved "the import[ation] of Western culture on an extensive scale" (Nitobe 1931: 27). Skilled political leadership of the time played a pivotal role in the success of Japanese modernization. The emerging political elite consisted of Satsuma and Choshu *han* members or those of the imperial household with close ties to the two clans. Power sharing was coordinated through Sanjo Sanetomi and Iwakura Tomomi, both court nobles, and a small selected group of young elite samurai. Modernization involved restructuring the educational system along the French model, importing Western dress, and adopting American and European technology. Politically, however, two camps existed. One camp, the Meirokusha, sought to revolutionize Japan through the wholesale adoption of Western value systems. Other political thinkers, like Motoda Eifu, favored the more socially conservative approach of adopting Western technological expertise but maintaining a more traditional Confucian-based political system (Shively 1965: 197).

Ultimately, political practicality mitigated the two extremes. On one hand, the Japanese political elite introduced Western culture to the upper-middle class, but simultaneously Western culture was highly alien to most Japanese. By the late 1870s, the pendulum for adopting Western cultural ideas lost its momentum and a more practical approach appeared which incorporated traditional Shinto, Buddhism, and Confucianism. The latter two, while imported from China via Korea, were reintegrated into Japanese national life during the Meiji Restoration. Umaji Kaneko (1931: 56) observed that

Confucianism, a sort of idealism with a practical moral code as its essential core, had become so perfectly integrated with the national character that the Japanese people were oblivious to its foreign origin. It is true to say therefore, that the imposing task involved in the Restoration of 1868 was founded upon the Confucian spirit. Furthermore, Confucian thought, in its idealistic form, is no doubt the basic spirit of the Japanese race.

Even with Western learning, Kaneko argued that Confucian idealism operated "below the surface" and held an "impregnable position" in Japanese life. He asserts that only "more superficial aspects of Western civilization which did not conflict with the Buddhist or Confucian spirit" were imported (Kaneko 1931: 57).

The Meiji Restoration did not significantly alter the traditionally hierarchical structure of power in Japanese society, but enhanced it and used it as an instrument for national integration. The Meiji Restoration set the stage for traditional Japan to operate in modernity. As Huntington (1996) stated, modernization strengthens traditional values in a rapidly modernizing society. During most of the Meiji Period up to 1900, the elites from the imperial household (the emperor and the Privy Council) competed against Choshu and Satsuma samurai bureaucrats and a small but modernizing military.

During the Meiji era, beginning with the 1880s, a movement toward political reform under the rubric of Japanese traditionalism took hold. The primary model for political reform had been Germany and England. England's democracy and Germany's statist model appealed to the Japanese elite inclined toward a strong state under elite leadership of senior bureaucrats, the imperial household, and the military. Reforms in education, culminating with the Imperial Rescript on Education (1890), enshrined a moral education based on Confucian principles that fostered education for state building. Although as early as 1873, government strictly regulated shipping as the government became increasingly involved in industrial production through an import substitution policy. Commerce, considered a dirty profession in Confucianism and still in its infancy, however, did not attract the best and the brightest of the samurai. Finance Minister Matsukata Masayoshi began a process of privatization in 1881 that led to the state's disposal of unprofitable industries (Beasley 1995: 107). These factories found their way into familiar *zaibatsu* hands including Mitsui and Mitsubishi. This was the beginning of an

enduring partnership between government and business, with bureaucrats who managed state enterprises entering into the business world.
Not until 1889 did Japan adopt a modern constitution, modeled after
the Bismarckian constitution. Emperor Mutsuhito bestowed the constitution as an imperial gift to the people reflecting the symbolic concept
of "*tenno*"—a deity bestowed from the heavens. The Meiji constitution
emphasized a strong central government that consolidated the elite's
power over Japan. Some argue that it led to Japan's future fascism (Hall
1968: 56–58). Hall notes that nationalism and the lack of opposition in
the newly created Diet (national assembly) was caused by a hidden "inner psychology of a people struggling for preeminence in a hostile
world" (Hall 1968: 59). Democracy without opposition, religious freedom
without a plurality of religions, and freedoms which exist in theory but
are circumscribed by social and political convention represented reality
for modernizing Japan.

Although the constitution protected private religious freedom, Shinto
became publicly associated with nationalism and civic duty (Hardacre
1989: 31). Religious rituals, symbols, and the emperor system simultaneously consolidated the Japanese elites' power. Simultaneously, they
gave the populace an identifiable nationality to buttress their traditional
orientations in dealing with a rapidly modernizing nation. In particular,
the role of the emperor as an absolute and sacred monarch embodied
the essence of the *kokutai* (organic state) by uniting people nationally with
an "us" versus "them" *Weltanschauung*.

However, the constitution contained more than traditionalism. In
many ways it enshrined a modern approach to government by embracing modern institutional forms of government, including a national assembly. The newly created national assembly, the Diet, embodied this
peculiar combination. It emerged out of a deeply socially conservative
era and possessed only advisory power. In many ways, both the Diet
and the constitution could not transcend traditionalism into modernity
because of their unique political context. In practice, the constitution and
Diet served the government's economic, political, and social modernization plan (Johnson 1995: 103–4; van Wolferen 1990; Hardacre 1989).

JAPAN RISES: IMPERIALISM AND THE
CONSOLIDATION OF THE BUREAUCRATIC-
AUTHORITARIAN STATE

Yukichi Fukuzawa, a leading 19th-century intellectual, was concerned
about the preservation of national sovereignty—China's loss of autonomy loomed large in the minds of the Japanese elite (Craig 1968: 118–
19). To "conquer the barbarians," Fukuzawa placed inordinate effort on
the eradication of traditional Confucianism through education. For him,

Confucianism was destructive to the necessary adoption of Western technology and knowledge. Over time, however, Fukuzawa—as if to mirror the changing undercurrent of Japanese intellectual thought—became increasingly acceptant of Japanese nationalism as part of the modernization effort. The emerging nationalism embodied many traditional sources of authority and solidified national unity contrasting sharply with the dissensus of party politics in Western (modern) democracies. To him, the emperor's leadership represented an apolitical and neutral competence for managing state affairs in contrast to the various *hans'* factional interests. By 1881, Fukuzawa lost belief in Western notions of natural and universal rights so imbedded in Western classical liberalism. Subsequently, he recognized that no functional equivalent of a moral code could be found in the traditional world that would be applicable in modernity. While he never resolved many contradictions seen in transitional societies, the historical development of his ideas illustrated some complex issues elites must address. This said, this historical story illustrates the plasticity of culture—its ability to promote modernization and protect traditional approaches.

While Fukuzawa believed in science, rational thought, and the need for Japan's modernization, the elites looked to traditionalism to find the normative basis for national construction in a modern era. Craig (1968: 147) states that the essence of the emperor came to manifest a modern reincarnated Japanese morality in the face of Western values. Socioeconomic modernization during the Meiji Period and beyond did not lead to the wholesale adoption of Western values. Traditionalism needed recreation in modernity for society to maintain an authentic Japanese identity.[2]

The political thoughts of Fukuzawa also showed how he, like Japan, emerged as products of traditionalism and modernity. For example, he believed that the partisanship of the Diet undermined nation-building and that the imperial household and the emperor embodied more than rules and laws—the essence of Japanese strength. In many ways, Fukuzawa was a renaissance Confucianist. He wanted to take the central Confucian principles and spirit and apply them toward modernization.[3] Fukuzawa, a complex intellectual giant from a minor samurai background who was influenced by Confucian thought and an understanding of Western science and philosophy, represented a microcosm of the Japanese paradox of modernity and traditionalism. Japan was becoming increasingly modern, but in many ways remained very traditional, just like Fukuzawa.

A series of developments in the 1870 to 1890 period suggested that the initial efforts at modernization and nation-building were successful. First, the establishment of political parties in the 1890 Diet elections and the end of extraterritoriality both followed the adoption of the Meiji Constitution. In the countryside, sporadic peasant uprisings occurred up to 1873, but gradually the local rural areas were incorporated into the national integration process. Local administration increasingly bureaucratized and consolidated in spite of the persistence of local traditional values. Lastly, the period of 1890 to 1910 witnessed a major change in Japanese social and political life based on its emergence as a global economic and military power. Its modernized military defeated China and Russia in the Sino-Japanese War (1894–1895) and the Russo-Japanese War (1904–1905) signaling Japan's arrival on the global stage. Domestically, the wars further unified the elites and cemented the mass' allegiance to elite-led modernization.

These two wars catapulted Japan into the ranks of modern nations with empires. These wars appeared to represent the fruits of nation-building and the desirability of a hierarchically structured Japanese elite system. Until 1890, modernizing governmental and political institutions to survive in modernity while maintaining a traditional core represented the elites' primary focus.[4] Both of these tasks involved a concerted effort to import Western ideas and indigenize them with traditional Japanese values. A shift toward balancing planned economic growth and political stability became the new focus of the state as modernization unleashed political and social conflict. The two wars facilitated the emergence of heavy industry—machinery and military weaponry in particular—which received significant government interest on the premise of national security. It laid the stage for significant government involvement in economic affairs in the late Meiji Period, representing a major shift from the previous move to privatize industry in the 1880s. The overall impact of the movement toward government involvement was the establishment of the foundation of the industrial state as we know it today.

During the late Meiji Period and the early Taisho Period (1912–1926), political power was in the joint custody of a clique known as the *genro*. The *genro* consisted of the elder guardian leaders from the Meiji Restoration period who exercised inordinate influence on politics. Many belonged to the Choshu and Satsuma *han*. As a social class, the *genro* permeated all avenues of political power. Table 5.2 lists some prominent leaders and their respective *hans* at the time of the Meiji Restoration. Many of them later became important junior figures of the *genro* class.

Many of the *genro*, as the modernizing element in Japanese society, occupied important positions in commerce, political parties, the military, and the bureaucracy. Their importance derived from official positions and social connections based on bloodlines and a vast network of alliances that operated in the background. Beyond the primary position that the *genro* played in the cabinet, they also participated in politics by organizing the first political parties. Two political parties, formerly the Jiyuto (Liberal Party) which became the Rikken Seiyukai in 1900, and the

Table 5.2
Major Leaders of the Meiji Restoration and Their Respective Clans

Name	Years	Affiliation
Sanjo Sanetomi	(1837–1891)	Imperial Court
Iwakura Tomomi	(1825–1883)	Imperial Court
Okubo Toshimichi	(1830–1878)	Satsuma
Terashima Munenori	(1833–1893)	Satsuma
Godai Tomoatsu	(1835–1885)	Satsuma
Saigo Takamori	(1827–1877)	Satsuma
Kuroda Kiyotaka	(1840–1900)	Satsuma
Matsukata Masayoshi	(1835–1924)	Satsuma
Takasugi Shinsaku	(1839–1867)	Choshu
Kido Koin	(1833–1877)	Choshu
Omura Masujiro	(1824–1869)	Choshu
Ito Harubumi	(1841–1909)	Choshu
Inoue Kaoru	(1835–1915)	Choshu
Yamagata Aritomo	(1838–1922)	Choshu
Hirosawa Saneomi	(1833–1871)	Choshu
Itagaki Taisuke	(1837–1919)	Tosa
Goto Shojiro	(1837–1897)	Tosa
Fukuoka Kotei	(1835–1919)	Tosa
Sakamoto Ryoma	(1835–1867)	Tosa
Eto Shimpei	(1834–1874)	Hizen
Okuma Shigenobu	(1838–1922	Hizen
Soejima Taneomi	(1828–1905)	Hizen
Oki Takato	(1832–1899)	Hizen
Okamoto Shonan	(1809–1869)	Kumamoto
Inoue Kowashi	(1844–1895)	Kumamoto
Katsu Kaishu	(1823–1899)	Tokugawa bakufu
Yuri Kimimasa	(1829–1909)	Fukui

Source: Hall (1970): 268.

Rikken Kaishinto (Constitutional Progressive Party) which, in turn, became the Rikken Seiyukai (Constitutional Friends Association), closely integrated with the *genro*. The latter two, founded by the influential Ito Hirobumi (of the Choshu *han*), and Rikken Seiyukai, founded by Okuma Shigenobu (of the Hizen *han*) who left the government earlier, represented the *hans'* political action vehicle. A "guided democracy" existed throughout the period of "Taisho Democracy" in the 1920s. It placed a heavy premium upon the "virtue and the wisdom of the ruling elite"

(Scalapino 1968: 251–52) and acted as patron-client political machines servicing the elites' political ambitions while simultaneously preserving and nurturing the organic state.[5]

The *genro* set the political pace leading up to "Taisho Democracy," and only their departure brought forth questions of political succession. Peter Duus (1968: 244) states that the *genro* failed because they did not plan for succession. He states that not a "single group of political heirs capable of succeeding to their mantle of prestige or their extensive personal connections" formed. From 1920 to 1932, party politics reflected the new atmosphere of the emerging democracy and a diffusion of political power. Suffrage was expanded by lowering tax requirements gradually and in 1925, political pressures resulted in the institution of universal manhood suffrage. Then socioeconomic change caused by industrialization increased the size of the restless proletariat. In the *genro*'s place, a variety of weak party leaders led the nation. These factors contributed to a decentralization of power and pluralism in party politics. Simultaneously, however, the early attempts to create national identity by the manipulation of cultural symbols and the drive toward modernization appeared too successful and by that legitimized the system's ideology and led to a violent conservative reaction.

Evolving mass democracy of the Taisho Period contributed to the non-party elites' manipulation of nationalistic symbols. Growing nationalism derived its fuel from the nexus of traditionalism and modernity. Modern mass politics in a traditional system, absent liberalism, combined with an increased concentration of political power in an autonomous military—which named its own ministers to the cabinet—set the stage for fascism in the 1930s.[6] Political power drifted to the bureaucracy and the military while political parties struggled to gain hold over important issues, including the budgetary processes of the military. From 1895 to 1922, the military was under the leadership of Marshal Yamagata of the Choshu *han* and under him, Tanin and Yohan (1934: 175) argue, the military had significant control over the imperial household. By the late 1920s, division among the Japanese political elite emerged, reflected in the vacuum created by the departure of the old *genro* who previously held the system together. The new rivalry pitted a new breed of politicians. These politicians sought to expand the Diet's power against the bureaucracy and increasingly powerful military. Within each political party, various politicians were far from united; they played off various remnants of the *genro* class, the military, the imperial household, and the bureaucracy by creating powerful personal networks.

Following the Universal Manhood Suffrage in May 1925, the Diet passed the highly antidemocratic Peace Preservation Act thereby making extreme leftist activities, including the organization of Marxist-inspired strikes, illegal and punishable. Feuding political parties representing remarkably similar nationalistic visions whipped up personal acrimony for public consumption. The establishment of universal manhood suffrage in 1925 did not lead to the vocal left's increased political power. The left remained a divided entity that fought over ideological lines (Duus 1968: 247). Public disdain for parliamentary conflicts and radical imported revolutionary movements, coupled with effective socialization by the state, made the Marxist ideology of class conflict unattractive to the masses. Not only did vocal leftism represent an impracticality in a political system controlled by the power elite, but traditional notions of public virtue made these parties unattractive alternatives. In Taisho Democracy, political elites never questioned the morality of nationalism, but instead the method of enhancing the *kokutai* (organic state) occupied public discourse. Therefore, any progressive democratization in the parties or party system was nullified by a highly conservative and centralized military, the bureaucracy, and the imperial household. Essentially, the debate involved technique rather than policy. Beasley (1995: 138) states

Since policy differences were comparatively unimportant in parliamentary life, and success depended more on striking deals than on debates, decisions, even by party cabinets, tended to be bargains made behind closed doors, not always in accordance with election pledges. Party loyalty was a rare virtue, office being put before principle.

Ultimately, the contradictions between the reality of conflict in modern institutionalized parliamentary politics and the tradition-based myths of the organic state became a powerful propaganda issue for nationalists. These nationalists used the notion of an organic state for political purposes.

The Rikken Seiyukai (Constitutional Liberal Party), a political party founded by Ito Harubumi (one of the Meiji era *genro*) dominated the party system from 1900 to 1937. Political parties during this time held a junior status to the military and the bureaucracy. Organized originally by the *genro*, patron-client loyalties guided these parties' behavior. They did not represent social cleavages, but naked elite ambitions and factionalism within parties remained rife. The Rikken Seiyukai was the majority party in Japan's prewar experiment with party government. It held a plurality or majority of the Diet seats in eight of fourteen elections from 1902 to 1937. The major rivals during that time were Kenseihonto (Orthodox Constitutional National Party), which later became Rikken Kokuminto (Constitutional National Party), from 1902 to 1912, and then Rikken Doshikai (Constitutional Like-Minded Thinkers' Association) and later Kenseikai (Constitutional Government Association), from 1915 to 1924. From 1928 to 1937, the Rikken Minseito (Constitutional Democratic

Party) and Rikken Seiyukai battled in a highly fractionalized and competitive two-way race for a majority of the Diet seats. The major distinguishing characteristic of these Taisho Democracy political parties consisted of their *han* affiliations and their maintenance of a nationalistic and conservative political outlook. Excepting the Japanese Communist Party, the ideological gamut was relatively indistinguishable. The parties at the time possessed a traditional and conservative ideological skewness. In other words, political development of parties in early-20th-century Japan failed to account for the emerging social cleavages within a party system. Increased labor instability, domestic calls for an expansion of Japanese imperialism abroad, and a sense of xenophobia at home clearly undermined the development of liberal democracy. The conservatives' policy response consisted of increasing the state's coercive capacity through the *Kempeitai* (military police) and the *Naimusho* (Ministry of Home Affairs). These two institutions of social control monitored the citizens' behavior and shut down illegal left-wing activities.

Japan's colonial success overseas fueled the demise of democracy at home and an atrophying of political institutions and civil society by fanning nationalism and increasing the power of conservative politicians and military officers. Overseas, the establishment of the puppet state, Manchukuo fostered militarism and aggression in China. In the latter half of the 1930s, the military came to play an instrumental role in the production processes. Large *zaibatsu* firms like Mitsui and Mitsubishi benefitted financially from Japan's increasing empire, as the sources of raw materials and markets increased. By 1941, with party politics reduced to an organization known as the *Taisei Yokusankai* (Imperial Rule Assistance Association), the power elite mobilized for war under the joint leadership of the military, bureaucracy, and corporate elite. Prime Minister Tojo Hideki represented the military, the dominant actor in the political system. The 1930s Japanese political economy consisted of a symbiotic relationship among the *zaibatsu*, the military, and the bureaucrats. Political parties were merely window dressing and pawns in the struggle for power among elites.

POSTWAR JAPAN: RISING FROM THE ASHES AND RECONSTRUCTING LEGITIMACY

The end of World War II and the subsequent emergence of the Cold War and the liberal–free trade regime affected the political development of Japan in previously unfathomable ways. This section of the chapter covers Japanese post–World War II political development beginning with the American occupation. The primary focus of this section is on Japanese culture, the developmental state (especially the role of elites), and the contemporary party system resulting from the interaction between the first two.

Three characteristics of post–World War II identify the essence of Japanese politics:

- the national government's promotion of economic growth through an alliance between the bureaucratic elite, political elite, and corporate elite by focusing on producer needs
- the use of economic policy for creating a conservative political order which contributes to high levels of political stability
- the cultural construction of economic, political, and social space by evoking traditional cultural values

These three attributes fit within the general pattern of the Asian Political Development Model in which economic growth operates as the engine driving change. Culture facilitates the transfer from one stage to the next when elites re-create traditions to manage the pull of the past and the push of modernity. The three characteristics, mentioned above, remain salient today although altered in form over time to fit the context of the times.

The pattern of Japanese politics, as described above, results from a continuity with the prewar Japanese system and from reforms initiated during the occupation. Japan—a nation that for so long prided itself on, and developed nationalism based on, historically continuous sovereignty—experienced military occupation for the first time during 1945 to 1952. American-based liberal democracy, embodying both procedural and substantive aspects, clashed with the nominally democratic Japanese system. The occupiers originally sought to make Japan a democracy by changing the political and economic system. They wanted to create a more level playing field with a deconcentration of economic and political power.[7] American reformers wanted more than procedural democracy; they wanted to change Japanese society at all levels. New political institutions, a pro-democratic political culture, and a more individualistic belief system required the dismantling of traditional symbols. Idealistic Supreme Command Allied Powers (SCAP) administrators believed that a democratic spirit must replace the prewar democratic facade. The occupation of Japan, the first of its kind in history, sought to democratize the country—both procedurally and substantively. Democratizing Japan, as a social engineering experiment, involved the transplantation of American constitutionalism and values to a nation whose elite core possessed a very different view of democracy. The Japanese elites operated under a very different belief; they believed that they could manufacture the consent of the governed through traditional culture.

Political and economic democratization reflected the core ideology of the occupation. Occupation directives came from SCAP headquarters at the Dai-Ichi Building. A large group of New Dealers headed by Colonel Charles Kades, some conservatives, and General Douglas MacArthur designed occupation policy. After the initial disarmament of the Japanese military, SCAP worked to democratize and economically rebuild Japan. They remained cognizant of American values, but also worked within the context of Japanese traditionalism. All SCAP authorities agreed on democratizing Japan, but exactly what that meant remained a point of contention between the New Dealers and the conservatives. The former wanted to reengineer Japan, while conservatives remained uneasy about dramatic economic change.

The democratization of Japan required the breakup of the *zaibatsu* that represented a significant concentration of economic power. Dismantling the *zaibatsu*, to create economic democracy, would create the economic bases for democracy. Destroying Japan's engine of economic growth, incidentally, runs counter to the research on the economic prerequisites of democracy (Moore 1966; Lipset 1959).

Economic deconcentration, to some occupiers, provided reassurance for peace. Throughout modern Japanese history, corporations colluded with the military and bureaucrats to sustain an undemocratic system. Corporations also exerted undue influence by participating in a collusive arrangement to monopolize economic power and to manipulate political power by providing funds to favored candidates and parties. By supporting the war effort abroad and contributing to legitimize a national security state, government rewarded corporations. The government suppressed unions and the political left.

American ideology of upward mobility and an aversion to deeply entrenched hierarchical social order made it necessary to dismantle these economic conglomerates. Many New Dealers who dominated the early years of the occupation believed that extreme concentrations of wealth would undermine democracy. Simultaneously, however, the plan to make a more egalitarian nation of small capitalists ran counter to Japan's historical quest for economic growth. In the past, the big *zaibatsu* drove economic growth. Can a nation—which emerged into the modern economic world by concerted government efforts and concentrated capital—rebuild itself into a nation of small and medium-sized capitalist entities? To what extent can a hierarchical society, with its rigid social caste system reflected in its economic and political construction, really become more democratic?

Additional questions about the tone of the occupation existed. Political reforms emanated from the top, again. This time, however, the impetus came from the SCAP headquarter's top levels, rather than from the *genro* or emperor. To what extent should Americans with Western values direct democratic consolidation? The American occupiers, despite the reservation of the more conservative administrators chose initially to work toward substantive democracy by leveling the economic and political playing field. Several political and economic reforms highlighted the move to break down the concentrated power, including land reform and the permission to establish independent labor unions and allow them to organize strikes. Enforcement of antitrust legislation dismantled many *zaibatsu*, and the removal of corporate and political elites who contributed to Japan's war-making capacity created greater political pluralism during the first stage of the occupation.

Political and cultural changes were also an important element of the occupation. Political changes involved adopting a new and more democratic constitution, while cultural changes involved introducing the Japanese to a more individualistic orientation to life through American mass culture. The democratic context for political changes enshrined in the occupation-drafted constitution resembled the U.S. constitution. The 1947 constitution brought sweeping changes in the rules and procedures for the nation's political institutions and the relationships among them. Correcting the flaws inherent in the Meiji Constitution reflected the occupiers' desire to craft democratic institutions. The highlights of the reforms included the weakening and remaking of the emperor as symbol of a secular state; abolishing the House of Peers, formerly based on peerage and nobility; making the popularly elected National Assembly the supreme organ of the state; adopting women's legal and political rights, including the right to vote; and inscribing the controversial Article 9 in the constitution, which made it unconstitutional to establish and maintain a military and to declare war.[8]

The occupation's initial phase went to extraordinary lengths translating the tenants of procedural democracy into substantive democracy. The political purge sought to remove senior leaders who shared an antidemocratic orientation with a new generation of leaders. SCAP removed politicians who collaborated with the wartime elite removed from power and prohibited them from participating in political life. SCAP released journalists and leftists from prison and legalized the Communist Party. Furthermore, American censors monitored the media and censored anything that condoned militarism or nationalism including personal correspondence.

Beginning in 1947, the Reverse Course altered the trajectory of Japanese political development forever. In a series of stunning reversals, SCAP shifted its focus from democratization to rebuilding the economy. Previously, Japan depended heavily on U.S. aid. The government spent large amounts on social projects and other bureaucratic work, while budget deficits threatened the health of the economy. Joseph Dodge, a Detroit banker, advised SCAP to restructure Japan's public finance system by increasing interest rates and balancing the budget. George Kennan chimed in and warned that the New Deal policies abetted a communist takeover. SCAP ended its encouragement of unions and leftists.

The Reverse Course also reempowered the bureaucrats, corporate elites, and wartime politicians. The *zaibatsu*, previously targeted with antitrust action, regained their economic freedom. New SCAP pragmatists saw the *zaibatsu* and political conservatives as instrumental for a stronger Japan. The results of the October 1952 elections show the cumulative effect of these reversals. Almost 40 percent of those politicians formerly banned from office-holding were reinstated to the Diet (Johnson 1982: 46).

Despite the American rhetoric of creating a democratic society, even before the Reverse Course, the Americans formulated occupation policies and the Japanese bureaucrats and politicians implemented them. (See Johnson 1982, chapters 6 and 7.) From the perspective of crafting democracy, using the existing Japanese bureaucratic structure decreased the prospects for genuine democratic reforms. Fundamental political reform required a transformation of Japanese society into one with a liberal philosophical base. Japanese politicians and bureaucrats, however, did not share American liberalism. Whenever Japanese politicians and bureaucrats implemented American-issued directives, they altered them to their benefit. However, SCAP should not be faulted for relying on existing Japanese bureaucrats and politicians. The sheer magnitude of the occupation required MacArthur and SCAP to use the existing bureaucratic apparatus for economic and political reforms. Besides, if SCAP used more direct administrative procedures, the Japanese would have believed that the new system constituted exclusively foreign intent.

Bureaucrats emerged relatively unscathed from the purge. The occupation's decision to purge other elites and to use the existing bureaucracy to implement change strengthened the bureaucrats' power. The emperor, a traditional symbol, was recreated and became a secular "symbol of unity of the Japanese people." The occupation relied on modern and traditional symbols, just like the Meiji Restoration.

The occupation successfully established the outlines of procedural democracy as enshrined in the constitution, but it did not alter the underlying power structure. It failed to create a more substantive democracy because it relied too much on traditionalism and the *regime ancien*. While the MacArthur constitution embodied the necessary procedures, it did not include those sufficient for preventing the reconcentration of economic and political power.

On several other fronts, the occupation produced mixed results, particularly in the bureaucratic reform area. Overall, the occupation failed to change organizational culture. The "old patterns of the Japanese bureaucracy—stratification, elitism, legalism, retirement practices, and the like—have proved to be singularly resilient" (Koh 1989: 65). As Chalmers Johnson (1982: 41) notes, the purges did not affect the economic ministries. In fact, the decline of the military, the purging of party politicians, and the breakup of the *zaibatsu* created a power vacuum within the elite structure. Ultimately, the bureaucrats catapulted themselves into power and led the consolidation of the bureaucratic-corporate stage of the model.

The Reverse Course also empowered conservative prewar parties— the Liberals (Seiyukai) and the Progressives (Minseito)—both with close corporate ties to Mitsui and Mitsubishi respectively during the Taisho Democracy years, became the only significant choices in the immediate postwar era. The recovering economy buoyed these reconstituted prewar parties to electoral achievement. The procurement boom brought forth by American war materiel purchases stabilized the Japanese economy and increased the legitimacy of the conservative coalition. When the occupation officially came to an end in 1952, Japan emerged changed by its encounter with the West again. However, it arrived relatively intact; the prewar elites established a long pattern of succession that lasted until the 1993 collapse of the LDP. Scholars and commentators refer to the long consolidated period of one-party dominant and LDP-centered party politics as the stability resulting from the 1955 system.

THE 1955 SYSTEM: LEGITIMATION MECHANISMS CONSOLIDATED

The hallmark of the 1955 system is the collusion among the components of the power elite: politicians, bureaucrats, and corporations. Originally, the 1955 system was engineered as a merger of the Hatoyama Liberals and Conservative parties out of fear that the Socialists would eventually gain a majority in the Diet. Over time, however, it came to reflect the degree to which entrenched interests expanded their influence in the postwar Japanese system. To create a large conservative umbrella party, factional differences required amelioration. The amalgamated LDP that emerged possessed factional differences and leaders relied on negotiated compromises to subdue them. As Tetsuya Kataoka (1992: 14) states, "The LDP's factions are frequently likened to independent parties with all their trappings: headquarters, independent sources of funds, candidates for prime minister, shadow candidates, shadow party administrations, and so forth." The factions became one of the central identifying features of the 1955 party system.

LDP's political dominance prevented a rotation of political power and delegitimized the collective opposition. The longer the LDP excluded opposition parties from formal decision making (although consensus was often attempted and reached on many issues in the Diet), the less the public trusted their capacity to govern, and the LDP's ties to the bureaucracy and the corporations became stronger. Meanwhile the opposition missed repeatedly its windows of opportunity, beginning with its failure to counter the political effects of a conservative umbrella party. Instead of forming a left-of-center coalition, the Socialist Party (the main opposition party) stood helpless. They failed to agree with the Communists or later with the Komeito (Clean Government Party) in the mid-1960s or 1970s. Instead, in 1960, the JSP splintered when its right wing departed and formed the more moderate DSP (Democratic Socialist Party).

The carefully orchestrated 1955 system relied on delicate alliances that held for their mutual interest in cooperating for Japan's full economic redevelopment. Corporate elites, the LDP politicians, and the senior economic bureaucrats engaged in traditional symbiotic mutual backscratching and crafted a reincarnated *fukoku-kyohei* ideology (strong army, prosperous nation into strong economic army, prosperous nation). In the 1955 system, however, wealth and strength came from the economy, rather than through an empire maintained by the military-industrial complex, as before the war.

By 1962, the developmental state, consisting of the essential elite actors, became firmly entrenched by the boom in export-related production during Ikeda's "Double Your Income" years. Only anti–AMPO (U.S.-Japan Security Treaty) demonstrations and the rise of postindustrial concerns, like pollution, threatened the elites' control over the system.[9] Despite these problems, the LDP's hold on power at the national level remained firm.

What was the structure of elite relations in the 1955 system and how was culture used to maintain the system? The 1955 system fits the context of the developmental state when particular attention is paid to the linkages among the three primary actors—bureaucrats, corporate elites, and politicians. The system, as this section will explain, parallels the bureaucratic-corporate stage (second stage) of the model. Besides the analysis of elite linkages, this section shows how traditional culture played a central role in maintaining the economic and political system. Figure 5.1 describes the relationship among the three actors below. It displays the linkages as mutual dependencies that form the core of this section's analysis.

Figure 5.1 depicts that relationships among the power elite originate from culture and require economic growth for maintenance. Because of a general economic decline in the 1990s in Japan, the model experienced serious stress. Increased corporate profit-maximizing behavior, at odds with the politicians' and bureaucrats' sociocultural orientation, also undermines the model's linkages. The effects of economic decline and exogenous forces causing economic rationalization will be discussed later.

Figure 5.1
Symbiosis among the Japanese Elites in the 1955 System

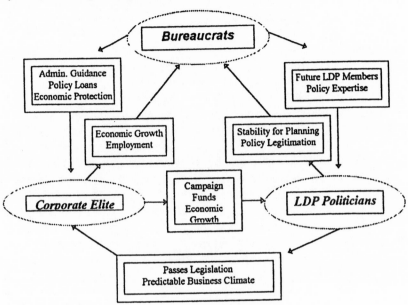

Source: Adapted partially from Tsurutani (1977): 108.

The model's third stage best describes the present Japanese political economy. In that final stage, economic rationality increasingly influences the political development process.

Bureaucrats

At the core of the model are the bureaucrats. The bureaucrats possess an *esprit de corps* by graduating from the same universities, primarily Tokyo University (Todai) and Kyoto University. Beginning in the Meiji Period, the Choshu and Satsuma *hans* depended on these two universities to train bureaucrats. According to Chalmers Johnson (1982), in 1965, 73 percent of the 483 department chiefs (*bucho*) were graduates of Todai. This trend, while less pronounced now, still exists. From 1981 to 1987, 83 percent of the administrative vice-ministers were from Todai, while another 10 percent were graduates of Kyoto University, leaving 7 percent for all the other universities combined (Koh 1989: 142). According to Tadahide Ikuta (1995: 39), the top nine ministries recruited 70 percent of their new hires from Todai in 1991, despite Prime Minister Miyazawa Kiichi's request for more diversified hiring patterns.

Enduring ties formed by colleagues at the same university also created an *esprit de corps* based on common cohort socialization. Upon graduation, they are hired together and promoted as a group into middle management, further enhancing those ties. Even when graduating classmates receive assignments to different ministries, the ties developed during one's educational years provide the social capital which lay the basis for future intergovernmental cooperation. Furthermore, other sources of these ties include arranged marriages, common birthplace, and financial wealth (Johnson 1982: 55–56). These enduring ties fortify the bureaucratic factions' arsenal when jurisdictional competition flares.

The power of the economic bureaucrats peaked in the 1960s and 1970s. During the 1960s and early 1970s, the annual Japanese economic growth rate exceeded 10 percent annually, further adding to increased morale among them. Bureaucrats were responsible for providing administrative guidance to the corporations and, especially in the early 1960s, policy loans. Administrative guidance involves many varieties, but generally it consists of advice, arbitration, and suggestions to the corporate elite. The purpose of the administrative guidance is to direct economic development and to harmonize growth, by that eliminating waste and excessive competition (Komiya 1986: 63).

Policy loans, another instrument used by MITI, provide economic bureaucrats with an avenue to control corporate behavior. Bureaucrats arranged these loans to loyal corporations that abided by administrative directives, unlike in Korea, where personal relationships became the primary factor for securing these loans. In Japan, the high savings rate allowed bureaucrats access to large sums of money at virtually zero interest. These loans reduced competition by targeting selected entry into particular product fields. Frequently, larger firms prevailed in their quest for low-interest loans and special import licenses. The number of entrants into particular markets remained controlled. Throughout the 1950s and 1960s, the Japanese bureaucrats provided these loans and bureau sponsorship which guaranteed the safety of investments. Bureau sponsorship reflects government confidence in the product and company, and many other banks flocked to these firms. Japanese economic protection, however, remained substantially different from the Eastern European command system. Whenever products or research and development failed to produce the desired results, economic bureaucrats intervened by organizing corporate mergers. Sometimes the bureaucracy suspended additional loans. While Japan's economy contained elements of a planned economy, it also embraced capitalist traits. The planned elements often reflect traditional sociocultural imperatives, while the capitalist elements mirror modern-market rationality. To remain eligible for government protection, corporations must produce a profit or enlarge market share.[10]

Economic bureaucrats looked at export-oriented firms in a particularly favorable light.

The bureaucrats also benefitted the ruling party. They provided the LDP with policy expertise in drafting appropriate probusiness legislation. The economic and political advice provided to the LDP lawmakers contained policy and technical planning information needed to maintain national economic growth. If the economy continued to grow and the nation experienced a constantly "expanding economic pie" (Tsurutani 1977: 42), the LDP could reasonably expect to do well at the polls. Once bureaucrats retired, they would join the LDP and run for office, publicly trumpeting their connections to the ruling circles of government.[11] The possession of *konne* (connections) provided a direct *paipu* (pipe) to the senior bureaucrats. Politicians functioned as intermediaries between the local constituents and the bureaucracy, so the electorate valued personal connections much more than ideology. These politicians, too, valued connections because they gave them the key to power. In return for consistent reelection, the elected official vigilantly maintained connections back home. For an aspiring representative, constituency and party service represent necessary tools for becoming an LDP *han* (faction) leader. One day, he may be rewarded with an important cabinet position or even a prime ministership.[12]

Corporate Elite

The corporate elite, in the second stage of the Asian Political Development model, exert important influence on the other elite actors, but their role remains secondary to the bureaucrats. They depend on the bureaucrats to fashion industrial policy and to provide the necessary regulatory atmosphere that benefits them. In particular, during the early 1950s and 1960s, the Japanese corporate elite lacked the capital base to expand production of new electronic products rapidly. In many ways, the corporate elites were beholden to the bureaucrats. During this period, many larger Japanese corporations maintained traditional-style management practices including employee involvement, enterprise unions (shop unions), and fairly egalitarian pay systems for male workers. As Kunio Okada (1993: 28) states, "Starting in the late nineteenth century, the entrepreneurs and managers of modern Japanese firms realized that Japan would suffer the same problem of labor alienation, with all of its dangerous consequences for their companies' survival and growth, if they allowed their companies to remain mere associations in the *gesellschaft* sense."

The Japanese *kaisha* (company) contained many traditional characteristics derived from Confucianism and Zen Buddhism. The traditional elements contributed to the corporations as social institutions instead of purely economic entities because a broad orientation toward a communitarian ethic existed (Durlabhji 1993: 69–72). Special benefits included lifetime employment for those employed by large corporate entities, bonuses, pay based on seniority, and sometimes housing assistance. On the other hand, the corporate environment places social pressures on employees, and *karoshi* (death by work) has become a social issue. The communitarian approach required significant sacrifices from employees, and social pressure played a role in shaping productivity.

To hold the paternalistic Japanese corporate system together, the corporate elite depended on government protection of the domestic market. Traditional communitarian values form the anchor for the government's paternalism toward corporations and corporate paternalism toward employees. At the corporation-to-employee level, traditional values helped the corporate elite in creating a strong sense of "my companyism" which made Marxist class agitation not only impractical but also alien to the climate fostered by a paternalistic labor-management system. The success of corporate paternalism subsequently weakened the attractiveness of the left-of-center political parties. At the government-to-corporate level, paternalism created a bureaucracy-led developmental state.

Bureaucrats benefitted from their paternalism when it came time to retire, at age fifty-five. Under the 1955 system, senior bureaucrats "descended from the heavens" (*amakudari*) and occupied positions on corporate boards and in management. Large corporations sought top-level economic bureaucrats for their connections to policy makers in their respective agencies. Those from ministries that regulated industrial and commercial interests commanded high salaries. Economic and regulatory agencies prided themselves in placing retired bureaucrats in desirable positions. Table 5.3 shows some *amakudari* positions assumed by top bureaucrats upon retiring from their ministry.

Initially, the corporations sought senior-level bureaucrats for their expertise and connections to their former ministry (Johnson 1995: 146–56). During the early stages of the postwar developmental state, corporations actively sought those individuals who gave them social capital for securing import licenses, policy loans, and regulation easements. However, more recently, placement of senior bureaucrats became more difficult with corporations showing recalcitrance in receiving bureaucratic castaways, especially as corporate autonomy increased in the 1980s bubble economy.

The Japanese corporate elite also gave politicians financial resources to wage their costly political campaigns and the LDP's internecine *habatsu* (factional) warfare. The powerful *zaikai* (elite financiers and business organizations), through the Keidanren (Federation of Economic Organizations), regularly funneled hundreds of millions of dollars into elections until the LDP's implosion in 1992. According to Yanaga (1968:

Table 5.3
Amakudari Positions of Senior-Level Bureaucrats from MITI and MoF*
(1970–1985) as Compiled by Albrecht Rothacher

Name	Ministerial Position	New *Amakudari* Position
Kuroda Makoto (MITI)	Vice-Minister for International Affairs	Advisor to Long-Term Credit Bank of Japan
Anraku Ryuji (MITI)	Director-General of Industrial Location and Environmental Protection Bureau	Advisor to Sumitomo Bank
Kurihara Shohei (MITI)	Vice-Minister for International Affairs	Vice-President, Toyota
Akazawa Shoichi (MITI)	Director General	Executive Director/Vice-President/Vice-Chairman with Fujitsu (1973–1983), Chairman, Japan External Trade Organization (JETRO)
Amaya Naohiro (MITI)	Vice-Minister for International Affairs	Executive Director, Dentsu Institute for Human Studies
Sumita Satoshi (MoF)	Administrative Vice-Minister	President Ex-Im Bank (1972–1979); Deputy Governor (1979–1984) and Governor (1984–1989), Bank of Japan (BoJ)
Hosomi Takashi (MoF)	Vice-Minister for International Affairs	Advisor, IBJ (1974–1981); Chairman, Overseas Economic Cooperation Fund (1981–1987); Nippon Life Insurance Research Institute

*MITI = Ministry of International Trade and Industry; MoF = Ministry of Finance.
Source: Rothacher (1993): 146–47.

69–70), the Japanese business community sought political stability and took refuge in the conservative LDP. The *zaikai* did not take the LDP's electoral dominance for granted; they hedged their future by supporting Socialists and Democratic Socialists. Funding leftist candidates also tempered their extreme radicalism. Overall, however, the most significant amounts went to the LDP. For example, in the 1952 general elections, Yanaga (1968: 80) stated that *zaikai* distributed the following amounts— Liberal Party, 150 million yen; Progressive Party, 93 million yen; Right Socialists, 15 million yen; and Left Socialists, 12 million yen.

By the 1960s, the Keidanren became exceptionally powerful after a series of failed national strikes, including the famous Miike coal mine labor impasse. That strike required suppression by national police and left labor docile and more cooperative with management (Allinson 1987: 391). Meanwhile, as the cost of electioneering increased in the 1970s and 1980s, the LDP became more dependent on corporate interests for funding the escalating costs of electioneering. Frequently, questionable funding reached the very top of Japan politics, as evidenced in the resignation and conviction of the powerful Prime Minister Tanaka Kakuei. Throughout the history of postwar Japanese politics, corruption charges were *de rigueur* in politics.

By the mid-1980s, van Wolferen (1989: 134) estimated the cost of maintaining an average *koenkai* (home constituency electoral support group), in non-election years, at $3 million. He also provides anecdotal evidence concerning the cost of maintaining a viable LDP with competing factions. In two months of fund-raising, one LDP Diet member officially netted $9.8 million in 1984. Corporations, through their financial muscle, propped up the LDP's often sagging popularity in the late 1960s and 1970s. This pattern of behavior is reminiscent of the prewar period, when political scandals proliferated.

Politicians

Politicians, the least respected of the three elite groups, remain a crucial component of the Japanese political development model. Throughout the duration of the 1955 system, their influence steadily increased along with that of corporations. While the bureaucrats' power reached its zenith and subsequently declined in the 1970s and 1980s, politicians and corporate elites increased their political leverage into the 1990s. The major strengths that elected officials bring to the political system consist of their ability to claim the mantle of democratic legitimacy. Beginning with the Meiji Diet and in the postwar Diet, elected politicians represented democratic accountability, being the only component of the power elite subject to popular contestations. Only elected officials could claim that their authority derived from a popular mandate. Other components also came to view the elected officials as indispensable for democratic linkage to the populace and for providing insulation from public pressure.

In the postwar system, elected officials' cooperation is essential in passing necessary legislation that reflected corporate and bureaucratic interests. However, without elected officials, the Japanese public would challenge the political system's legitimacy. The LDP, as the major political party, performed vitally important functions in the 1955 system by seemingly linking citizens to the policy-making process and by integrating the power elite.

Meanwhile, opposition parties also served an important function as a safety valve for pent-up frustration. Their existence checked the arrogance of the LDP and prevented the overall system from being perceived as unresponsive. During the 1950s and 1960s, the political radicals consisting of students, laborers, and environmentalists pointed to the excesses of the developmental state. Radical groups' dissent also played an important but perhaps an unintended role by forcing the LDP to recognize their concerns. The LDP co-opted nearly all of their concerns as a part of its hegemonic strategy (Calder 1988). The opposition parties, therefore, guaranteed the long-term sustainability of the system and helped the cause of political quiescence.

The power elite's need for legitimacy increased the power of politicians as their role in policy making grew. Primarily beginning in the late 1960s and continuing to the present, but especially during Tanaka Kakuei's tutelage, Diet members became more autonomous of the bureaucrats and the corporate elite and developed independent sources of policy expertise.[13] Diet members acquired their own policy expertise instead of relying exclusively on research from bureaucratic agencies or corporate think-tanks. These *zoku-giin* (policy clan representatives) met regularly with their bureaucratic and industrial counterparts. The Parliamentary Affairs Research Council (PARC) or *Seichokai* serves as a venue to match *zoku-giin*'s expertise with the appropriate bureaucratic ministry and to deliberate policy options. The politicians and the bureaucrats form a *zoku* (policy family or clan) with the purpose of deliberating policy changes and managing the administrative and legal aspects of pending legislation. Seniority (number of times reelected) and factional strength are the deciding rules for determining LDP committee assignments. Thus factions covet and orchestrate memberships of individual politicians into the best *zoku*.

The best *zoku* are those with influence over large sums of government funds, including construction, posts and telecommunications, industrial policy, and industry. In this system, the retired bureaucrat transfers his personal connections and modern technical expertise to his elected post and assumes a position among fellow *zoku-giin*. In addition to corporations, factions within political parties seek former bureaucrats to strengthen their policy area. Under the system of factional rivalry, each LDP faction specializes in specific policy areas and recruits the appropriate former bureaucrat. Control over many policy tribes translates into factional strength, which in turn increases its standing within the party and attracts increased corporate contributions. A strong faction can then increase its influence over the nominations of key ministers and ultimately capture the prize of Japanese politics—the prime ministership.

POLITICAL DECAY? ADVANCEMENT TO THE THIRD STAGE

The end of the 1955 system began with subtle incremental changes and below-the-surface turmoil in the 1970s. The changing international system and required responses produced political fallout. Internationally, increasing global competitiveness brought scrutiny of the successful Japanese export-led growth strategy. *Endaka* (overvalued yen) phenomenon began in 1972 after the United States abandoned the Bretton Woods systems and floated its currency. The overvalued yen led to Japanese economic distress in labor-intensive sectors of the economy, particularly steel. The emergence of the NICs (Newly Industrialized Countries) put pressure on Japanese manufacturers contributing to increased offshore production. Domestically, years of sustained economic growth unleashed new social phenomena concerning quality of life issues and an aging population that required social services. The consensus that existed in the 1955 system broke down as the size of the economic pie grew more slowly.

Two themes dominated domestic politics in the 1980s and 1990s, both resulting from the overall change in macroeconomic conditions and social structure. These themes reflected the extent to which the power elite in Japan must operate under changed conditions. One theme—"internationalization" (*kokusaika*)—suggested that Japan, an insular island nation, needed to open its economy and culture and become *futsuno kuni* (like the rest of the world). The implicit message was that Japan is not unique or special in contrast to other countries. Cultural construction of society since the Meiji Restoration was just that, an elite-inspired ideology of *Nihonjinron* (study of theories of Japanese uniqueness). While it provided the Japanese with identity and nation-building tools, it ran counter to the universalistic nature of globalization. The ideology, while useful for constructing the developmental state, embraced particularism and traditional sociocultural norms. Japan succeeded in modernizing its economy, but not its culture, and globalization asserted pressure for cultural change. As in the late Tokugawa Period, Japan again found itself feeling inferior and on the defensive.

The second theme, decentralization, emerged from years of a strong, centralized unitary form of government. The developmental state's successes overly centralized the political and economic system and made Japan unable to adjust to structural changes in the international economy (Ozawa 1994). Decentralization was also part of the move away from the LDP-bureaucracy dominated government embodied in the 1955 system to make Japan more democratic. These changes contributed to the ultimate demise of the LDP's invincibility in the 1993 general elections. This section of the chapter traces the economic, political, and social changes that Japan experienced against the background of calls for decentralization and internationalization to draw tentative conclusions about the trajectory of Japanese political development. Then the implications for the Asian Political Development Model are addressed.

The global recessions of 1974 to 1976 and 1979 to 1982, induced by two successive oil shocks, shattered the public's confidence in the conservative coalition government. Coupled with this, the Japanese economy was experiencing a protracted slowdown as it matured; growth rates of 7 percent to 10 percent became untenable. The growth rate declined to around 4 percent while increased foreign pressure mounted on Japan to reduce its trade surpluses, by that undermining the export-oriented growth strategy of Japan's developmental state. In particular, the Cold War's end exacerbated Western perceptions of Japan's trade surpluses. During the Cold War, U.S. and Japanese leaders viewed security and economic interests as integrated. The United States willingly overlooked Japan's trade surpluses in return for military bases and allegiance to the West. Japan benefitted economically in return for weak international sovereignty. After the end of the Cold War, these two issues became delinked. The United States began increasingly to view economic security as separate from military issues. The United States, through its Super 301 provisions, attempted to manage Japan's export-led growth policies.[14] Domestically, economic globalization severely affected the conservative establishment because it undermined the sociocultural imperatives of the developmental state with many corporations in textile and consumer electronics having to farm out production to Southeast Asia throughout the 1990s.

On the business front, corporations lost domestic protection for automobiles (especially foreign parts), consumer electronic devices, and even major government construction projects. The Kansai International Airport project received fierce *gaiatsu* (foreign pressure) to open the bidding process to foreign firms.[15] While Kansai Airport's construction remained virtually closed to foreign firms, foreign pressure successfully opened the Japanese rice, beef, and many consumer products markets. These changes displayed the extreme difficulty Japan faced in maintaining a closed economic system based on sociocultural imperatives.[16] Increased foreign consumer goods' penetration and higher domestic wage rates contributed to hollowing out the Japanese economy in certain industrial sectors that relied on intensive labor.

Japan's persistent trade surpluses drove up the yen's value and contributed to land speculation in the 1980s. *Endaka* (highly valued yen) meant that Japanese products would cost significantly more than cheaply produced goods from the NICs. From the perspective of the Keidanren, the bureaucrats and politicians' effectiveness in representing their interests in a globalizing economy came into question. Powerful business interests began to question the necessity to fund political parties. At one point after the 1993 elections, Keidanren claimed, in an unprecedented move, that it was no longer going to provide the LDP with campaign contributions. Even the restoration of the LDP in the 1996 elections did not lead to the resumption of close ties between the LDP and corporations. For example, in February 1997, automakers rebuffed LDP demands for $806,000 in campaign donations and complained that the party failed to meet the needs of automakers. They also stated that a strong NFP (New Frontier Party) (*Shinshinto*) provided an effective counterbalance to the LDP (*Nikkei Weekly*, February 24, 1997, p. 1).[17]

Beginning in the 1970s, Japan also experienced noticeable social changes common to all industrialized nations—primarily the greying of the population and concerns over budgetary constraints imposed by aging (*rojinka*). Additional concerns included increased drug use, crime, and signs of economic inequality and increased unemployment. Unemployment reached unprecedented levels of more than 3 percent and the official rate in 1999 increased to over 4.3 percent. The unofficial unemployment rate, however, remains considerably higher. Much corporate deadwood remains from years of sociocultural practices that promoted lifetime employment. In times of growth, sociocultural imperatives were sustainable through high domestic prices and export earnings, but in times of contraction they derailed recovery. The international financial community and organizations (e.g., the WTO) and multilateral trade negotiations made adherence to these imperatives difficult.

During the 1970s, the political component underlying the 1955 system also began to collapse. The LDP no longer appeared as invincible as it once was. The primary cause of the LDP's legitimacy problems related to "money politics," as a series of scandals tainted the public image of the party. The most serious of these, the Lockheed Scandal, concerned Tanaka Kakuei. Another major scandal, the Recruit Scandal in 1988—implicated virtually every high-ranking LDP politician of every LDP faction. The scandals, in effect, had the consequence of upsetting the traditionally accepted convention of rotating prime ministerships among the various factions and ultimately led to the fissure in the LDP.

The disintegration of the political element of the 1955 system was gradual, but ended in a shattering climax. In 1993, a weakly unified coalition of seven political parties consisting of the DSP (Democratic Socialist Party), CGP (Clean Government Party—Komeito), SDPJ (Social Democratic Party Japan—formerly named Japanese Socialist Party), and a whole host of younger and restless LDP defectors drove the LDP out of power. At its onset, the new coalition seemed impossible; wide ideological differences among its participants made a consensus unlikely. The new government, formed under Hosokawa Morihiro on 6 August 1993, lasted just about nine months. After the revelation of alleged campaign loans from the *yakuza* (Japanese crime syndicate), Hosokawa resigned. In a circus of prime ministers that followed, Hata Tsutomu lasted just two months.

Ozawa Ichiro's attempt to exclude the Socialists from a newly organized coalition called *Kaishin* (Innovation), led to their withdrawal of support from the Hata government. In a move that surprised most conventional observers of Japanese politics, the Socialists joined with the remaining lepers to form a coalition government under Murayama Tomiichi, a Socialist. He became the first Socialist prime minister since Katayama Tetsu in 1947. However, the LDP dominated the cabinet's most important portfolios and the Socialists became increasingly marginalized after the 1996 elections that restored an LDP prime minister in Hashimoto Ryutaro. During the tumultuous 1989–1996 period, Japan had seven prime ministers.

Some in the Japanese public heralded the decline of the LDP as the beginning of a more democratic party system. With declining bureaucratic influence and a rising alternative to the LDP, it appeared that these predictions had some merit. However, even as early as 1993, Karel van Wolferen (1993) suggested that political change was merely illusory and that significant change in the party system was not in the making. In many ways, his predictions were correct. The bureaucrats still maintain significant control over policy making and this tendency increased during the LDP's internal turmoil. On the other hand, decision making among the elites did become more pluralist or immobilist (depending on one's perspective) according to Allinson (1987: 405–6). Each elite actor developed its own constituency and vested interests that were mutually exclusive. Japan, in the advanced period or third stage of the political development model, experienced greater political pluralism among the elites. Yet, it remains unlikely that these changes would translate into greater political choices for the average Japanese voter.

The new political party formed as an alternative to the LDP, Shinshinto (Japan New Party), consisted primarily of former LDPers, and it remarkably resembled the LDP itself. In many ways, Japan went from a one and one-half party system to a new variation of a system that includes little significant political opposition. The 1996 elections mortally wounded the left-of-center parties. After the elections, party leaders mentioned the Socialists disbanding while the Japanese Communist Party remained peripheral. In the end, the LDP came back triumphantly, but the distribution of the political power among the elites changed in favor of the corporations. They seemed able to operate in a more globalized Japanese economy without political and bureaucratic encumbrances. As for the political left, political ineptness and ideological intransigence prevented it from adjusting to the social and economic changes that Japan experienced. Union membership declined throughout the 1980s and 1990s with government privatizing public corporations which contributed a large number of Sohyo members. Sohyo (a Japanese labor federation consisting of public employees), a major supporter of the Japanese Socialist Party, suffered when the conservative government privatized the National Railways. One scholar, sympathetic to the political left, wrote, "Today the ideology of organized workers as such has lost any autonomy and any reforming impulse it once might have possessed. It has fused completely with the national common sense of neoliberal Japan" (Kumazawa 1996: 81). This comment echoed Karel van Wolferen's point that the "LDP, bureaucrats, and businesses applaud the plans for Rengo [a more moderate union] and helped them along" (1989: 71). He also said that the "further domestication of enterprise unions" and Rengo's call for a moderate national umbrella of unions would lead to the expansion of the LDP's constituency base (72). All these changes helped the Japanese power elite deal with the competitive pressures of globalization by rationalizing the Japanese economy.

Domestically, global changes resulted in social and economic changes being forced on Japan. These global capitalist forces seriously affected the way politicians, bureaucrats, and corporate elites colluded in making policy.[18] Overall, in many ways, the political economy continues to undergo rapid change. The present prime minister Ryutaro Hashimoto and his successors must decide the extent to which the economy should harmonize itself with the rest of the world. Politicians and many bureaucrats resist economic harmonization. Socially, harmonization could potentially lead to the loss of balance between modern and traditional symbols. Such a loss may contribute to the deconstruction of Japanese society.

Japan remade itself repeatedly to function in a modern context: political and economic change during the Meiji Period, imperial democracy in the late Meiji through early Showa Periods, and "democratization" through the U.S. occupation. Each time, Japan rejected Westernization and instead chose to incorporate selected characteristics of the West, essentially maintaining its traditional, although changing, culture. When the current political turmoil subsides, the LDP's lock on power will likely be broken. However, expectations of significant changes toward a liberal democracy are unlikely given the current power structure. The present system still favors the conservative elite, perhaps more now than ever before, given the political left's atrophic condition. Power may become more diffuse among the conservative elite, but it will not increase interest-group participation. As two conservative parties jockey for electoral superiority, some competition will infuse into the political system, but the likelihood of altering the existing alliance of bureaucrats, corporations, and conservative politicians remains low.

NOTES

1. For a survey of early Japan see Hall (1970).

2. Without national identity, modernization in Japan and other East Asian nations would produce political ungovernability. The lack of national identity may be a culprit for economic stagnation in the Philippines, Papua New Guinea, and many African countries.

3. Fukuzawa said (Craig 1968: 143), "We must truly admire them [referring to the *shishi*: men of spirit bent on preventing foreign intervention in Japan through assassinating Japanese leaders sympathetic to barbarians] for their spirit of love for country. Our position is no different. We only want to change the form of their patriotism and apply it to the present." In many ways, this was characteristic of the adaption of Confucianism to a more modern era.

4. McNelly (1969: 370–71) notes that political institutions in Japan draw from traditionalism because they formed around the monarchy.

5. Scalapino (1968: 253) strongly argues that the ruling elite accepted "Western-style parliamentarism as the wave of the future" during this pre-Taisho era. However, here, the distinction between form and essence is necessary. It is likely, given the modernization process in Japan, that parliamentary government was in fact accepted in terms of procedures. However, the essence of the Japan polity—of the modernization period up to 1890 and the consolidation period to the end of the Meiji era (1912)—is that power was highly concentrated in traditional patterns of patron-client relations and various alliances between industrialists and specific *hans*, for example. Culture in this instance, made the adoption of the essence of liberalism unfathomable because of its conflict with traditional Japanese values and behavior. The political parties of the time were a product of Japanese culture and the economic modernization process. This is hardly analogous to the Western experience in which democratic institutions were constructed to limit the power of government rather than to centralize and strengthen it.

6. Hardacre (1989: 122) argues that the Imperial Rescript on Education (*Kyoiku Chokugo*) possessed "supercharged symbolic value" because "It made loyalty and filial piety into absolute, universal values that could not be questioned or subordinated to anything else." The purpose of the rescript was to create a public morality distinct from Western influences but connected to Confucianism. The rescript was copied and sent to all elementary and secondary schools where students were required to memorize it and celebrate in the monthly ceremonial readings of the scroll. "These ceremonies soon developed into elaborate school rituals of paying homage to the rescript and the imperial photo," and "Shinto priests were mobilized in the distribution of the rescript and in the standardization of the rites" (122).

7. For good survey accounts of the U.S. occupation of Japan, see Robert E. Ward and Sakamoto Yoshikazu, eds. (1987), *Democratizing Japan: The Allied Occupation* (Honolulu: University of Hawaii Press) or John Curtis Perry (1980), *Be-*

neath the Eagle's Wings: Americans in Occupied Japan (New York: Dodd and Mead). For an interesting account from a Japanese elite perspective see Yoshida (1962), *The Yoshida Memoirs: The Story of Japan in Crisis* (Boston: Houghton Mifflin).

8. See Reischauer (1995: 103–11) for a summary of occupation policy.

9. Postindustrial concerns became salient beginning in the 1960s and continuing throughout the 1970s decade. Taketsugu Tsurutani (1972, 1977) identified these as "rights" oriented issues including specific entitlements, postmaterialist issues including those pertaining to the environment, and the politics of identity. The opposition political parties were able to capitalize on these issues at the local level, especially in the larger cities and in regions specifically affected by these pollution-related issues, such as Minamata or Yokkaichi. On the national level though, the progressive era did not lead to a fundamental shift in the dynamics of the party system. While part of the explanation may be that the LDP's continuous electoral advantages in rural overrepresentation made it impossible for the opposition to obtain a majority, some credit must be given to the tenacity of the LDP in terms of their organizational savvy (through their *koenkai* or local support groups). Another important factor promoting the longevity of LDP rule is the party's ability to address traditional concerns such as economic growth and sociocultural imperatives.

10. Johnson (1995: 62) asks, "Is the Japanese economy capitalist?" Matsumoto [author of *Kigyo-shugi no koryo* (*The Rise of the Japanese Corporate System*) as stated by Johnson] attacks this question from several interesting points of view. "Just as a monarchy can have a democratic government, a country can have a formally capitalist system—private property, joint stock companies, markets—and yet not be capitalist." Then Johnson, in paraphrasing Matsumoto (63), points to "enterprise unionism, seniority wages, career job security in upper-tier exporting companies for male heads of households, and the lack of a serious political role for labor in Japan" as encouraged by the bureaucracy as reasons why the Japanese economic system contains elements of command economy.

11. According to Rothacher (1993: 145), about one-third of all LDP members of the Diet are former bureaucrats with 25 or more years of government service.

12. The position of the prime minister in itself is not coveted as much as the social capital one can develop by holding the position and performing a power-brokering role. Power-brokering varies from one prime minister to another dependent upon the extent to which he is beholden to the interests which placed him there in the first place.

13. However, it should be duly noted that elected LDP officials' dependence on corporate contributions increased as the position of the Dietperson becomes more valuable to the maintenance of the overall political system.

14. Super 301 resulted from the Omnibus Trade and Competitiveness Act of 1988 and targeted those nations which engaged in unfair trading practices as determined by the USTR's (U.S. Trade Representative) office. The USTR had authority to place violators on a list of unfair traders and recommend retaliatory measures until the violating nation remedied the problem.

15. See *The Economist* (1987: 60–61) on details about the extent of American construction firm's exclusion from the bidding process. The Japanese bidding system for construction projects is notorious for the *amakudari*-type patron-client relations, which rely on a closed bidding system where only Ministry of Con-

struction–approved firms can submit bids. According to the *Wall Street Journal*, December 12, 1990, a partnership group consisting of a Japanese, German, and American firm was awarded the exclusive contract for baggage handling at Kansai International Airport, somewhat ameliorating the ire of U.S. trade officials seeking expanded opportunities for American firms in Japan.

16. Specifically regarding the construction business, the bureaucratic-corporate nexus is well entrenched through the *amakudari* system. Johnson (1995: 108) notes that "every major company in the Japanese construction industry . . . had at least two directors from the Ministry of Construction [as advisors and deputy department chiefs]" indicating the extent to which sociocultural imperatives are still quite strong in the construction industry. The construction industry is also notorious for large campaign contributions to LDP Dietmembers and its connection to the Japanese *yakuza* (mafia or crime syndicates) pointing to many interesting media stories concerning corruption and speculations of underworld-money politics.

17. Shinshinto, led by former LDPers Hata Tsutomu and Ozawa Ichiro, is an amalgamation of former LDP members who defected; CGP—Clean Government Party (Komeito); and Democratic Socialist Party (DSP), who banded together to present themselves as an alternative conservative party to the LDP. While this party has not clearly identified how it differs on issue positions from the LDP ideologically, it has recently taken policy stances opposed to the LDP. Issues such as decentralization and the consumption tax are major issues that the Shinshinto addresses. The entire post-1992 political party system culminated from the anticipated changes to the electoral system, which reduced the number of proportional representation seats under the multimember district system from 511 to 200 and created 300 single-member districts. Smaller political parties feared possible extinction under the new system; some of the political parties rationalized the need to band together, resulting in the umbrella party, Shinshinto.

18. For example, see Sandra Sugawara, "For Japan Inc., Beginning of the End," *Washington Post*, March 9, 1997, pp. 1 and 23, or Yutaka Kosai, "Reform No Longer an Option, but a Necessity," *Nikkei Weekly*, February 3, 1997, p. 7. Both articles argue that the present system of centralized control exerted by the bureaucrats is no longer beneficial and harms the future of the Japanese economy and society's social needs.

6

South Korea:
Imperfect Legitimation
Leads to Democracy?

Ruthless? Is this the same Kim Dae Jung who was for years the great hope of democrats and human-rights activists everywhere? Is this the same man who served years in prison, house arrest or exile for opposing dictators? Is this the Kim Dae Jung nominated a staggering 11 times for the Nobel Peace Prize, the man who everyone thought would be for South Korea what Nelson Mandela is for South Africa? The short answer is no. But in his 12 months in office, President Kim has unquestionably had to be tough. He has issued marching orders to the heads of South Korea's biggest corporations like he was an army drill sergeant addressing so many raw recruits. His dealings with the opposition Grand National Party (GOP) range from simple political hardball to alleged acts which, if found to be true, would get him impeached in some other countries. . . . How did Kim do it [get the economy back on track]? He bullied people; he twisted arms.

"Asia's Tough Guy" (1999)

SOUTH KOREA: DISSONANCE OF CULTURAL
CONSTRUCTION AND IMPERFECT LEGITIMATION

South Korea presents an interesting test for the political development model because of similarities and differences with Japan.[1] Japan characterizes a case in which the power elite successfully managed to construct a political order by balancing the traditional, charismatic, and rational-legal aspects of authority. Nevertheless, South Korea displays primarily a charismatic mode of authority. In Japan, the power elite more successfully constructed a conservative political system by co-opting political dissent and promoting modernization as a loosely defined ideology. To accomplish this, the Japanese power elite used traditionalism by recasting it for a modern world.

Korean political development, in contrast to the Japanese model, draws from a greater continuity to an authoritarian past coupled with a popular tradition of vehement protest to authority. The central paradox of Korean political development is tension between elites in society that sought to impose order and subjects who resisted it. A strong state juxtaposed against weak legitimacy characterizes Korean politics, states Lucien Pye (1985: 219). State power, in South Korea, intruded the life's private sphere so much that the state earned the term "overdeveloped state" (Im 1987: 249). In Japan, high levels of governmental acceptance nurtured and strengthened the state's insularity. In contrast, the Korean state increased its coercive capacity to overcome low legitimacy. As a result, the Korean state relied primarily on excessive force to maintain the system, which resulted in the decay of political institutions.

Despite the striking differences between the Japanese and Korean cases, many similarities between the elites' political and economic structure and behavior exist. Some of these similarities resulted from Korea's colonization (1910–1945) and the administrative and economic socialization to which the Japanese subjected the Koreans. Part of this case study explores the effects of colonialism on contemporary Korean political development.

Korea's recent democratization provides organization themes for structuring this case study within the Asian Political Development Model. The major themes of the Korean case examined in detail are the following:

• South Korean elites were never able fully to create an organic state embodying *Gemeinschaften*.

• Circumstances surrounding the aftermath of the Korean War made the military elite the primary actor in politics because national survival allowed the military to expand.

• South Korean economic legitimation provided limited positive effects because it failed to rely on the appropriate mix of modern and traditional elements. Instead, it relied on a combination of repressive and charismatic mechanisms.

KOREA BEFORE AND DURING THE JAPANESE OCCUPATION

From 1392–1910, the long-lasting Chosun dynasty governed Korea and placed Confucian legal and bureaucratic systems at the center of its political structure. In particular, the *Yangban* (aristocratic class) organized society along strict hierarchical Confucian lines (Eckert et al., 1990: 95–

96). While the royal court functioned along Confucian philosophy, rural villages manifested a surprising degree of traditional egalitarianism (Janelli 1993: 37–39). Roger Janelli (1993: 37) argues that even in the 1950s to 1970s, informalism and egalitarianism dominated rural life because the central government administered the villages only indirectly. One government program that sought to change this was the Saemaul Movement (New Community Movement) discussed later in greater detail.

However, in 1876, Korea opened its economy to Japan. By the turn of the century, the ineptitude of the Chosun dynasty to maintain Korea's sovereignty in the face of mounting foreign pressure became clearly apparent. In part, this failure indirectly resulted from the Chosun dynasty's inability to use Korean traditionalism and nationalism as a defense against Western pressures that sought to undermine the traditional and Confucian-based system. In 1894 to 1895, the Tonghak Rebellion sought to reignite Korean nationalism by introducing a modernization plan, but the "state" feared this form of political expression and sought to squelch it. According to Chong-Sik Lee (1965: 21–23), the Tonghak's syncretism in intermingling Confucianism, Buddhism, Taoism, and Catholicism resulted from a xenophobic and isolationist reaction to the West's division of China. The rebellion signified a spirit of urgency to modernize Korean society and the extent to which the Chosun dynasty was politically incapable of accomplishing this. The assistance of mostly Chinese troops quelled the rebellion, but the Japanese also sent a small contingent of troops to contain Chinese influence over the Korean government. Japan attempted to gain control over the Korean government, but Russian security influences checked Japanese ambitions temporarily. The Russo-Japanese War (1904–1905) eliminated that check and allowed the Japanese to create a Korean protectorate in 1905. Japan then annexed Korea in 1910.

Japanese colonization until 1945 affected significantly Korea's domestic and international politics that emerged in the post–World War II period. The brutality which characterized relations contributed to the present-day love-hate relationship of the two countries—similar to the former European colonies' relationship to their colonizers. In particular, the emerging Korean elite received Japanese language and culture training as Japan began forcefully assimilating Koreans into the Japanese empire by 1942, although as second-class Japanese. To this day, Japanese mass cultural preferences remain popular in Korea long after the occupation has ended despite government restrictions on Japanese media. The masses, however, experienced more Japanese brutality and expressed greater disdain and hostility toward the Japanese than the elite who tended to cooperate with the occupation. Domestically, the colonization played an instrumental role in the political development of the post–Korean War era.[2]

First, Japanese colonization delegitimized the Korean military elites on nationalistic grounds because many participated in a Japanese-trained officer corps in the Kwangtung Army or the Japanese army assigned to China. As Jon Huer (1989: 52–53) notes, South Korea never possessed an indigenous military regiment. Instead, the factional rivalry relied on past service classification—service to the Japanese, Manchurian, or Chinese military—to determine lines of loyalty in the politicized 1950s' Korean army. During the early years of the Korean Republic after World War II, President Syngmun Rhee (1948–1960) played off various factions. Meanwhile, an indigenous junior officer corps emerged and resented the senior officers attached to the three factions.

The dominant colonial-era senior officers exerted disproportionate influence until 1961, when Major General Park Chung Hee and Colonel Kim Jong-pil overthrew the short-lived democratic government of Chang Myon. The new and ambitious junior officers opposed the entrenched influence of these senior officers and decided to launch a coup. By the middle to late 1950s, promotions slowed and junior officers blamed the foreign-trained senior officers. The younger officers expressed contempt toward their poorly trained and hastily promoted superiors and envied their rapid rise during the army's formative years. General Park and Colonel Kim arrived with a nationalistic orientation geared toward modernizing the Korean economy through rapid industrialization guided by strong leadership. The military, according to this vision, was to play a pivotal role in Korean modernization.

Second, Japanese colonialism left a sense of mistrust toward strongly centralized authority, although, paradoxically, the Korean elite knew of no other form of administration given their previous training. The partition of Korea into north and south was not only geographical but also had significant implications for the distribution of leadership. In North Korea, Kim Il Sung and his comrades opposed Japanese occupation and could legitimately claim to be nationalists. However, in South Korea, many military and political elites collaborated with the Japanese and lacked legitimacy to the nationalist claim. Thus the legitimacy of the South Korean elites, as a whole, was questionable because of their inability to wave the anti-Japanese symbol of Korean nationalism. Syngman Rhee represented an exception, since he had opposed Japanese colonization and upon becoming president in the 1950s refused to resume relations with Japan. However, the legacy of Japanese colonization continued to be felt even prior to President Park. Colonial Korea's socialization and education robbed them of their identity and sensitized them to Japanese culture, in particular magazines and newspapers, which became popular trend setters (Eckert et al. 1990: 392).

After the end of the occupation, the Japanese-trained officers and bureaucrats controlled the levers of power. For example, during Rhee's administration from 1948 to 1958, the commander of the army was always a general who had served either in Japanese-controlled Manchuria or in the Japanese Army itself (Huer 1989: 54). Also, Donald MacDonald (1990: 17–18) pointed out the large number of Japanese-trained Korean bureaucrats, especially at the lower ranks of the colonial administration. During the occupation, the Japanese controlled the top bureaucracy, and Japanese-trained Korean civil servants filled lower-level positions. These Koreans later formed the core of the country's administrative capacity.

General Park Chung Hee typified the political elite of the time. A product of Japanese socialization during the colonization period, Park went to extraordinary lengths to display his nationalism. Yet, this is surprising given his background. As a captain in the Manchurian Army, Korea's colonial experience shaped his world view. Fluent in Japanese, he also received training in a Japanese officer's school. In many ways, when he seized power in 1960, he was the quintessential Japanese militarist displaced in Korean culture. Reflecting his Japanese predilections, he worked to normalize Korea-Japan relations by seeking to reestablish the elites' connections to the former Japanese colonial administrators. Many Japanese elites who participated in the Korean occupation held important positions of authority in postwar Japanese economic and political life (Eckert et al. 1990: 392). Park's positive image of Japanese industrialism and militarism placed him at odds with the Korean nationalist sentiments of the majority who suffered most from the occupation.

Primarily in the early period of the occupation, Korean students and nationalists staged strikes and demonstrations that the Japanese military and police suppressed ruthlessly. In contrast to Park, most Koreans resented Japanese colonization. Instead of relying on the indigenous resistance experience, Park derived his modernization *cum* nationalist inspiration from Japan's Meiji Restoration and industrialization. In particular, for economic organization, he looked to the Japan of the 1930s—strong state controls and the *zaibatsu*'s economic concentration—as a model for Korea. The Park model fit the first stage of the Asian Political Development Model outlined in Chapter 4.[3]

SOUTH KOREA FROM 1960 TO 1979: HARD AUTHORITARIANISM DOMINATES

The central paradox of Korean politics during the Park Chung Hee dynasty juxtaposed the state's centralized authority against a long tradition of vehement protest. During this period, the student movement constantly called for greater political liberalization and an end to authoritarianism. Freedom, as embedded in the philosophy of Western democratic ideals, however illusive, had an inherent appeal to many Korean students and workers. The greater the authoritarianism in Korea, the greater this urge for freedom became. The Korean state, however, continued to repress the masses. In the 1960s, the governance formula switched from a reliance upon traditional law and order to a mix of authoritarianism and economic growth. The peculiar idiosyncracies of the Korean developmental state, as discussed later, point to an important distinction in approach. Rhee relied on Korean nationalism, but Park combined nationalism with an authoritarian Japanese political and economic model.

Students and urbanites protested Rhee's attempt to fix the March 15, 1960 elections to his favor. Then, public pressure led to drafting a new constitution with subsequent elections on July 29, 1960. This important election consolidated the destruction of Rhee's Liberal Party and the triumph of the opposition Democratic Party. Later, the Democratic Party, led by Chang Myon, split into two factions in August 1960, leading to a period of party politics characterized by instability, corruption, and gridlock (Henderson 1988: 34). The military took advantage of the instability by launching a successful coup on May 16, 1960. Parliamentary government and constitutionalism ceased, and in their place a military junta consisting of thirty colonels and brigadier generals formed the core of government decision making (Henderson 31).

After Park seized power, he sought to create a 1930s Japanese-style industrial state, with strong control exerted from above. To Park, the 250 officers involved in the coup mirrored the Meiji Restoration carried out by the Satsuma and Choshu clans. Furthermore, according to James Cotton (1991b: 207), "He sought a moral, administrative, and a cultural renaissance in Korea to deliver it from weakness and undue foreign influence." To accomplish this task, Park labored to create an economic and political order based on his idea of Korean culture and his own charismatic personalism. His economic and political construction of society, however, left a large group of students, laborers, artists, and intellectuals disempowered and alienated. Furthermore, his economic policies starved the Cholla region of investment and growth and thereby created regional disparities and regional distrust of the national government. Park relied extensively on the state authoritarian techniques, especially the Korean Central Intelligence Agency (KCIA) and the military to silence the opposition. Both entities sought to expand their influence and curried favor with the president. The military and national police disrupted student and labor protests while the KCIA infiltrated these groups to keep Park abreast of any impending protests.

Internationally, Park found a natural ally in the American national security establishment. Over the years, the United States provided its vital security ally with officer training, military aid for procurement, and materiel that allowed the repression of dissenters. Rhee, followed by Park, and then Chun, frequently used national security to legitimate their

brutality against domestic enemies with only limited American protes-
tation. Whenever the North Korea threat would flare up, or domestic
instability would rise in response to the undemocratic nature of the Park
regime, the national police and the military intervened. North Korea became a "national red flag" or a new symbol manipulated by the Korean
elite to justify a strong military and martial law. The traditional order
and stability symbols, the argument goes, were necessary. The Korean
government simply could not tolerate the polarization characterized by
parliamentary politics and democracy.

The Park system shaped successive regimes by laying the precedent
for political conduct. Later, this affected successive democratic consolidation in the posttransition period after 1987 by establishing an entrenched political and economic elite. The Korean elite during the Park
Chung Hee era consisted of the bureaucracy, the military, corporations,
and the hegemonic DJP (Democratic Justice Party). Together, they set the
rules, the patterns of interaction, and the procedures for the political
system by using culture and modernization. The rules, patterns of interaction, and procedures stated above are the central concern of this section. In particular, the interrelationships between culture, economy, and
politics are relevant within the context of the Asian Political Development model.

In contrast to elite pluralism exhibited in the Japanese case, where the
bureaucracy, corporations, and LDP politicians all jockeyed for power
reflecting a collective orientation to power, the Korean elite operated
under a strictly hierarchical model. President Park and the military assumed the leadership role, and the bureaucracy, corporations, and DJP
remained subordinate to them. The Korean bureaucratic-authoritarian
system that developed during the Park period—in contrast to the Japanese system that relied on rational bureaucratic controls supplemented
by patron-client networks—relied primarily on the personalism of Park
and his connections to various industrialists. Weberian bureaucratic ra-
tionalism assumed a secondary role in the planning process in Korea
because the personal charisma of Park overrode bureaucratic expertise.
Park's personalism often determined the degree of a regulations' enforcement and the extent of benefit distribution. For example, in disbursement
of policy loans, Park's personal approval of a corporate leader went a
long way toward a corporation's obtaining funds. Government's coercive
power required subordinated corporations to modify their behavior to
fit political expectations.

The weakest political institution, the party system, remained significantly and purposely underdeveloped in the Park era. However, despite
their weaknesses, political parties participated in multiparty elections beginning in 1963. The ruling party of President Park, the DJP, maintained
hegemony over the party system. Without DJP control, multiparty elec-

tions could not continue because Park would have ended party politics for fear of losing power democratically. The ruling elites controlled and managed opposition on a short leash. Unlike the Japanese case, however, the DJP faced significant challenge from the New Democratic Party (NDP) and resorted to vote rigging, police harassment of opposition candidates, infiltration of campaigns, and other measures to delegitimize the political opposition (Han 1990). In the Korean system, power—in a Confucian sense—emanated from the leader with the political system organized around him. The behavior and actions of the primary actors of the model were based on their relationship to Park Chung Hee. Corruption and electoral fraud became analogous to the "noble lie" in Plato's republic.

PARK: THE CHARISMATIC LEADER AND CULTURAL CONSTRUCTION

Initial reaction to Park Chung Hee's seizure of power in 1960 was ambivalence. The public viewed the democratic government of Chang Myon as too chaotic. To many, it displayed the worst tendencies of parliamentary democracy in a society already dominated by potentially explosive conflict. However, Park also possessed legitimacy problems. He was not elected to office but became president through a military junta and by that lacked the legal-rational source of legitimacy. As a result, he relied on his charisma and personalism to construct legitimacy within the Korean power elite. In many ways, he succeeded in co-opting the elites but proved less successful in winning over the loyalty of the average citizen.

Park realized from the very beginning the importance of nationalism in the nation-building process.[4] Immediately, he seized upon "industrialization" as a symbol to increase the level of his government's legitimacy. (Incidentally, all East Asian nations exercised economic legitimation, beginning with Japan during the Meiji Restoration.) In Korea, just as in the other East Asian nations, rapid industrialization benefitted primarily the corporate and military elite. Citizens, however, gradually received benefits from the trickle-down effects of a modernizing economy. Park probably reasoned that workers would be less inclined to riot and more likely to overlook the regime's illegitimate origins if economic growth benefitted the average citizen.

Park realized that the economic problems experienced in South Korea required a multipronged approach, one that combined charismatic, traditional, and rational economic planning methods. He believed that while Confucianism had positive factors that could propel industrialization, it also possessed a host of negative ones (Nam 1994: 4–5).[5] The government used the major positive influences, including value placed on education and deference to authority. For example, the *Saemaul Un-dong* (New Community Movement) in the 1970s attempted to modernize the condition of the peasants by instilling a modernization mentality.[6] The economic components of the program produced mixed results, but its political significance reflected tradition's use in modernization. Instead of relying strictly on modern values to improve agricultural productivity, the movement used Confucianism for economic development and national integration. As a result, the traditional organic notions remained preserved and uneroded. Pye (1985: 224) comments,

Given the capacities of the Koreans, who like the Chinese, can divorce ideological rhetoric from practical calculations, it seems surprising that the government continues to spend so much effort to promote the ideology when practical payoffs are what count in the countryside. Yet, ideology remains a necessary fig leaf for power in a Confucian culture. The lasting commitment of the government to the *Saemaul Undong* movement must therefore be understood as a manifestation of the need to strengthen the legitimacy of the state which in its dependence upon outside support may seem to some to be less legitimately nationalistic than North Korea.

By 1979 economic troubles mounted, and Park recast the *Saemaul Un-dong* movement and applied it to industrial labor-management relations. He sought more cooperation between labor and management by calling for many more enterprise-style unions to weaken the more radical national FKTU (Federation of Korean Trade Unions). In the spirit of nation-building, corporations and workers must compromise key positions. According to his expectations, workers must provide greater loyalty and dedication to the firm while corporations should increase wages and benefits and provide better work conditions. To facilitate cooperation, government provided tax breaks, low interest loans, and supported KEA's (Korean Employer's Association) position that Labor-Management Councils at the firm level should handle labor-management issues (Rhee 1994: 118–19).

On the business-government front, the first two economic matters that Park addressed included adjusting the national credit supply and controlling emerging business entrepreneurs. He addressed the problem of capital by nationalizing banks in 1961 and ending interest rate controls on savings. Corporations cooperated in return for dismissal of mounting corruption charges accumulated during the Rhee period (Bello and Rosenfeld 1992: 50–52). Also, to provide the corporate elite with direction, he proclaimed his intention to rapidly industrialize the economy through *Suchul ipquk* (nation-building through exports) and thereby switched economic policy toward export-led growth rather than Rhee's Import-Substitution-Industrialization (ISI) Plan (Cho 1994; Im 1987; Jones and

Sakong 1980). These changes supported the country's First Five Year Plan and subsequent plans. The plans' emphases consist of the following, as summarized below (Cho 1994: 30–31):

• The initial direction of industrialization should be light manufacturing with the focus shifting to heavy industry only after income and employment is increased from the former.

• Through five year plans, the primary onus for leadership and control should rest with the government. The market must employ other means than market mechanisms.

• For major business decisions that impact the greater economy, the government must have the final decision-making authority.

• Foreign capital should be utilized vigorously; export earnings will pay for this.

• Moderately high levels of inflation are tolerable, as are regional differences and maldistribution of income in the early stages.

The First Five Year Plan produced mixed results; the overall economic picture improved, but the actual results fell short of government goals. However, it succeeded in placing the bureaucracy, particularly the Ministry of Industry and Trade (MIT) and the Economic Planning Board (EPB), in charge of economic planning. Because of increased bureaucratic intervention in the economy, the bureaucracy's power increased significantly compared to the corporate elite. The economic structure constructed by Park and his economic bureaucracies subjected the corporate elite to rules with all the awards and punishments associated with compliance and noncompliance.

Throughout the 1960s, Park consolidated his political control by placing the colleagues of the Korean Army's Officer Candidate School (OCS), second graduating class in particular, to key ministerial and administrative positions. Kim Jong-pil, Park's confidante, and his colleagues from the eighth OCS, also received a disproportionate share of positions.[7] Kim Jong-il, as Park's chief political strategist, organized the Democratic Republican Party (DRP) for the dual purpose of democratic accountability and electoral access vehicle for former military officers (Huer 1989: 84–85). Kim equipped the DRP with a developmental ideology and used its apparatuses to employ military allies and assist in President Park's reelection.

The Second Five Year Plan (1967–1971) initiated the shift toward heavy industry and petrochemicals, and government-business relations further strengthened. Government became involved in microeconomic planning by controlling access to capital through launching new corporations in targeted industries and by engaging in large-scale infrastructural projects. For example, the government helped found Pohang Iron and Steel

Corporation and completed construction of the Seoul-Pusan highway and the Seoul-Inchon highway (Cho 1994: 36–37). Also, government bureaucrats controlled access to foreign capital, and they frequently put together corporate rescue package loans when large corporations faced insolvency (Cho 1994: 36). The primary problem under the early years of Korean industrialization was a scarcity of capital; interest rates often exceeded 25 percent and most of the capital came from abroad. Government economic policies and tools (e.g., license for capital goods imports, preferential credits, free trade zones, tariff exemptions, and government projects) promoted its dominance over corporations who groveled to survive (Cho 1994: 36; Song 1994: 136–37). The scarcity of foreign capital required government controls over access and use, based on corporate contribution to export growth. Connections to the leadership also helped in securing capital.

During the Second Five Year Plan, the average rate of economic growth for the year 1967 to 1971 was 9.7 percent in contrast to the 7.0 percent target (Song 1994: 130). Government planning succeeded beyond the expectations of the planners, and that led to the increased legitimacy of economic planning and high levels of authoritarianism became accepted as a necessity. However, such increased legitimacy existed primarily among the Korean power elite and not generally among all members of society. The Korean developmental state could not capitalize on industrialization to ignite a traditional ideology of *Gemeinschaft* because growth could not effectively eliminate accumulated hostility toward the government.

Despite the questionable effectiveness of developmental-state tactics in producing greater political legitimacy, the Korean government lacked any other comprehensive approach. Therefore, it had to continue its course. After somehow orchestrating his reelection in 1971, Park wanted to refocus economic mobilization efforts on heavy industry and the chemical industry in the Third Five Year Plan (1972–1976). However, for reelection, Park needed to amend the constitution to allow a three-term president. While Park successfully amended the constitution in 1969, Kim Dae Jung, the chief opposition candidate, garnered 46 percent of the popular vote concentrated in the Kwanju region. With Kim campaigning on the economic slowdown and increased in regional disparities, Park found himself threatened and held accountable to the public. The economy slowed from 15 percent growth in 1969 to 7.9 percent in 1971, resulting in stagnant wages. Clearly, Park realized that a shift from relatively low value-added products to significantly higher value-added products, as stated in the Third Five Year Plan, provided the only long-term economic solution. Potential economic failure and ability to destabilize the government dominated the concerns of the power elite. Park and the elites felt the presidential election proved that they could not take his longevity in office for granted.

Besides economic insecurity, military conflagrations with the North reemerged after Nixon announced a partial troop withdrawal from South Korea. Domestically, Park's political machinations and student desire for reunification led to violent student protests. Parked responded by clamping down again. Following a declaration of a state of emergency on December 6, 1971, and a subsequent martial law proclamation, he introduced a new constitution. The Yushin Constitution (Revitalization Constitution) captured the turn of political orientation toward increased authoritarianism and governmental centralization. (Park probably thought that the Yushin Constitution reflected the spirit of the Meiji Constitution.) The new constitution significantly increased the repressive nature of the state and centralized presidential power for national mobilization to fight the twin wars of postwar Korea: modernization and the threat from the North.[8] Haggard and Moon (1993: 76) summarize the effects of the Yushin regime on the major actors of the Korean elite:

Under the Yushin regime, executive authority was further consolidated, and opposition forces were either co-opted or neutralized, insulating the economic domain from social protest. A realignment of power also took place in the ruling circle. The ruling Democratic Republican Party was transformed into a mere appendage of the executive. Park's personal power was strengthened, the political and administrative role of the Blue House [office of the Korean Presidency and his residence] dramatically increased, and bureaucrats gained unprecedented power as the National Assembly was marginalized. The Yushin regime opened a new era of state-society relations in which state dominance was increased through new legal-institutional arrangements.

The new constitution laid the framework for South Korea's authoritarian state to broaden its reach and deepen its intrusion into the country's civil society and economy. From 1972 to 1979, the Park regime's character became increasingly authoritarian. Park handsomely rewarded those who cooperated but severely punished opponents. Government supported loyal *chaebols* (large privately held corporations that dominate the Korean economy) by mitigating labor restlessness and by providing low interest loans, special import licenses, and tax breaks. However, unlike the decade of the 1960s, the new Yushin system concentrated economic power even more than the old system.[9] According to Haggard and Moon (1993: 79), "Between 1972 to 1979 more than 60 percent of policy loans and 50 percent of general bank loans went to one hundred business groups." The greater the dissatisfaction with the Park regime among students, laborers, and Christians,[10] the more these groups became critical of the corporate elite for their close ties with the government.[11] In response, Park concentrated economic and political power into fewer hands to maintain control over the nation's political and economic development.

By 1979, South Korea experienced phenomenal economic growth under authoritarian political leadership. GNP per capita increased from $80 in 1960 to $1,589 in 1980, far exceeding Park's personal goals for the nation. However, years of rapid economic growth left severe economic dislocations. In particular, the Kwangju region (southwest Korea), suffered from years of neglect after World War II and that produced a potentially explosive situation. Despite years of repression, dissident pressures increased as Koreans became more sophisticated consumers of political information. Perhaps because of the highly coercive nature of the Korean state, the legitimacy of the Park regime was low outside those who directly benefitted from his rule. Unlike the Japanese political system, where the prime minister could claim democratic legitimacy, the South Korean government failed to fully legitimate itself and continued to use force and electoral manipulation as primary methods for maintaining power. Then in 1979, the economy again showed signs of over-extension, and Park anticipated even harsher retaliation against dissidents and protestors.

Suddenly, on October 26, 1979, Korean CIA director Kim Jae Kyu assassinated Park. Apparently Kim felt personally and professionally betrayed by the president and believed that he must liberate Korea from authoritarian rule. While Park's authoritarianism sparked economic modernization, his Korean-style democracy promoted the decay of political institutions and mechanisms for addressing the divisions in society. Political parties, the legislature, and the judiciary lost their independence and became tools of legitimation. In particular, Park's regime manipulated the security threat from North Korea and strong economic growth to hold the country together through a combination of ideologically charged economic nationalism and terror. Park also experimented with controlled participation. For example, he encouraged the formation of the National Conference for Unification (NCU) consisting of 2,000 to 6,000 nonpartisan members who ostensibly worked for national unification with the North. In reality, however, this institution took advantage of nationalist sentiments and increased the power of the president. The NCU elected the president (without debate) and one-third of the members of that institution also served in the National Assembly (Sohn 1989: 48–50). In assessing Park's contribution to nation building, Chalmers Johnson (1987: 144) summarizes:

Had Park, in the early 1970s, retired to Taegu and assumed the role of senior statesman supervising his carefully chosen successors (that is, had he become a Korean genro, not on the Meiji model but on that of Yoshida Shigeru in Oiso), he would be hailed today as the greatest Korean Leader of modern times—and would probably still be alive (he was only forty-four at the time of the coup in 1961).

By the end of the Park regime, South Korea was on its way to becoming an industrialized nation. Politically, it possessed a strong state, but it was anchored by Park's charisma and personalism. Underneath this shell, however, a strong bureaucracy developed. Yet the gap between the mass and the elite remained a serious problem for state legitimation in South Korea. Because Park failed to craft a succession plan, the seeds for future conflict were sown.

KOREA AFTER PARK: DEMOCRACY FROM THE ASHES OF THE DEVELOPMENTAL STATE?

Park's death represented an opportunity for democratic politics to take hold finally. Interim President Choi Kyu Hah, formerly prime minister under Park, revoked emergency decrees and declared a general amnesty. However, political pressures continued to mount and the government rapidly lost control over the political environment. Student dissidents and laborers erupted in protests demanding political reform and greater wages for workers in addressing persistent inflation and stagnant wages. They called for the resignation of the former regime's key players, including the new KCIA director General Chun Doo Hwan and Prime Minister Shin Hyon Hwak. After Kim Dae Jung's rearrest, his base region, Kwangju, erupted in the most severe civil protest Korea ever experienced.

On April 15, 1980, the infamous Kwangju Massacre took place, where government troops fired on civilian protesters killing upwards of several hundred people (Han 1989: 283). Meanwhile, informal political power shifted toward a clique of senior military officials bent on restoring stability. The eleventh class of the Korean Military Academy (KMA) which included Generals Chung Ho-yung and Roh Tae-woo (who later became president after Chun Doo-Hwan) played a pivotal role. Chun gained control over the military, took over the KCIA, and made many arrests of political leaders, including those loyal to Park (Cotton 1991b: 210–11). Clearly, the South Korean elite did not possess the kind of cohesion that characterized the Japanese elite in the postwar period. In many ways, Korean politics, before the 1987 transition to democracy and during this period, resembled the chaos of Japanese politics in the early 1930s. Political intrigue and showmanship by individuals characterized this period, showing the military's powerful influence. However, absent a central unifying leader (e.g., the emperor) or any cultural consensus, the manifestation of the model's bureaucratic-authoritarian stage displayed greater elite disunity and higher political instability than in Japan. The Japanese emperor, as the spiritual and political symbol, helped bureaucratic and military cooperation in the 1920s and 1930s and emotional healing after World War II. Korea simply did not have an emperor representing traditional unity. Korean politics of the post–Korean War era represented a dissonance between mass political culture and elite culture. Elites failed to inculcate the kind of political culture necessary to maintain their legitimacy. As a result, the incomplete Korean mass political culture, from an elite perspective, contributed to only partial elite legitimacy.

The cultural gap between elites and masses reflected a partial construction of politics and economics. The inherent instability in such a system could not endure permanently. In many ways, the silent coup by Chun represented the last gasp of the military to remain the focus of power in Korean politics. After Chun banned all political parties, declared a state of emergency, and placed many political leaders under a political purge, repression brought temporary peace again. These measures, however, weakened political parties again (Han 1990: 327). In August 1980, Chun Doo Hwan was formally elected as president by the NCU, and in October of that year, a referendum approved a new constitution resembling the Yushin Constitution. A provision of the new constitution called for a seven-year term for President Chun.

President Chun declared that he would be a one-term president, after which time, power would be transferred to another leader through democratic means. Chun's rule institutionalized the DJP as South Korea's hegemonic party and reasserted state power over the corporations in the early 1980s. This represented a fundamental shift from the emerging trend of corporate parasitism of the government. Government was losing control over corporations as they increased their power through foreign earnings and, by overborrowing capital, forced the government to put together rescue packages of virtually insolvent firms. Concerns over the expanding corporation's political role and their increasingly concentrated national economic presence caused the political elite to restructure the economy after the severe recession in the 1979 to 1981 period.

Clearly Korea in the 1980s was a different place from Korea in the 1960s. Internationally, competition was increasing as globalization spread, while domestically, the public's political sophistication increased after years of social and economic improvement. With a highly literate population and a politically savvy electorate, the idea of an authoritarian government seemed anachronistic. Chun's modest liberalization maneuvers altered the political and economic system permanently.

A period of uncertainty affected the symbiotic relationship between business and government in the 1980s. Government increased pressures for domestic economic liberalization in response to international competitiveness that made some HCI (Heavy and Chemical Industries) uncompetitive. The government simply could not continue to subsidize these firms (Moon 1994: 147). Once again, the government rewarded corporate cooperation and punished resistors. Resisting firms, such as Hyundai and Kukje, refused restructuring their product lines, refused mergers, or otherwise refused to follow government directives. Politically, putting pressure on the *chaebols* was popular, as many Koreans resented the concentration of economic wealth that these companies represented. Given the low level of Chun's legitimacy, such populist moves drew support from a politically disaffected public.

While it appeared that the state disengaged itself from the economy, in reality, it exercised prudent economic rationalization to improve *chaebol* productivity at the next level of higher-value-added production (i.e., automobiles, semiconductors, and computer chips). At the same time, however, government coercion, cajoling, and frequent intimidation of *chaebols* emboldened the FKI (Federation of Korean Industry) to protest against the government. For the first time, the corporate elite exercised its power by criticizing government vocally, breaking the long tradition of corporate acquiescence to government pressure. Simultaneously, however, Chun and his party began to solicit large sums of money from the *chaebols* as political contributions (Bello and Rosenfeld 1990: 72–73). These funds created party and presidential financial dependence on the *chaebols* and undermined the bureaucracy's attempt at continued economic rationalization. The huge infusion of capital thwarted economic rationalization and introduced greater political considerations for crafting policy.[12] Paradoxically, Chun and the DJP's need for campaign capital gave the *chaebol* significant leverage for manipulating policies and regulations and, in effect, placed the regulated in the driver's seat. The balance of power among the bureaucratic and corporate elites suggests an emerging parity between the two, suggesting the possible premature movement to a higher stage of elite political development. The global (exogenous) factors of globalization affected the distanciation of time and space by compressing the pace at which Korea maneuvered through the later stages of the model.

By the middle of the 1990s, corporations exerted significant influence on politics. In December 1996, the ruling New Korea Party (NKP)—a descendant of the DJP—forced passage through the National Assembly, of a new labor law that ended lifetime employment by allowing layoffs. Simultaneously, the government strengthened the Agency for National Security Planning (formerly KCIA). Amid increasing labor and student protest, a senior government official stated: "We should grow out of the myopic perspective of seeing the intelligence agency as something that threatens democracy. We are creating a new framework for the intelligence agency to combat communist activities."[13] Given the increasingly emaciated condition of the North Koreans and the nation's looming economic collapse, the attempt to strengthen the intelligence agency seems anachronistic. It shows that even with a Democratic National Assembly and a civilian president, the need for a strong centralized government through coercive measures persists.

With more institutionalized political parties in the 1990s, the role of the military continues to decline. The bureaucracy and corporations continue to play a major role in politics. In 1987, 1992, and 1996, democratic elections occurred. Elected the first civilian president in 1992, Kim Young Sam promised national healing and an end to corruption in politics. It appeared that South Korean politics experienced a previously unknown level of democratic consolidation. Yet, in many ways, the pattern of Korean politics resembles the Japanese scenario today. The DLP (Democratic Liberal Party), which became the KNP (Korea New Party), traces its roots to the ruling military-bureaucratic elite, just as the LDP traces its history to the military-bureaucratic alliance of the late Taisho and early Showa periods. The KNP was established by a merger of Roh's DJP and two opposition parties—the Reunification Democratic Party (RDP) and Kim Jong Pil's New Democratic Republican Party (NDRP)—just as the union of the Liberal and Democratic parties in Japan established the conservative LDP hegemon. Furthermore, the present KNP represents a grand conservative party, filled with factional rivalry, just like the LDP. Two opposition groups, the United People's Party (UPP) founded by Chung Ju Yung—the founder of the Hyundai *chaebol*—and the Democratic Party (DP) do not represent a significant threat to the established hegemonic NKP. Both the Korean and Japanese political systems stabilized the electoral component of the political system by creating a hegemonic party. Political change in both countries is guarded by the power elites with set rules for the political and economic game.

However, the Korean political system differs from the Japanese system on several accounts. The unprecedented election of Kim Dae Jung as president in December 1997, displayed the weakness of the Korean state and an instance when democracy in Asia triumphed. While it is uncertain whether he will successfully maneuver the country through recession and political turmoil, his accession signaled Korea's entry into uncharted waters.

Korean politics also remains much more volatile than Japanese politics in part because the national security threat from North Korea, while diminished, still exists. The tradition of labor activism and authoritarianism, furthermore, remains much stronger in Korea than in Japan. Unlike Japan, which was more successful in integrating the various regions of its nation, South Korea continues to exhibit major regional differences and subsequently distrust toward a strong central government.

Also, regionalism continues as a major factor determining electoral performance of the parties. Regional rivalry coupled with perceived grievances around issues involving substantive democracy continues to divide the national elite. For example, the sentencing of former presidents Chun Doo Hwan to death and Roh Tae Woo to twenty-two and one-half years in prison for the Kwangju massacre and acceptance of corporate funds suggested that political tables could turn quickly against those who lose power.[14]

Legitimacy of the Kim Young Sam regime remained low, especially in the aftermath of the new 1996 labor laws. The Asian economic crisis of 1997 affected South Korea particularly severely and contributed to Kim Dae Jung's victory. A weak economy, political corruption, and other developmental state–related problems continue to chisel away the state's legitimacy.[15] While it remains unlikely that South Korea will return to its "hard authoritarian" days, the regime's long-term stability remains questionable. If the South Korean government starts IMF (International Monetary Fund) ordered economic rationalization, the level of political dissatisfaction will grow. However, given the mismanagement that occurred recently, the public's skepticism of government is justified. Kim must find some way to balance traditional and modern tools of legitimacy creatively and depart from the past authoritarian tactics, or the volatility of Korean politics will continue. Unfortunately, the tradition of authoritarianism and democracy as modernity remain at the base level mutually exclusive. While he can claim legitimacy through the democratic mantle, he will need to reform recalcitrant bureaucratic and economic systems.

NOTES

1. Prior to 1945, "Korea" refers to both northern and southern Korea. After 1945, both Korea and South Korea refer to southern Korea.

2. See Lee (1963) and Cummings (1984).

3. Some scholars compare the Korean system of the 1960s and 1970s to Japan in the 1920s and 1930s. Many noted that exposure to Japanese colonialism, when Japan itself emerged as a global industrial power under the *zaibatsu* movement, provided the Korean elite with a Japanese model of development for emulation. For example, see Johnson (1987) and Eckert et al. (1990), especially chapter 20.

4. Two slogans used frequently by Park were *Jaju Guk-Bang* (self-standing military) and *Jarip Gyong-Je* (self-sufficient modern economy).

5. According to Nam (1994), the major tenets of Confucianism discouraged the development of a strong nation because they denigrated the military and commerce and worked to benefit the guardians who claimed to represent national interests. However, he also noted the importance of obedience and education and the virtue of public service.

6. Given the large and ongoing migration to urban areas, particularly Seoul, the infusion of modern values ultimately would make the transition easier for

farmers. A more critical view of the program is provided by Bello and Rosenfeld (1990: 80–85). They argue that the program was a miserable failure of central planning because it indebted the farmers while the government dictated production without meeting the costs of modernizing and maintaining tin roofs. Furthermore, they argue that the program was intended to create a false sense of nationalism after years of rural neglect to increase the regime's legitimacy in the countryside.

7. Johnson (1987: 153) argues that many of the military officers presided over public corporations and utilized their military management techniques in running many of these high risk enterprises established by the Korean government.

8. For the chronology of events surrounding the establishment of the Yushin Regime, two sources provide excellent historical accounts: Haggard and Moon (1993), primarily pp. 73–77, and Han (1989), principally pp. 320–26.

9. Soon (1994: 42–43) noted that one feature of the Yushin economic system was the establishment of the general trading firm modeled after the *sogo shosha* in Japan which linked together the production, distribution, and marketing of a product under the umbrella of one large corporate firm. This is another example of how Park attempted to transplant the Japanese economic model on the Korean nation.

10. For more about the role of Christians in the South Korean protest movement, see Sohn (1989), especially pp. 56–64.

11. Apparently, the Park regime went to extraordinary lengths to legitimize itself internationally believing that overseas acceptance would contribute to increased domestic tranquility. The Korean government's budget expanded the *chaebols'* profits dramatically. Flush with capital, the Korean elite attempted to purchase legitimacy abroad. According to Cumings (1996a, 1996b), both the Korean government and corporations in close cooperation orchestrated a carefully planned strategy of targeting and funding American academics and Korea Studies Centers to solicit positive coverage and less critical exposure of the Park regime.

12. According to Bello and Rosenfeld (1990: 73), firms that refused to cooperate fully with campaign fund raising were dismantled and they provide the example of the Kukje–ICC group, a firm primarily engaged in the steel and textile industry. Politically cooperative firms were allowed to purchase components of Kukje–ICC.

13. See "Strike Idles 100 Major S. Korean Firms," *Washington Post*, December 27, 1996, pp. 1 and 28.

14. Later the sentences were reduced on appeal to life for Chun and seventeen years for Roh. Upon election, Kim Dae Jung announced pardons for both men.

15. See B.C. Koh, "South Korea in 1996," *Asian Survey*, 37 (1): 1–9.

7

Thailand: Weak State but High Levels of Legitimacy

> Our preliminary study suggests that businessmen now can influ-
> ence politics and policy both particularistically and, what is more
> significant, collectively. This, together with other advantages, such
> as increasing social prestige, employment and investment decision-
> making power, and heavy representation in parties, Parliament, and
> the cabinet, makes business a nonbureaucratic group with substantial
> political power in Thailand today.
>
> Anek Laothamatas (1988: 470)

THAILAND AND THE ASIAN DEVELOPMENT MODEL

Thai state-society relations compared to those in Japan and Korea reveal
three different system dynamics within the Asian Political Development
Model. Japanese state-society relations exemplify the existence of a
strong state and corresponding high levels of state legitimacy; Korea,
possesses a strong state but comparatively low levels of legitimacy. The
Thai state, like the Japanese state, successfully maintained high levels of
legitimacy. However, unlike Japan and South Korea, Thailand's state displays weaker characteristics on two accounts. First, while the Japanese
and Korean states possess a strong developmentally oriented bureaucracy, Thailand does not. Second, the Thai state's existential logic is not
organic, but pluralist, with frequent competition within a pluralist elite.
These fundamental differences in state-society relations account for significant variations in the Thai democratic consolidation process contrasted with Japan and Korea.

A comparatively weak state in Thailand reflects on the different kind of democracy emerging in that country.[1] Military-led modernization and a powerful rural pull context define Thai political development. The political development of Thailand shows a consensus on the traditional elements of political culture but pluralism in the economic modernization processes and political questions concerning it. Thai political pluralism stems from the lack of a consensus on economic and political modernization. As Steven Scholsstein states (1991: 171),

Thai politics has about as many descriptions as it does participants. Some call it a "prism," through which many different political views are refracted. Others call it a "triangular partnership," which includes the king, the military, and the political parties. Or a "rectangular partnership," which includes those three components plus the competent Thai bureaucracy (also frequently referred to as the "four pillars" of Thai politics). Or a "pentagonal partnership," which includes those four plus the Buddhist Sangha, Thailand's powerful monastic order.

How are greater levels of pluralism seen in the Thai political scene? To what extent is the Asian Political Development Model a useful heuristic device for explaining Thai political development? These questions require an exploration of two ideas, which this case study covers extensively: the relationship between modernization and traditionalism and the idea of distanciation, as applied to Thailand.[2]

One characteristic that explains the pluralistic nature of Thai politics is the exacerbation of the rural and urban caused by the changing distanciation within the country. Thailand's economic and political modernization reflects its latest development in contrast to Japan and South Korea. In the Thai case, international structures and norms created much more profound effects on its development. Specifically, Thailand's extremely rapid socioeconomic change and the changing global economy's structure over the past 20 years imposed a different set of constraints and catalysts on the developmental state. Successful economic takeoff began in Japan in the 1870s; in Korea in the 1960s with President Park; and in Thailand, it began in the 1970s and picked up momentum in the 1980s. While it took Japan approximately forty years (by 1910) to become a fully industrialized nation, it took Korea more than thirty years (by 1990). Thailand's successful modernization process started in the mid- to late 1960s; past attempts under the monarchy and Phibul Songram (during and after World War II) did not lead to rapid economic modernization.

The rapid advance of global technology affected Thailand's pace of modernization by speeding up the process that required a greater concentration of political power for leadership. Thailand faces greater challenges to modernize compared with Japan or Korea. New nations face

greater difficulty adjusting to the changing pace of technological innovation abroad and must compete to find a niche in a system with rigid
rules. The technological advances by OECD (Office for Economic Cooperation and Development) nations signify the hardening of the international political economy's structure and division of labor. The gap
between the developed and underdeveloped nations becomes increasingly more difficult to bridge with exponential technology advances that
leave the have-not nations even more destitute. Developed nations now
have technological advancements far beyond those that Japan faced in
the 1900s or Korea faced in the 1980s in the steel and consumer products
industries, respectively. Today, Thailand needs to produce computer
chips and quickly establish R&D (research and development) mechanisms, at a minimum, to catch up with the West and other newly industrialized countries (NICs). Simultaneously, higher level technology
transfer becomes more difficult, and the technical human resource demands of developing economies become more difficult to satisfy. In other
words, the task of economic modernization is becoming increasingly
more difficult, and political systems experience increased stress by the
"new paradigm of modernization."

The political implication of shrinking distanciation is the abrupt im-
position of a modern cultural world upon Thailand's traditional society,
much more so than in Japan or even Korea. Therefore, Thailand is a
dichotomous nation: Bangkok is modernized and the rural areas are far
removed from the hustle and bustle of the capital. Unlike Japan or Korea,
most Thais still live in rural areas, by that giving the country's politics
a unique rural-urban political cleavage.

Of the three countries, Thailand is still in the infancy of economic
development, and this represents itself in the initial stages of the Asian
Political Development Model. Relative weakness of the bureaucracy (i.e.,
economic ministries), coupled with strong military traditions, increasing
corporate interests, persistence of rural demands, and personality-based
political parties point to simultaneous congruence and divergence from
the Asian Development Model. The historical continuity and future of
Thai politics represented by the political actors and their changing relationships show that politics, "Thai style," is a curious blend of traditionalism and modernism. As in South Korea and Japan, recreating
tradition in modern Thailand gives connections and continuity to the
past while modern values abet rapid industrialization and social transformation of the nation. Relying on the culture-as-tool box analogy again,
modernization in Thailand also involves the selective use of traditional
symbols. Traditional symbols in modern Thailand, such as the monarchy,
reflect both traditional and modern values. Others, such as the institution
of slavery in Thailand, no longer legally exist.[3]

THAILAND BEFORE SARIT: ESTABLISHING "THAINESS" IN MODERNITY

The fusion between Therevada Buddhism and the monarchy characterized the traditional political culture of Thailand until 1932. In Japan and Korea, the influence of Confucianism permeates the cultural construction of a political order, while in Thailand, Buddhism represents a functional equivalent. The traditional Thai system, much like the Confucian-influenced Sinic systems of Japan and Korea, possessed characteristics compatible with a strong hierarchical system of governance.[4] Analogous to Plato's organic society, hierarchy was quite rigid or "profoundly vertical" in traditional Thailand (Siffin 1966: 31). As David Elliot states (1978: 47), "Ideological practices of the pre-capitalist Thai social formation recognized a stratification of society in which each individual found himself set within a fairly narrow spectrum."

The traditional bureaucracy, once formed, reflected the unity of monarchy and Buddhism and revolved around deference to authority, patron-client relations, and personalism centered around the king (Girling 1981: 38–40; Sifflin 1966: 33). Charisma and traditionalism complemented each other in crafting legitimacy in a traditional Thailand where an imposed hierarchy from Bangkok created a stable social order with political stability throughout the kingdom.

The traditional Thai system faced pressure from abroad. Western intrusions into Indochina forced the Thai to confront modernity, and the once stable political system experienced punctuated development in response to outside forces. Accommodation best describes Thai strategy toward foreign threats. During the King Monghut (Rama IV) reign (1851–1868), Thailand opened up to the West and signed a commercial treaty in 1855 with Britain after the preceding king, Phra Nang Klao (Rama III), established diplomatic relations with Britain in 1826.[5] King Monghut observed British control over Burma and parts of China and feared that Thailand would lose its independence if it failed adequately to address the Western threat. King Monghut's major contribution consisted of meeting the "western threat," just as the Meiji Restoration thwarted Japan's colonization. King Monghut exercised a cautious policy of satisfying the economic needs of the West by providing raw materials and a market for manufactured goods. Simultaneously, he established a more centralized authority by improving transportation systems, relying on the natural waterways, and through economic modernization by developing trade and modern coinage. In addition, he introduced his son, King Chulalongkorn to Western ideas through the services of a private tutor (Siffin 1966: 50). However, the monarchy was essentially an institution with a conservative outlook and emphasized gradual, rather than rapid social and economic change. A concerted attempt to transform Thai society was not forthcoming from the monarchy, unlike the Meiji Restoration or the Park Chung Hee period.

King Chulalongkorn (Rama V) reigned from 1868 to 1910 and turned the table of diplomatic and commercial relations with Great Britain and France to his country's favor. The modernization of political structures, including fiscal and legal reforms, and the establishment of a bureaucracy, gradually improved Thailand's negotiating status with the West. Initially, however, Thailand lost about one-third of its territory, suffered from extraterritoriality, and was forced to open virtually the entire domestic market to foreign goods. These factors made the development of indigenous industry all but impossible.

The most important changes influencing political development that took place during Chulalongkorn's reign were the development of a paid civil service and the creation of the ministerial form of government. The latter resulted from the observations of Prince Devawongse who visited England at the Queen's Silver Jubilee and studied British government and its functional differentiation. Despite the legal-rational nature of bureaucracies, the initial Thai bureaucracies reflected the traditional element of the monarchy. According to Siffin (1966: 58–60), blood lines tied loyalists. The polygamous activities of King Monghut (94 children) and his predecessors resulted in offspring who filled the highest positions of the bureaucracy (Siffin 1966: 94–95). The criterion of loyalty over merit reflected the traditional culture of *Gemeinschaften*. A traditional mechanism contributed to bureaucratic control. By placing selected royalty into the Thai bureaucracy, the monarchy controlled the independence of the bureaucracy. When Chulalongkorn passed away, Thailand had successfully ended extraterritoriality and improved its communication system and fiscal system despite these bureaucratic drawbacks.

A period of instability followed Chulalongkorn's departure. Kings Vajiravudh (Rama VI) (1910–1925) and Prajadhipok (Rama VII) (1925–1935) lacked the charisma and organizational skill of Monghut or Chulalongkorn. They failed to build on the previous legacy of monarchy-directed modernization. In the famous 1932 coup, a group of junior officers and a few selected senior officers seized power under the guise of modernizing Thailand for the 20th century. Years of monarchial control ended abruptly and power shifted to military officers who looked to the military and the bureaucracy for carrying out the modernization program.

The two primary leaders—Phibul Songgram and Pridi Phanomyong—played instrumental roles in the 1932 coup and shaped Thai politics for the next three decades. Both Phibul and Pridi met as students in Paris (Kobkua 1995: 10–11) and believed that government needed to direct and control the political and social development of Thailand. To them, leadership provided the key in developing a Thai development model and for resisting Western influence. Logically, this would prevent it from being colonized. The new elites recognized that the monarchy's gradualist approach prevented Thailand from pursuing a more direct approach in reacting to Western pressure. They believed that the political system remained too traditional for dealing with a modern world. Their solution consisted of modernizing the Thai bureaucracy and creating a modern state that respected Thai traditions. To them, modernization required focused leadership—the political will to preserve some culture characteristics and the will to adopt others from abroad.

A group of several senior officers and a large coterie of disaffected junior officers mounted a poorly organized, amateurish coup on June 24, 1932. Nonetheless, they succeeded in gaining control over the country, and King Prajadhipok acquiesced to become a constitutional monarch and then subsequently abdicated his throne in March 1935. In the new system, the newly adopted constitution and National Assembly signified a diversification of power and a departure from "traditional politics." However, to the coup plotters, diversification of power meant a greater role for the military. The legacy of the 1932 coup remains the politicization of a largely inefficient military.

After the establishment of the 1932 system, a period of instability followed. During that time, Phibul strengthened his position by strengthening his network within the military and by successfully suppressing a royalist counter-coup in 1933. Phibul's rise to power began a long tradition of military involvement in Thailand's government, either directly or as a power broker. The military organized the first political party, the People's Party that dominated the National Assembly. After Phibul strengthened his position by becoming prime minister, he used his charisma and his personal network to remake Thai society according to his vision for a modern Thai nation. As Kobkua (1995: 17) states, "It can be said that the years 1939–1941 were Phibun[bul]'s finest hours. He had power, political and military, the support of his colleagues and the nation, and success beyond the wildest dreams of any Thai leader, past or present."

Phibul possessed the power to change single-handedly the destiny of Thailand. Throughout the remainder of his regime he consolidated power by marginalizing the National Assembly and by choosing predominantly military officials to ministerial portfolios (Kobkua 1995: 18). Phibul emerged as a dictator who claimed to rule with the people's consent, and he drew on his charisma for legitimation. In many ways he fit the definition of an authoritarian populist demagogue. Then, in some ways, he was a social engineer, skillfully balancing traditionalism and modernity as bases of personal power.

However, Phibul was not an authoritarian without a vision; he was a skilled strategist at managing political differences in order to accomplish his goal of modernization. He molded domestic and international politics to his liking. Thailand needed a strong leader to tackle growing international uncertainty and later the specter of Japanese encroachment. Phibul, the charismatic pragmatist, adeptly used international crises (i.e., Japanese expansion and World War II) to construct an organic nation. International crisis legitimated his modernization program and his authoritarian approach to governance characterized by his suppression of political dissent. His modernization approach aimed to authenticate traditional "Thainess" while simultaneously embracing modern culture and industrial techniques of production.

On another dimension, Phibul worked hard to eliminate long-established traditional practices by pointing out their backwardness. He attempted to construct a modern economic, social, and political system by drawing on pieces of tradition and by choosing the appropriate cultural tools. His eclectic approach de-emphasized that which he deemed harmful, bolstered favorable characteristics, and imported from abroad what appeared missing.

What distinguished Phibul's comprehensive modernization program, and to what extent did these changes endure after World War II? Nationalism and modernization represented the core belief of Phibul and the military officers. Collectively, they believed in transforming the cultural and social values among the masses. From 1933 to 1944, Phibul worked to modify standards of personal dress, eating, social skills, and individual thinking. At a societal level, he constantly invoked the greatness of the Thai nation. Even during Japanese collaboration, beginning in 1942, he justified it by claiming that the Thai-Japan partnership would strengthen Thailand by restoring territory previously lost to Great Britain. However, his partnership with the Japanese remained uneasy. A controlling leader, he zealously guarded against Japanese intrusion into domestic politics. Phibul resisted Japanese attempts to control and manipulate political events in Thailand (Thamsook 1977). Thus, the Japanese distrusted him.

While Phibul's social modernization programs appeared authoritarian and perhaps petty, in retrospect they successfully mobilized the population by instilling a sense of national unity and spirit of *Gemeinschaft*. Some changes, including the adoption of the name "Thailand" to replace "Siam" in 1939, or the inauguration of a new national anthem, created a collective psychology of national progress. Another example is the *Rattha Niyom* (Cultural Mandates of the State). These decrees and slogans, attest to the mobilizational orientation of Phibul.[6] The twelve *Rattha Niyom* are listed in Table 7.1.

Three examples illustrate the extent of social engineering during the Phibul regime.[7] Article 4 of the Royal Decree in 1940 stipulated the following as subversive to national prestige (Kobkua 1995: 115): "unnecessary noise or improper language or behavior that ridicules those who

Table 7.1
The Twelve *Rattha Niyom* from 1939 to 1942

1. On country, people, and nationality
2. On protecting the country's security
3. On the name of Thai honorific names
4. On respecting and saluting the national flag, national anthem, and royal anthem
5. On using indigenous products rather than imports
6. On the tune and words of the national anthem
7. On calling the Thais to build their nation
8. On the royal anthem
9. On the Thai language and the duty of good citizens
10. On the dress style and appropriate clothing
11. On the daily work routine of Thais
12. On the treatment of children, the aged, and the handicapped

Source: Based on Numnonda (1977): 23.

try to promote the national customs; forceful acquisition of space such as on buses or at ticket windows or at theater entrances; vandalism of public properties by writing on improper places; bathing along public roads." Social conformity and clearly defined norms crafted from traditional culture and a dash of modernity gave the Thai citizens a psychological feeling of impending modernity and progress.

Another example of social engineering dealt with eating betel nuts, as cited in Numnonda (1977: 33):

The government turned its attention to eliminating the old custom of chewing betel-nut because it consider [sic] the habit a deep national disgrace which had to be stamped out and the people practising it had to be condemned. They looked like they had blood over their mouths and because of their blackened teeth, they generally appeared ugly and older than their age. Besides, this custom encouraged spitting on roads and sidewalks.[8]

The *Wiratham*, or national code of valor, gives one last example (Numnonda 1977: 36–37) of attempted social engineering which also combined modern and traditional elements. The following are the fourteen points as cited in Numnonda (1977: 37) and Kobkua (1995: 124):

1. The Thais love their nation more than their lives.
2. The Thais are great warriors.

3. The Thais are hard working in agriculture and industry.
4. The Thais enjoy a good living.
5. The Thais are well dressed.
6. The Thais speak according to what their hearts say.
7. The Thais are peace lovers.
8. The Thais worship Buddha more than their lives.
9. The Thais honor their children, women and the aged.
10. The Thais follow the Leader.
11. The Thais grow their own food.
12. The Thais are best to their friends and worst to their enemies.
13. The Thais are honest and grateful.
14. The Thais leave behind property for their children.

Attempts at overt social engineering ended in 1944 when Seni Primoj and Pridi (two prominent members of the Free Thai exiled movement) overthrew Phibul. The legacy of Phibul's leadership reflected in the increased reputation of the military as a "law and order" institution. The groundwork for future military intervention was laid. Meanwhile, before Japan's imminent defeat, the People's Party's fissure into two factions— one pro–Allied powers and another pro-Japan—contributed to the ouster of Phibul. Many saw Phibul as a Japanese collaborator.

Pridi formed a new government immediately after World War II by working with the new prime minister, Seni Pramoj. The Pridi faction's constituency base consisted of students, artists, and intellectuals while Phibul drew his support from the military, which he constantly exalted. Pridi played an instrumental role in rewriting a more democratic constitution (he was a legal scholar by training) which barred active military participation in politics (Kobkua 1995: 188). Through elections, Pridi's Constitution Front (Naew Rathammanum) and its coalition partner Co-operation Party (Sahacheep), controlled a significant majority of seats. In the semidemocratic system that Pridi established, the military felt denied its legitimate role. The disgruntled military formed the base of a conservative-royalist alliance, which in the 1947 coup restored Phibul into power. Once back in power, Phibul tried to return to the early 1940s system. He stamped out the chaos associated with parliamentary government and restored the military's and his own personal honor, tarnished during Pridi's rule. (Tried as a war criminal and a Japanese collaborator, Phibul was acquitted in 1946.)

Marshal Sarit Thanarat, the senior military commander during the decade of political turbulence (1948–1957), became nationally prominent. Political turf-battles during the decade pitted one faction against another. Rivalry between the executive and the court royalists, dedicated to increasing the monarchy's power, displayed the fundamental weaknesses of the state during this period.[9] The stage emerged for highly competitive, elite-based politics, dominated by the military, monarchy, parties, and corporate elites. The urban and rural cleavages divided the elites of the nation.

INSTITUTIONALIZED MILITARY DOMINANCE UNDER SARIT AND SUCCESSORS (1957–1973)

Bureaucratic-authoritarianism characterized the period 1957 to 1973 when relations between the military elite and bureaucracy became closer and more symbiotic. During this period, the military relied on the bureaucracy for essential technical advice and administrative functions. Meanwhile, the military protected its "honorable and patriotic tradition" by designating prime ministers, cabinet members, and selecting candidates as potential members of the National Assembly. Simultaneously, the military class involved itself in politics and administration and thereby maintained a large share of the Thai budget.

External support and conditions bolstered the defense forces during this period. Much of the military's external support derived from the ongoing Indochina conflict and the threat of communism, on which Sarit always capitalized. From 1950 to 1975, the United States supported the national security state in Thailand—just as it had supported the one in South Korea—by training officers and providing military assistance (Elliott 1978: 129–33).[10]

The short-lived interim rule of Thanom Kittikachorn ended by a counter-coup led by Marshal Sarit in 1958. He controlled the military through years of coalition building. Sarit moved swiftly to consolidate power, banning political parties, jailing dissidents, and controlling the press. His contributions to nation building, however, were threefold:

• He increased the importance of traditionalism in Thai politics by embracing traditionally accepted values and by that introducing sociocultural norms into policy making while also introducing modern elements, including planning as evidenced by Five Year Plans.

• He restored the power and respect of the monarchy.

• He continued the idea of crafting a distinctive "Thai polity."

Sarit's approach to social, economic, and political development, while highly idiosyncratic and based on personalism,[11] led to greater economic development and a stronger role for technocrats (Thak 1979). He believed that, as prime minister, his leadership, based on traditional patron-client relations, was akin to that of a father to his children. Hierarchical orientation, enforced by traditional notions of obedience and loyalty, represented the two most important characteristics used to cultivate a renewed sense of urgency for modernization (Muscat 1994: 87–88). In contrast to Thai traditionalism, he believed Western liberalism caused social chaos because of its discontinuity with Thai tradition (Muscat 87–88). Western liberalism is antithetical to the strong concentration of power required to orchestrate late development, and Sarit recognized this fact.

During this military-dominated period, the trajectory of political, social, and economic development assumed a mix of the personalistic basis of Marshall Sarit and the legal-rational elements of technocrats. Political and economic development embodied a Saritian *modus vivendi* by fusing Thai traditionalism and religion with Western-based ideas of modernity and progress. (In Thailand, traditionalism and Buddhism, like Confucianism and traditionalism in Japan and Korea, became integrated and mutually reinforcing.)[12] He sought to increase his legitimacy and used traditional notions to promote social change by relying on the pull of tradition and the push of modernity.

Sarit orchestrated the First Five Year Plan (1961–1966) and strengthened the economic bureaucracies in a show of modern administration. The economic technocrats gradually replaced the military elites who lacked the technical knowledge to implement these plans. These technocrats, however, initially lacked the appropriate expertise too and resulted in only modest success. Even to this day, the technocrats remain weak in the Thai developmental state. During the plan's years, the development of the infrastructure (especially transportation and utilities) as it related to agriculture, occupied importance (Muscat 1994: 95). The government increased expenditures on rural projects, and later this would become a valuable resource for rural network-based patron-client acts of "pork barrel Thai style" into the 1990s (Robertson 1996).

The introduction of business elites as central political players and the exclusion of labor represent other consequences of a Thai-style developmental state. Unlike the cases of Japan and South Korea, Thailand's developmental state manifested structural weaknesses, both in personnel and in a lack of autonomy from the ruling military elite. The state could not create the kind of industrial targeting or policy loans that made the state-led strategy a success in Japan, Korea, or even Taiwan. Instead, third-wave late industrializers—Malaysia, Philippines, and Thailand (Japan represents the first wave and Singapore, Taiwan, and South Korea the second wave)—came to rely predominantly on foreign investment from industrialized nations. As a result, economic planning bureaucracies of the third wave exerted less control over the economy than first- and second-wave nations. The Thai government relied more on private enterprise activities to propel economic development.[13] Clearly, the role of the state in Thailand, beginning with the Sarit days, points more toward macroeconomic management than microeconomic intervention. Thai industrial policy, in contrast to microeconomic management in Korea (Amsden 1989) or in Japan (Johnson 1987, 1982), represented an overall strategy of macroeconomic management (Laothamatas 1995: 211).

Sarit's developmentalist approach hinged on the use of comparatively low-cost Thai labor, similar to the early days of Japanese and Korean economic development. Quickly, he banned strikes and weakened the labor movement by jailing its leaders. Economic growth, in particular labor intensive industrialization, promoted rapid migration of people seeking employment to Bangkok. Thais flocked to industrial development zones around the city, creating the many urban infrastructural problems of Bangkok today. These workers' wages, however, remained artificially low in contrast to Western labor, because industry and government prohibited them from organizing independent labor unions.

Japanese, Korean, and Taiwanese firms that took advantage of special development zones emulated the "home grown" enterprise system within these newly established Thai subsidiaries. The phenomenon of a politically weak left came to reflect Thailand's political landscape, too. Despite the proliferation of political parties in Thailand, beginning with the 1973–1976 failed democracy, few represented or allied with labor unions. As in the Korean and Japanese cases, labor-oriented parties are virtually nonexistent in Thailand. Workers had difficultly becoming a major political force because they arrived on the political scene after elites solidified the rules of competition.

The Thai developmental state's macroeconomic policy led to greater elite pluralism by empowering bureaucrats, politicians, and corporate elites much earlier than in the Korean or Japanese cases. Unlike the Japanese or Korean state, the Thai state remained weak and political currents changed rapidly. The monarchy represented the only source of constancy. Therefore, when corporations became involved in the political process by using their financial resources, the state could not fend them off through coercion. Instead, the weakness of bureaucrats and elected officials required that the corporate elite rapidly join them.

Lastly, the Thai developmental state allowed the military full access to political parties. This allowed them to refrain from conducting coups, in the long term, and to focus on political parties as alternative vehicles for political interest articulation. The military during this period actively worked to secure their electoral future.[14] By 1973, Thailand possessed the requisite elite actors identified in the bureaucratic-authoritarian stage of the Asian Development Model. However, it lacked the kind of concentration of power seen in Japan, based on a consensus among elites, or in Korea in the Park era, through coercive instruments.

FROM AUTHORITARIANISM COMES SEMI-DEMOCRACY AND THE "NEW POWER ELITE": 1973 TO PRESENT

Vacillation between civilian and military leaders characterize most of the period from 1973 to the present. Many scholars suggest that Thailand evolved from a bureaucratic-authoritarian system toward a semi-democracy (Neher and Marlay 1995; Quiggley 1995; Muscat 1994; Dhiravegin 1988). One noticeable difference between the previous years (1957–1973) and the new era (1973–present) was the increased institutionalization of elections. Elections occurred more regularly without annulment by coups. Elections gained some degree of legitimacy for all elites because the Thai public increasingly accepted the political participation of former officers in preference to the coups of active military generals. The power elite in Thailand found elections useful because they legitimized the elite's rule and gave them a mechanism for managing pluralistic tendencies. For citizens, they provided a popular mechanism that elites found less threatening than Western-style democracy.

From the military's perspective, launching a coup became too costly because it became an insufficient mechanism for legitimately ruling the country. As Derek Tonkin, the former British ambassador to Thailand stated (Tonkin 1990: 287), "The increasing sophistication of the Thai public and the realities of an industrializing society have made military coups as an acceptable alternative to elections no longer a tolerable option." As members of the power elite, military officers had to work within the party system by nominating some of their own or by forming their own parties. The military's overall power declined as its monopoly on political power dissipated, and it had to compete against rural and urban professional politicians. Meanwhile, some business and bureaucratic elites turned to politics as a means to obtain political power, further weakening the military's monopoly.

Beginning in 1973 and lasting until 1976, a period of instability characterized by student protests and labor activity ended the Sarit system. Signaling the sunset of military power, in 1992, King Bhumipol intervened and requested that the army share power with the emerging Bangkok urban middle class represented by the Democrat Party. The economic transformation begun under Sarit provided greater participation by a more politically sophisticated middle class. This trend continued to increase so that by 1992, when a suddenly retired General Suchinda Krapayoon became prime minister, the public protested in Bangkok streets, recognizing the threat to their democratic ideals (Neher 1994b). Consequently, Suchinda lasted only about a month and resigned in May after protests brought Bangkok to a virtual halt.

By 1992, politics operated through political parties on a procedural level with citizens developing respect for democratic ideals. Substantively, however, political parties to this day have not adequately or accurately accounted for the needs of the country's emerging industrial labor population or urban residents. Rural residents have gained representation although rurally oriented political parties, just as those directed toward urbanites, are vehicles for the power elite. Accordingly, Thai politics became more substantively democratic than the other two cases. However, the members of the power elite still permeate the formation and operation of political parties, something that fits within the expectations of the general Asian Development Model. Given the trend toward increased party competition and a decline in the overt powers of the military, to what extent do Thai politics fit the Asian Political Development Model?

As demonstrated and discussed in Chapter 4, Thailand differs from the norm of the East Asian model because of high fractionalization levels inherent in its party system. Similar to other Asian parties, however, Thai political parties also represent a narrow band of socially derived interests, including bureaucratic, military, and corporate ones. Unlike all other East Asian political systems, however, the major Thai political parties and the competition characteristic of the party system reflect some pluralistic orientations of elites. The three primary elites in the model, the military, bureaucrats, and the business community, are well represented in Thai political parties. The political system also shows a significant tilt toward the Asian political model by manifesting the simultaneous effects of traditionalism and modernization.

Political parties show the simultaneous effects of traditionalism and modernity. These three characteristics need addressing:

• military interest represented in elections and parties (combination of modern and traditional politics)
• business involvement in elections and parties (modern politics)
• rural interests in elections and parties (tradition recreated for modern politics)

Political parties and the military share a long history in Thailand. Traditionally, generals established political parties for legitimation purposes and for providing the military a dominant voice in policy making. For example, generals founded seven of the more than fifteen significant political parties. The Democrat Party (DP), founded in 1946, currently draws its support from a combination of military officers and urban professionals. Another significant party, the Chart Thai (Thai Nation) originated from Thanom's United Thai People's Party and drew its support primarily from the rural northern section of the country. Other promilitary parties include the Thai Citizen (Prachakorn Thai) and Social Action Party (SAP). These promilitary parties and citizen disapproval of coups effectively terminated the military's violent intervention in politics. This trend represents a significant improvement in political liberalization. However, business intervention in politics raises several major concerns about Thailand's future political development. According to Laothamatas (1988: 454) approximately half of all cabinet members in the 1980s came from the business world, showing the increasing influx of business tycoons into the Thai power elite. The blurring line between the state and corporations poses a significant problem. Who will regulate them?

Ethnic Chinese political participation reflects a positive trend. Since many corporate elites have Chinese backgrounds, the empowerment of corporations means greater participatory rights of Chinese corporate elite. Their recent inclusion points to increased pluralism within the power elite. For the first time since Phibul, in the 1940s, systematically excluded non-Thai participation, the Chinese—who are now almost fully assimilated into Thai life—could participate fully (Nicro 1993: 175). Through intermarrying Thai nationals and developing monied connections in Southeast Asia, local tycoons increased their financial capital and bought votes, positions, and opportunities for more money (Dhiravegin 1988: 89–90). Given the continued globalization of Thailand's economy, the influence of the corporate elites will increase as they find new opportunities for building financial capital and political resources. Greater wealth among the business elite hastened their political participation through specially created interest groups, including the Thai Bankers Association, Thai Chamber of Commerce, and the Association for Thai Industries (Laothamatas 1995: 203). Overall, the corporate elite's position, as it emerged from clientelism toward a greater influence over the government, points to a rough fit with the second stage of the Asian Political Development Model. However, significant limitations exist, including the weakness of the state and elite pluralism. These factors make state insularity less likely. Therefore, the Thai developmental state does not resemble the Japanese or Korean version.

The rise of rural political networks, however, displays counterevidence regarding the placement of Thailand in the bureaucratic-corporate stage. Through their vote-buying tactics, based on patron-client relationships and the traditional values of loyalty, rural politicians increased their power in the National Assembly (Robertson 1996). Given that most Thais still live in rural areas and given the pluralistic nature of the power elite, these politicians exert significant influence over the political system.

An example of rural politics which still dominates the political scene is that of Chavalit Yonchaiyudh (present prime minister) and Banharn Silpa-archa (former prime minister). Both derive vast support from rural

Thailand. Banharn, in particular, is notorious for his traditional-style politics with his social network well entrenched in the home province of Thonburi. However, the degree to which the power of rural politicians will continue for the future is far from certain. As migration to the city continues and rural Thais become gradually more modern, the present pervasive extent of the patron-client ties will decline but may not entirely fade. One study in particular, by LoGerfo (1996), suggests that significant differences in values between rural and urban Thais exist. Given the continually increasing income gap between urban and rural residents, political representation for rural areas and any pork it may provide is beneficial for national integration. On theoretical grounds, such a system—whether in this case or in Japan with rural electoral over-representation—agrees with substantive democracy, assuming that urbanites are not excessively harmed.

In summary, Thailand presents a difficult case for the model, straining its internal logic. Thai cultural background differs significantly from Japan's and Korea's and the pattern of economic development also deviates from them. Given the cultural differences between a Confucian-traditional society and a Buddhist-traditional society, and the weak control exerted by the Thai state over the developmental process, the country fits the model loosely.

NOTES

1. Based partly on Neher (1992) and updated with Quigley (1995); and Banks et al. (1996), *Political Handbook of the World* (New York: McGraw-Hill), section on Thailand, from 1932 to 1997 Thailand experienced 19 coup attempts (13 successful), 22 different prime ministers (average tenure of about three years), 51 different cabinets, 15 new constitutions promulgated, and 21 general elections held.

2. According to Anthony Giddens (1984: 377), time-space distanciation is "the stretching of social systems across time-space, on the basis of mechanisms of social and system integration." Increased communications, technology, and transfer of information led to a shrinking of time-space continuum in which "space" and "time" between locales decreased and led to a rapid speeding up of social phenomena. See Harvey (1989).

3. On an interesting side note, one can only wonder the extent to which ideas of traditional Thai slavery exist in present-day Bangkok's sex trade.

4. Elliot (1978: 47) notes that hierarchy in traditional Thai society developed from the need for a strong government and eventually placed the king at the center of religious observance. Religion sanctioned hierarchy through the rituals performed by the priests, which with the king present, would signify the unity of the kingdom and provide it with social stability. For more information, see Riggs (1966), especially pp. 65–77.

5. The early account of Thai political history is based primarily on the following four sources: Riggs (1966); Sifflin (1966); Girling (1981); and Muscat

(1994). Robert Muscat's account of Thailand's encounter with the West differs from the other three authors who begin with Rama III, while Muscat mentions initial contact with Rama IV in 1855.

6. The decrees were of two kinds—those decreed by the government and then those declared by royal decree. Phibul made sure that the monarchy remained a central part of the ceremonial aspects of Thai society. The utilization of the monarchy in this fashion demonstrates how he used traditional sources of authority to his benefit.

7. The decrees were of two varieties: those decreed by the government and those declared by royal decree. Phibul made sure that the monarchy remained a highly visible ceremonial part of Thai national life. The utilization of the monarchy in this fashion demonstrates how Phibul used traditional sources of authority to consolidate power and govern.

8. Coincidentally, many of these prohibitions and attempts at social engineering are similar to measures presently used in Singapore where gum chewing and spitting is subject to fines.

9. Neher (1994b: 55) develops the theme that Thailand's government represents a strong state insulated from independent actors. The theme developed in this case study suggests the contrary. The Thai state never developed the kind of insularity and general cohesiveness indicative of either Japan or South Korea. Thailand represents a co-opted state, especially with rural politicians and the corporate elite of Bangkok assuming control over the political system for their personal benefit.

10. Direct U.S. military presence in Thailand was stabilized between 27,000 and 44,000 troops from 1966 to 1974 (Elliott 1978: 131) as part of Vietnam War efforts.

11. Sarit's personal ideology consisted of paternalism, as discussed, and anti-communism (Girling 1981: 169).

12. For example, the Buddhist-centered notions of communitarianism and egalitarianism consisted of programs of health care for the elderly, reduced utility rates and school charges, and other populist programs (Muscat 1994: 84).

13. Additionally, the globalization of the economy, which accelerated rapidly from the 1970s, makes the effectiveness and probability of strong developmental-state apparatuses extremely unlikely.

14. Samudavanijia (1989: 324) states that during the period from 1976 to 1982, the budget of the military included a secret fund, part of which was used for political purposes such as political activities. Given the loosely organized nature of Thai political parties, it is likely that some of the money drifted toward campaigns.

8

Conclusion: Cases and the Asian Development Model

Modern societies have much in common, but they do not necessarily merge into homogeneity. The argument that they do rests on the assumption that modern society must approximate a single type, the Western type; that modern civilization is Western civilization. This however, is false identification. Virtually all scholars of civilization agree that the Western civilization emerged in the eighth and ninth centuries and developed its distinctive characteristics in the centuries that followed. It did not begin to modernize until the eighteenth century. The West, in short, was Western long before it was modern.

Samuel Huntington (1996: 30)

CRAFTING ASIAN POLITICAL DEVELOPMENT: LOOKING AT THE PAST TO PREDICT THE FUTURE

Significant political change occurred in East Asia since the developmental state placed economic growth and socioeconomic modernization at the center of public policy. East Asian political changes over the past ten years need careful examination within a cultural and historical context, rather than through the lens of Western political development. In the three case studies, the differences in the role of culture and developmental state activities explained how these countries democratized differently. Also, each of these three countries dealt with the encroachment of the West quite differently. This, too, affected the democratic trajectory because modernization's success reflected developmental state strength. Despite these differences, the general pattern of political development as presented in the Asian Political Development Model holds well.

In all three of the case studies, the political elite used traditionalism to create economic and political systems that mirrored elite social values. Simultaneously, leaders adopted modern ideas, including the Weberian notions of legal-rational bureaucracies, to mobilize middle class aspirants. However, in all three cases, the elites selected carefully the cultural elements essential for constructing their vision of a good society. Social engineering played an important role in the acculturation of the public to modernity.

The developmental state crystallized more firmly in Japan than in Korea or Thailand. In postwar Japan, each political elite contributed to the interlocking directorate's structure, which made policy consensuses easier. Korea possessed a more hierarchically differentiated elite structure, and the triangular interlocking relationships evidenced in Japan were absent. Therefore, the developmental state in South Korea retained a much more charismatic element. In Thailand, unlike Japan or South Korea, the developmental state reflected a significant degree of pluralism. Thai pluralism emerged over time as new political elites gained access to the levers of power, but this occurred before the developmental state developed fully. As a result, the Thai developmental state never matured.

The shape of democratic consolidation in all three countries represents the dominance of the conservative elements who participated in the formation of the developmental state. Incidentally, the observation holds for all seven countries in this study. All East Asian political systems manifest an exclusion of the political left because the developmental state weakened or prevented the formation of independent labor unions. However, in Japan, the conservative coalition's success in managing the Western threat through modernization created the hegemonic form of democratic consolidation. Hegemonic democracy in postwar Japan experienced relatively high levels of elite legitimacy. In the Korean case, low levels of governmental legitimacy meant that authoritarianism prevented the establishment of a democracy until 1987. After a period of transition, the election of Kim Dae Jung may signal the end of the old conservative establishment. Also, democratic consolidation in South Korea also suggests that the conservative remain powerful. Unlike Japan, however, Korea will continue to manifest high levels of periodic turbulence in its political system because the elites were never able fully to legitimate themselves. In Thailand, the military successfully integrated themselves into political parties while new actors, such as the business elites and rural-based politicians participate in a chaotic party system. A traditional symbol of national unity, King Bhumipol, gives a necessary continuity with the past. In all three countries, the kind of democracy emerging combines the traditional elements of social hierarchical stratification with indigenized Western norms of procedural democracy.

Asian democracy then, unlike its Western counterpart which derived its bases from the liberal tradition, originates from Asian traditionalism and the modern experiences of the developmental state. The essential characteristics of procedural Asian democracy include conservative party dominance, the heavy intervention of the corporate elite into politics, and the exclusion of the political left. Regarding substantive democracy, Asian elites acted on traditional communitarian values. They created, for example, full employment in South Korea and Japan. In all three cases, an emphasis on relatively equal access to education remains a foundation of social and economic policy. Poverty and income inequality throughout the seven countries in this study, except Thailand, Malaysia, and the Philippines, declined over time as these countries' economies grew rapidly. For Thailand, Malaysia, and the Philippines, no one knows the long-term direction of poverty and income trends, but if Japan, Singapore, Taiwan, and South Korea provide a clue, it is likely that the poorer countries will ultimately have similar results. Given the concentrated nature of political power, one would not expect altruistic policies to result if elites are entirely self-interested and lacking a communitarian moral philosophy. However, in Asia, traditional notions of community and an organic view of society mitigate such self-serving behavior.

THEORETICAL IMPLICATIONS

This research examined East Asian political development and concluded that democratic consolidation takes into account the varied historical and cultural experiences of countries. The evidence in this research points to an alternative form of democracy, one that evolved from the developmental state. Leaders of the developmental state use culture, both traditional and modern, as a source of legitimacy. Frequently, Western notions of democracy, based on the idea of party competition, fail to take form in East Asia. In particular, the political weakness of the left reflects the unique interplay of culture, economics, and politics.

When political scientists speak of democratic consolidation, they need to examine the historical and cultural context of the ongoing process carefully. Failure to do that results in the inability to extract meaningful conclusions about each of these societies. Simultaneously, with a grossly general model of political development, the theories fail to decipher the differences between Western and Asian political systems.

As demonstrated in the case studies, culture plays an important role in political development. Many scholars focus exclusively on institutional rules and procedures and do not account for differences caused by cultures. The use of traditional and indigenous cultural symbols complemented modernity, which elites imported from abroad. The particular mix of tradition and modernity varied from one nation to another depending on whether existing traditional culture supplied appropriate tools for economic modernization. No society relies exclusively on traditionalism or modernity because socioeconomic modernization requires that the transformational leader balance the need for identity and change. Without traditions, a society cannot be stable, and without progress, no leader can maintain society's allegiance. Modernizing is clearly a difficult and perilous task for leaders.

As societies modernize, they must deal with the impact of socioeconomic change. Two aspects of concern are pressures from the masses and changes within the elite structure. Modernization changes attitudes among the masses and empowers and weakens specific elites. The challenge for political leadership revolves around facilitating change and maintaining continuity. Asian leaders rely on economic growth and guided democracy to maintain their societies.

This research also explored the connections between economic and political development and the intermediary role that cultures play. An appropriate balance between economic and political development ensures political stability and continued economic development. Elites who successfully lead their nation in economic development experience a higher level of legitimacy. However, as the South Korean case shows, legitimacy based on economic growth faces uncertainty in times of economic turmoil.

The distinction between economics and politics in East Asian societies does not exist as it does in the West because the elites' legitimacy draws heavily from economic growth. The connections between economic and political development are complex and multifaceted. The pressing need for modernization and the initial disparities in opportunities concentrated economic and political power in an elite. The structure of Asian power resembles an interlocking directorate with the military, bureaucratic, corporate, and political elites participating in politics. Over time, however, the dominant actors change according to economic needs and modernization's socioeconomic impact. Elected political leaders remain consistently weaker than other elites.

International events and the global economy also shaped Asian politics. To achieve rapid growth and to resist communism, elites persecuted labor unions and other leftists during the Cold War era. The developmental state systematically excluded the political left by co-opting them. They also suppressed the creation of independent labor unions and tarnished their reputation by pointing to communist potential to destroy long-established traditions. An economically revolutionary developmental state required a politically conservative and evolutionary atmosphere that insulated the power of the economic bureaucracies and the corporations from excessive public pressure.

All these factors point toward a distinctly Asian pattern of political development. It relies on modernity of the developmental state and the traditionalism of a *Gemeinschaft*. Given the imperialism of the West, Asia's response considered the need for national survival as the paramount goal of the state. Protecting traditionalism, however, did not preclude Asia from adopting and adapting Western ideas. One such idea is democracy, which elites adapted to Asian conditions.

The relationships among economy, culture, and politics are incorporated into the Asian Development Model. Economic modernization through the developmental-state framework provides the driving mechanism for political development. Asian leaders resisted Western neocolonial pressures and looked to Japan's economic model for successful examples of balancing tradition and modernity. Therefore, Japan's modernization effort, beginning with the Meiji Restoration, provides the empirical groundwork for the Asian Political Development Model. Not surprisingly, East Asian political development shared important and similar characteristics with Japan. The strong ruling class' hegemony and a dominant political party remain a distinctive feature of Asian political systems. In particular, the Thailand and Japan cases point to a triangular elite configuration while in Korea, a hierarchical power structure exists. In all three cases, the conservative elites weaken political dissent by focusing on economic growth and by allowing adjustments of power within the elite configuration. Economic, military, and bureaucratic elites use political parties as vehicles to legitimacy. Political parties in Asia, then, were not institutionalized as independent entities for providing the necessary institutional check on the existing power elite. The ruling conservative parties throughout East Asia did not exist as countervailing forces to the established elite, but instead were part of them. Therefore, democratic consolidation means less party-system competition and a party system dominated by a hegemonic conservative party existing as an appendage to the state. Elections represent more of a plebiscite than a genuine vehicle for political change.

TOWARD ASIAN-STYLE DEMOCRACY OR LIBERAL DEMOCRACY?

The dominant concern among East Asians is not democracy but the preservation of social order and good government (Bell 1995b: 17). Democracy is a foreign import, developed in the West, and marketed to the East. At the same time, global society views democracy as a sine qua non of modernity. Thus, while Western liberal democracy cannot be applied to Asia without modifications, Asian leaders remain sensitive to Western notions of liberal democracy. Political development of democracy takes place within a historical and cultural context. In order for democracy to survive, context provides necessary modifications to a

Western form of government. The examples of newly independent nations show this. Many African and Asian nations that used the blanket adoption approach quickly abandoned the parliamentary system of government. Philosophically, Confucianism, Buddhism, and traditionalism can effectively become part of Asia's democratic experience. Unlike democracy in the West, which enshrines individual liberty, Asian democracy would tilt toward the community, possess aspects of paternalism, and place a premium on social order. These philosophical orientations support the traditional notion of *Gemeinschaft* as the basis of governance. Under traditional Asian forms of social organization, hierarchy and strictly defined societal roles promote social order. The political system reflects traditional Asian social organization with political elites playing an important role in guiding democracy.

The idea of elite-guided democracy fits well with communitarian notions of elderly respect and meritocracy by gerontocracy. The wisdom of elders is a valuable asset to anchor democratic practices in past traditions and to temper the potential for tyranny of the masses. Given the organic propensity of traditional Asian societies, much of which still exists today, political elites can construct a more meaningful polity if they allow individuals greater participation. Policies in such a system would be more reflective of substantive democracy, and the decision-making process would protect the integrity of Asian notions of organic communities. The poor levels of political party institutionalization undermine possible progress toward substantive democracy.

Now that many Asian nations are industrialized, the past undemocratic and frequently brutal practices undermine long-term political development. The concentration of power within the power elite is harmful to the traditional values of Asian societies if large segments of the population, such as labor groups, continue to receive inadequate representation. Instead of the present corporatism without labor, Asian leaders have a moral responsibility to address these concerns. Failure to do so will only lead to greater political instability.

Some degree of concentrated economic power is necessary for late modernization. However, the extent to which this power becomes a corruptive force in politics represents a significant threat to Asian democratic consolidation, especially because it affects the most crucial citizen-to-government link: the political parties. Not only does it affect the electoral strength of parties, it also makes Asian democracy substantively undemocratic by affecting the equitable application of rules. Furthermore, policy decisions that emanate from such a system favor the power elites over the masses. At some point, such policies no longer reflect a communitarian perspective and may become exclusive to it. Concentrated economic power remains a defining characteristic of Asian economic development. While corporate interests deserve a role in politics, their activities should not hamper the participation of other interests, including labor, rural residents, minorities, environmental groups, and women's rights groups.

One aspect of Asian politics not addressed by this research was unconventional participatory forms. Unconventional participation reflects the failure of the political system to address emerging issues. Riots, protests, and student demonstrations reflect the extent to which Asian political systems remain insular from the masses. Elites must work to construct an inclusive political forum. Enterprise unions, for example, despite their shortcomings, are widely used in Asia to reflect a communitarian perspective geared towards a consensus. Is it possible to improve their role in the political process? Can Asian nations avoid the antagonism that the West experienced through destabilizing conflict revolving around the worker-owner cleavage? Past attempts at political construction suggest the possibility of such an alternative. Can society transform economic nationalism into political nationalism for creating indigenous democratic political systems for each respective society?

Yet, the phenomenon of rapid economic growth is a double-edged sword because economic growth is part and parcel of nationalism; nationalism has an ugly side. For example, nationalism caused by economic modernization led to the rise of the fascist Japanese state in the 1930s. In the future, China's emerging nationalism can prevent its centrifugal tendencies resulting from regional imbalances in development. Under a militarized and nationalistic China, elites will likely use modern and traditional symbols to hold together a nation beset with disintegrative tendencies.

On the other hand, nationalism could lead to the healthy rejection of elements of Western culture that would weaken indigenous culture and lead to political decay. Rightfully, many Asians are proud of their economic and cultural accomplishments over the past 30 years, and that feeling is probably increasing. Emerging Asian nationalism can reconcile the pull of tradition and the push of modernization for new and younger generations. The key to its success lies in helping Asians to construct indigenous approaches to political, social, and economic meanings of existence. In that regard, the recent economic problems of East Asia and the consequent pressure to adopt IMF-sponsored economic solutions appears short-sighted. These reforms will undermine the sociocultural basis of the economies and weaken the power elite. The success of the reforms ultimately depends on how elites can manage them constructively.

Managing the future of Asia will require even greater attention to traditional and modern identity symbols. As the pace of global change hastens, what can prevent the globalization process from undermining one's identity? Globalization also pushes people to assume that the Western democratic experience is something Asia should emulate. Even many younger Asians think so. Yet, Asia remains Asian in many ways. It is not the West nor can it be the West, and that is the uniqueness of Asia. Its rich history of culture and traditions continue to affect economic and political construction. The search for identity, as Koreans, Japanese, Thais, and Filipinos, will intensify, just as Asians begin to ponder what makes them Asian. The globalization of culture and economy forces those living in non-Western societies to ask these particularistic questions. To some extent, this is already happening, as reflected in the values of the Asian Generation X. According to a recent article, society successfully transmits conservative Asian values from one generation to the next.[1] Western values exist in Asian youth, but Asian values dominate according to the article in the *Far Eastern Economic Review*. It stated:

Still, whether conducting surveys or stumbling over anecdotal evidence, academic and private-sector analysts say the similarity of views expressed by Asia's Generation Xers is almost uncanny. In survey after survey, interviewees stress the importance of family, jobs, saving for the future, caring for older relatives and other such traditional values. Such supposed Western imports as individualism or a more relaxed attitude towards premarital sex are unequivocally rejected.

In the future, embracing Asian values would not mean that human rights can be violated or that women cannot participate in politics. Traditional Asian values seek to embrace the community, and if these became community values, democracy in Asia will change. If elites refuse to realize this, then they fail in their task of managing traditional and modern symbols inherent in the development process. The elites' responsibility should be to suggest and educate, not hijack the political process for their own interests. If the present political elites can construct political and economic systems embodying changing Asian values, the result is likely to be unprecedented improvement in the political, economic, and social lives of its citizens. As Daniel Bell (1995b: 40) concludes:

Prodemocracy forces [in East Asia] relying on moral persuasion will most likely not succeed by founding their political programme on our (alleged) essential interest in personal autonomy, or by emphasizing desirable outcomes commonly thought to result from democratic procedures, but a 'communitarian' argument for democracy, namely, the idea that democracy protects and facilitates communal ways of life, is worthy of special attention.

However, failure of elites to adopt more democratic attitudes and change political systems accordingly can be catastrophic. Built-up pressures will destabilize the system by creating a sudden political meltdown whenever economic growth slows dramatically. The recent economic meltdown shows that this has already occurred in Indonesia. Another scenario consists of the gradual weakening of political community, something that Singapore is currently experiencing. Broadening the bases of legitimacy, beyond economic legitimation, is necessary if Asian nations are to avoid this scenario.

NOTE

1. See "Rock Solid," *Far Eastern Economic Review*, December 5, 1996, pp. 50–52.

Bibliography

Allinson, Gary D. 1987. "Japan's Keidanren and Its New Leadership." *Pacific Affairs* 60 (3): 385–407.

Almond, Gabriel A., ed. 1974. *Comparative Politics Today: A World View*. Boston: Little, Brown.

Almond, Gabriel A. and James S. Coleman. 1960. *The Politics of the Developing Areas*. Princeton, NJ: Princeton University Press.

Almond, Gabriel A. and Sidney Verba. 1963. *The Civic Culture: Political Attitudes and Democracy in Five Nations*. Princeton, NJ: Princeton University Press.

Amsden, Alice. 1989. *Asia's Next Giant: South Korea and Late Industrialization*. New York: Oxford University Press.

Anderson, Benedict. 1983. *Imagined Communities: Reflections on the Origin and Spread of Nationalism*. London: Verso.

Apter, David E. 1965. *The Politics of Modernization*. Chicago: University of Chicago Press.

Arat, Zehra. 1991. *Democracy and Human Rights in Developing Countries*. Boulder, CO: Lynne Rienner.

———. 1988. "Democracy and Economic Development, Modernization Theory Revisited." *Comparative Politics* 21 (1): 21–36.

Aronoff, Myron. 1983. *Culture and Political Change*. New Brunswick, NJ: Transaction Books.

Asian Development Annual Reports. 1972, 1973, 1975, 1976. Manila, Philippines: Asian Development Bank.

"Asia's Tough Guy." 1999. In *AsiaWeek* [online], February 26, at http://pathfinder.com/asiaweek/99/022b/cs1.html.

Banks, Arthur. 1971. "Modernization and Political Change." *Comparative Political Studies* 2: 405–18.

Banks, Arthur et al. 1975–1997. *Political Handbook of the World*. Binghamton, NY: CSA Publications.

Barber, Benjamin. 1984. *Strong Democracy: Participatory Politics for a New Age.* Berkeley: University of California Press.

Barnes, Samuel. 1994. "Politics and Culture." In *Political Culture and Political Structure: Theoretical and Empirical Studies,* ed. Frederick Weil. Greenwich, CT: JAI Press, pp. 45–64.

Beasley, William G. 1995. *The Rise of Modern Japan.* New York: St. Martin's Press.

Bell, Daniel. 1995a. "The Asian Challenge to Human Rights: An East-West Dialogue." Paper presented at the American Political Science Association Annual Meeting, Chicago.

———. 1995b. "Democracy in Confucian Societies: The Challenge of Justification." In *Towards Illiberal Democracy in Pacific Asia,* ed. Daniel Bell et al. New York: St. Martin's Press, pp. 17–40.

Bello, Walden and Stephanie Rosenfeld. 1990. *Dragons in Distress: Asia's Miracle Economies in Crisis.* San Francisco: Institute for Food and Development Policy.

Black, C.E. 1966. *The Dynamics of Modernization.* New York: Harper and Row.

Bollen, Kenneth. 1993. "Liberal Democracy: Validity and Method Factors in Cross-National Measures." *American Journal of Political Science* 37: 1207–30.

———. 1980. "Issues in the Comparative Measurement of Political Democracy." *American Sociological Review* 54: 612–21.

Brint, Steven. 1994. "Sociological Analysis of Political Culture: An Introduction and Assessment." In *Political Culture and Political Structure: Theoretical and Empirical Studies,* ed. Frederick D. Weil. Greenwich, CT: JAI Press, pp. 3–44.

Calder, Kent. 1988. *Crisis and Compensation: Public Policy and Political Stability in Japan, 1949–1986.* Princeton, NJ: Princeton University Press.

Chipello, Christopher J. 1990. "Kansai Airport Gives Contract to Three Firms— Inclusion of U.S. Company May Aid Talks on Access to Projects in Japan." *Wall Street Journal,* December 12.

Cho, Sun. 1994. *The Dynamics of Korean Economic Development.* Washington, DC: Institute for International Economics.

Cohen, Anthony. 1985. *The Symbolic Construction of Community.* New York: Tavistock.

Compton, Robert. 1996. "Rapid Industrialization and the Environment in Asia: Prospects and Problems." *Asian Profile* 24: 347–54.

Cotton, James. 1991a. "The Limits to Liberalization in Industrializing Asia: Three Views of the State." *Pacific Affairs* 64: 311–27.

———. 1991b. "The Military Factor in South Korean Politics." In *The Military, the State, and Development in Asia and the Pacific,* ed. Viberto Selochan. Boulder, CO: Westview Press, pp. 203–20.

Craig, Albert M. 1968. "Fukuzawa Yukichi: The Philosophical Foundations of Meiji Nationalism." In *Political Development in Modern Japan,* ed. Robert E. Ward. Princeton, NJ: Princeton University Press, pp. 99–148.

Crozier, Michel et al. 1975. *The Crisis of Democracy: Report on the Governability of Democracies to the Trilateral Commission.* New York: New York University Press.

Cumings, Bruce. 1996a. "South Korea's Academic Lobby." Occasional Paper no. 7. Cardiff, CA: Japan Policy Research Institute (JPRI).

————. 1996b. "Korean Scandal, or American Scandal?" Occasional Paper no. 20. Cardiff, CA: Japan Policy Research Institute (JPRI).

————. 1987. "Origins and Development of the Northeast Asian Political Economy: Industrial Sectors, Product Cycles, and Political Consequences." In *The Political Economy of the New Asian Industrialism*, ed. Frederic Deyo. Ithaca, NY: Cornell University Press, pp. 44–83.

Curtis, Gerald. 1971. *Election Campaigning, Japanese Style.* New York: Columbia University Press.

Dahl, Robert A. 1971. *Polyarchy: Participation and Opposition.* New Haven, CT: Yale University Press.

————. 1961. *Who Governs? Democracy and Power in American Cities.* New Haven, CT: Yale University Press.

————. 1956. *A Preface to Democratic Theory.* Chicago: University of Chicago Press.

Dator, James. 1969. *Soka Gakkai, Builders of the Third Civilization: American and Japanese Members.* Seattle: University of Washington Press.

Dawson, Raymond. 1981. *Confucius.* Oxford: Oxford University Press.

DeCalo, Samuel. 1990. *Coups and Army Rule in Africa*, 2nd ed. New Haven, CT: Yale University Press.

Deutsch, Karl. 1961. "Social Mobilization and Political Development." *American Political Science Review* 55: 493–514.

Deyo, Frederic. 1989. *Beneath the Miracle: Labor Subordination in the New Asian Industrialism.* Berkeley: University of California Press.

————. 1987. *The Political Economy of the New Asian Industrialism.* Ithaca, NY: Cornell University Press.

Dhiravegin, Likhit. 1988. "Demi-democracy: Thai Politics and Government in Transition." In *The Changing Shape of Government in the Asia-Pacific Region*, ed. John Langford and K. Lorne Brownsey. Halifax, NS: Institute for Research on Public Policy, pp. 83–100.

Diamond, Larry et al., eds. 1989. *Democracy in Developing Nations: Asia.* Boulder, CO: Lynne Rienner.

Downs, Anthony. 1957. *An Economic Theory of Democracy.* New York: Harper.

Durlabhji, Subhash. 1993. "The Influence of Confucianism and Zen on the Japanese Organization." In *Japanese Business: Cultural Perspectives*, ed. Subhash Durlabhji and Norton E. Marks. Albany, NY: SUNY Press, pp. 57–80.

Durlabhji, Subhash and Norton Marks, eds. 1993. *Japanese Business: Cultural Perspectives.* Albany, NY: SUNY Press.

Duus, Peter. 1968. *Party Rivalry and Political Change in Taisho Japan.* Cambridge, MA: Harvard University Press.

Duverger, M. 1954. *Political Parties: Their Organization and Activity in the Modern State.* London: Methuen.

Dye, Thomas and L. Harmon Zeigler. 1972. *The Irony of Democracy: An Uncommon Introduction to American Government.* Belmont, CA: Duxbury Press.

Eckert, Carter J. 1993. "The South Korean Bourgeoisie: A Class in Search of Hegemony." In *State and Society in Contemporary Korea*, ed. Hagen Koo. Boulder, CO: Westview Press, pp. 95–130.

Eckert, Carter J. et al. 1990. *Korea: Old and New History.* Seoul, Korea: Ilchokak Publishers.

Eckstein, Harry. 1988. "A Culturalist Theory of Political Change." *American Political Science Review* 82: 789–804.

The Economist. 1987. "Kansai Airport: Tail-End Charlies." August 22, pp. 60–61.

Edelman, Murray. 1964. *Symbolic Uses of Politics*. Urbana: University of Illinois Press.

Elkins, David and Richard Simeon. 1979. "A Cause in Search of its Effect, or What Does Political Culture Explain." *Comparative Politics* 11: 127–45.

Elliot, David. 1978. *Thailand: Origins of Military Rule*. London: Zed Press.

Finer, S.E. 1988. *The Man on Horseback: The Role of the Military in Politics*, 2nd ed. Boulder, CO: Westview Press.

Flanagan, Scott. 1987. "Value Change in Industrial Societies." *American Political Science Review* 81: 1303–19.

Friedman, Edward, ed. 1994. "Democratization: Generalizing the East Asian Experience." In *The Politics of Democratization: Generalizing East Asian Experiences*. Boulder CO: Westview Press.

Fukui, Haruhiro et al., eds. 1985. *Political Parties of Asia and the Pacific*. Westport, CT: Greenwood Press.

Fukuyama, Francis. 1995. "Confucianism and Democracy." *Journal of Democracy* 6 (2): 20–33.

———. 1992. *The End of History and the Last Man*. New York: Free Press.

Funabashi, Yoichi. 1993. "The Asianization of Asia." *Foreign Affairs* 72: 75–85.

Gamer, Robert. 1976. *The Developing Nations*. Boston: Allyn and Bacon.

Geertz, Clifford. 1973. *The Interpretation of Culture: Selected Essays*. New York: Basic Books.

Giddens, Anthony. 1984. *The Constitution of Society: Outline of the Theory of Structuration*. Cambridge: Polity Press.

Gillis, Malcolm et al. 1983. *Economics of Development*. New York: W.W. Norton.

Girling, John L.S. 1981. *Thailand: Society and Politics*. Ithaca, NY: Cornell University Press.

Haggard, Stephen and Tun-jen Cheng. 1987. "State and Foreign Capital in the East Asian NICs." In *The Political Economy of the New Asian Industrialism*, ed. Frederic Deyo. Ithaca, NY: Cornell University Press.

Haggard, Stephen and Chung-in Moon. 1993. "The State, Politics, and Economic Development in Postwar South Korea." In *State and Society in Contemporary Korea*, ed. Hagen Koo. Ithaca, NY: Cornell University Press, pp. 51–93.

Hagopian, Frances. 1996. *Traditional Politics and Regime Change in Brazil*. New York: Cambridge University Press.

Hall, David L. and Roger T. Ames. 1987. *Thinking Through Confucius*. Albany, NY: SUNY Press.

Hall, John Whitney. 1970. *Japan: From Prehistory to Modern Times*. New York: Dell Publishing.

———. 1968. "A Monarch for Modern Japan." In *Political Development in Modern Japan*, ed. Robert E. Ward. Princeton, NJ: Princeton University Press, pp. 11–64.

Halpern, Manfred. 1963. *The Politics of Social Change in the Middle East and North Africa*. Princeton, NJ: Rand.

Han, Sung-Joo. 1990. "South Korea: Politics in Transition." In *Politics in Developing Nations*, ed. Larry Diamond et al. Boulder, CO: Lynne Rienner.

Hardacre, Helen. 1989. *Shinto and the State, 1868–1988.* Princeton, NJ: Princeton University Press.
Harvey, David. 1989. *The Condition of Postmodernity: An Enquiry into the Origins of Cultural Change.* Oxford: Blackwell.
Henderson, Callum. 1998. *Asia Falling.* New York: McGraw-Hill.
Henderson, Gregory. 1988. "Constitutional Changes from the First to Sixth Republics: 1948–1987." In *Political Change in South Korea,* ed. Ilpyong J. Kim and Young han Kihl. New York: Paragon House, pp. 22–43.
Higgott, Richard A. 1983. *Political Development Theory.* London: Croom Helm.
Hobsbawm, Eric and Terence Ranger. 1983. *The Invention of Tradition.* Cambridge: Cambridge University Press.
Hofheinz, Roy and Kent Calder. 1982. *The Eastasia Edge.* New York: Basic Books.
Hsu, Leonard Shihlien. 1975. *Political Philosophy of Confucianism.* New York: Harper and Row.
Huer, Jon. 1989. *Marching Orders: The Role of the Military in South Korea's "Economic Miracle," 1961–1971.* Westport, CT: Greenwood Press.
Hui, Po-Keung. 1995. *Overseas Chinese Business Networks: East Asian Economic Development in Historical Perspective.* Ph.D. dissertation, State University of New York, Binghamton, no. 1587.
Huntington, Samuel. 1996. "The West: Unique, Not Universal." *Foreign Affairs* 75: 28–46.
Huntington, Samuel. 1993. "The Clash of Civilizations?" *Foreign Affairs* 72 (3): 22–49.
———. 1991. "Religion and the Third Wave." *National Interest* 24: 29–42.
———. 1991b. *The Third Wave: Democratization in the Late Twentieth Century.* Norman: University of Oklahoma Press.
———. 1971. "The Change to Change: Modernization, Development, and Politics." *Comparative Politics* 3: 283–322.
———. 1968. *Political Order in Changing Societies.* New Haven, CT: Yale University Press.
———. 1965. "Political Development and Political Decay." *World Politics* 17 (3): 386–430.
———. 1957. *The Soldier and the State: The Theory and Politics of Civil-Military Relations.* Cambridge. MA: Belknap Press.
Ikuta, Tadahide. 1995. *Kanryo: Japan's Hidden Government.* New York: NHK Publishing.
Im, Hyug Baeg. 1987. "The Rise of Bureaucratic Authoritarianism in South Korea." *World Politics* 39 (2): 231–57.
Inglehart, Ronald. 1990. *Culture Shift in Advanced Industrial Society.* Princeton, NJ: Princeton University Press.
———. 1977. *The Silent Revolution: Changing Values and Political Styles among Western Publics.* Princeton, NJ: Princeton University Press.
Inoguchi, Takashi. 1991. "The Nature and Functioning of Japanese Politics." *Government and Opposition* 26 (2): 185–98.
Ishibashi, Michiro and Steven R. Reed. 1992. "Second-Generation Diet Members and Democracy in Japan: Hereditary Seats." *Asian Survey* 32: 366–79.
Jackson, Karl D. 1989. "The Philippines: The Search for a Suitable Democratic

Solution, 1946–1986, " In *Democracy in Developing Countries: Asia*, ed. Larry Diamond et al. Boulder, CO: Lynne Rienner, pp. 231–66.

Jameson, Sam. 1997. "Japan's Amoeba Politics." Working Paper no. 29. Cardiff, CA: Japan Policy Research Institute (JPRI).

Janda, Kenneth. 1970. *A Conceptual Framework for the Comparative Analysis of Political Parties*. Newbury Park, CA: Sage Publications.

Janelli, Roger L. 1993. *Making Capitalism: The Social and Cultural Construction of a South Korean Conglomerate*. Stanford, CA: Stanford University Press.

Japan Statistical Yearbook, nos. 38, 39, 40, 41. 1989, 1990, 1991, 1992. Tokyo: Office of Prime Minister, Bureau of Statistics.

Johnson, Chalmers. 1997. "Perceptions vs. Observations, or the Contributions of Rational Choice Theory and Area Studies to Contemporary Political Science." *PS: Political Science and Politics* (30) 2: 170–74.

———. 1995. *Japan: Who Governs?* New York: W.W. Norton.

———. 1994. "Capitalism: East Asian Style." Limited Distribution Paper for members of the Japan Political Research Group.

———. 1987. "Political Institutions and Economic Performance: The Government-Business Relationship in Japan, South Korea, and Taiwan." In *The Political Economy of New Asian Industrialism*, ed. Frederic Deyo. Ithaca, NY: Cornell University Press, pp. 136–64.

———. 1982. *MITI and the Japanese Miracle*. Berkeley: University of California Press.

Johnson, Chalmers and E.B. Keehn. 1995. "The Pentagon's Ossified Policy." *Foreign Affairs* 74: 103–14.

Jones, Eric. 1994. "Asia's Fate: A Response to the Singaporean School." *National Interest* 35: 18–28.

Jones, Leroy P. and Il Sakong. 1980. *Government, Business, and Entrepreneurship in Economic Development: The Korean Case*. Cambridge, MA: Harvard University Press.

Kaneko, Umaji. 1931. "A Survey of Philosophy in Japan, 1870–1929." In *Western Influences in Modern Japan*, ed. Inazo Nitobe et al. Chicago: University of Chicago Press, pp. 56–69.

Kataoka, Tetsuya, ed. 1992. *Creating Single-Party Democracy*. Stanford, CA: Hoover Institution Press.

Katz, Richard. 1998. *Japan: The System That Soured*. Armonk, NY: M.E. Sharpe.

Keyes, Charles et al. 1994. *Asian Visions of Authority: Religion and the Modern States of East and Southeast Asia*. Honolulu: University of Hawaii Press.

Kim, Dae-Jung. 1994. "Is Culture Destiny? The Myth of Asia's Anti-Democratic Values." *Foreign Affairs* 73: 189–94.

Kim, Jae-On and Charles Mueller. 1978. *Introduction to Factor Analysis*. Newbury Park, CA: Sage Publications.

King, Gary et al. 1994. *Designing Social Inquiry: Scientific Inference in Qualitative Research*. Princeton, NJ: Princeton University Press.

Klingemann, Hans-Dieter et al. 1994. *Parties, Policies, and Democracy*. Boulder, CO: Westview Press.

Kobkua, Suwamnathathat-Pian. 1995. *Thailand's Durable Premier: Phibun through Three Decades—1932–1957*. Kuala Lumpur, Malaysia: Oxford University Press.

Khoo, Boo Teih. 1996. *Paradoxes of Mahathirism*. Princeton NJ: Princeton University Press.

Koh, B.C. 1997. "South Korea in 1996." *Asian Survey* 37 (1): 1–9.

———. 1989. *Japan's Administrative Elite*. Berkeley: University of California Press.

Komolsiri, Chakarin. 1995. *Globalization and Local Voices: Globalists, Fusionists, and Resistors among Thai Intellectual Elites*. Ph.D. dissertation, State University of New York at Binghamton, no. 1560.

Kumagai, Fumie. 1995. "Familes in Japan: Beliefs and Realities." *Journal of Comparative Family Studies* 26: 135–63.

Kumazawa, Makoto. 1996. *Portraits of the Japanese Workplace*, trans. Andrew Gordon and Mikiso Hane. Boulder, CO: Westview Press.

Langford, John W. and K. Lorne Brownsey. 1988. "The Changing Shape of Government in the Asia-Pacific Region." In *The Changing Shape of Government in the Asia-Pacific Region*, ed. John Langford and K. Lorne Brownsey. Halifax, NS: Institute for Research on Public Policy, pp. 1–20.

Laothamatas, Anek. 1995. "From Clientelism to Partnership: Business-Government Relations in Thailand." In *Business and Government in Industrialising Asia*, ed. Andrew MacIntyre. Ithaca, NY: Cornell University Press.

———. 1988. "Business and Politics in Thailand: New Patterns of Influence." *Asian Survey* 28 (4): 451–70.

LaPalombara, Joseph. 1971. "Political Science and the Engineering of National Development." In *Political Development in Changing Societies*, ed. Monte Palmer and Larry Stern. Lexington, MA: D.C. Heath.

Lawson, Kay. 1980. *Political Parties and Linkage: A Comparative Perspective*. New Haven, CT: Yale University Press.

Lee, Chong-Sik. 1963. *The Politics of Korean Nationalism*. Berkeley: University of California Press.

Lee, Heng. 1994. "Uncertain Promise: Democratic Consolidation in South Korea." In *The Politics of Democratization: Generalizing East Asian Experiences*, ed. Edward Friedman. Boulder, CO: Westview Press.

Lerner, Daniel. 1958. *The Passing of Traditional Society: Modernizing the Middle East*. Glencoe, IL: Free Press.

Levy, Martin J., Jr. 1966. *Modernization and the Structure of Societies: A Setting for International Affairs*. Princeton, NJ: Princeton University Press.

Lijphart, Arend. 1984. *Democracies: Patterns of Majoritarian and Consensus Government in Twenty-One Countries*. New Haven, CT: Yale University Press.

Lipset, Seymour Martin. 1994. "The Social Requisites of Democracy Revisited." *American Sociological Review* 59: 1–22.

———. 1959. "Some Social Requisites of Democracy." *American Political Science Review* 53: 69–105.

Lipset, Seymour Martin et al. 1993. "A Comparative Analysis of the Social Requisites of Democracy." *International Social Science Journal* 45: 155–75.

Lipset, Seymour and Stein Rokkan. 1967. *Party Systems and Voter Alignments*. New York: Free Press.

LoGerfo, Jim. 1996. "Attitudes toward Democracy among Bangkok and Rural Northern Thais." *Asian Survey* 36 (9): 904–23.

Lowi, Theodore. 1969. *The End of Liberalism: Ideology, Policy, and the Crisis of Public Authority*. New York: Norton.

MacDonald, Donald Stone. 1990. *The Koreans: Contemporary Politics and Society*. Boulder, CO: Westview Press.

Mahbubani, Kishore. 1995. "The Pacific Way." *Foreign Affairs* 74: 100–111.

———. 1992. "The West and the Rest." *The National Interest* 25: 3–12.

Mainwaring, Scott et al. 1995. *Building Democratic Institutions: Party Systems in Latin America*. Stanford, CA: Stanford University Press.

Martz, John D. 1997. *The Politics of Clientelism: Democracy and the State in Colombia*. New Brunswick, NJ: Transaction Publishers.

Mazrui, Ali. 1990. *Cultural Forces in World Politics*. London: J. Currey.

McCloud, Donald G. 1995. *Southeast Asia: Tradition and Modernity in the Contemporary World*. Boulder, CO: Westview Press.

McNelly, Theodore. 1969. "The Role of Monarchy in the Political Modernization of Japan." *Comparative Politics* 1 (3): 366–81.

Michels, Robert. 1962. *Political Parties: A Sociological Study of the Oligarchical Tendencies of Modern Democracy*. New York: Free Press.

Mills, C. Wright. 1956. *The Power Elite*. New York: Oxford University Press.

Moody, Peter R., Jr. 1988. *Political Opposition in Post-Confucian Society*. New York: Praeger.

Moon, Chung-in. 1994. "Changing Patterns of Business-Government Relations in South Korea." In *Business and Government in Industrializing Asia*, ed. Andrew MacIntyre. Ithaca, NY: Cornell University Press, pp. 142–66.

Moore, Barrington. 1967. *Social Origins of Dictatorship and Democracy: Lord and Peasant in the Making of the Modern World*. Boston: Beacon Press.

Muscat, Robert J. 1994. *The Fifth Tiger: A Study of Thai Development Policy*. Armonk, NY: M.E. Sharpe.

Myrdal, Gunnar. 1971. *Asian Drama*. New York: Pantheon Books.

Nam, Duck Woo. 1994. "Korea's Economic Takeoff in Retrospect." In *The Korean Economy at a Crossroad*, ed. Sung Yeung Kwack. Westport, CT: Praeger, pp. 3–20.

Neher, Clark D. 1994a. "Asian Style Democracy." *Asian Survey* 34: 949–61.

———. 1994b. *Southeast Asia in the New International Era*. Boulder, CO: Westview Press.

———. 1992. "Political Succession in Thailand." *Asian Survey* 32 (7): 585–605.

Neher, Clark D. and Ross Marlay. 1995. *Democracy and Development in Southeast Asia: The Winds of Change*. Boulder, CO: Westview Press.

Neumann, Sigmund. 1956. *Modern Political Parties*. Chicago: University of Chicago Press.

Nicro, Somrudee. 1993. "Thailand's NIC Democracy: Studying from General Elections." *Pacific Affairs* 66: 167–82.

Nitobe, Inazo. 1931. "Two Exotic Currents in Japanese Civilization." In *Western Influences in Modern Japan*, ed. Inazo Nitobe et al. Chicago: University of Chicago Press, pp. 1–25.

Noble, Gregory W. *Collective Action in East Asia*. Ithaca, NY: Cornell University Press.

Numnonda, Thamsook. 1977. *Thailand and the Japanese Presence, 1941–45*. Singapore: Institute of Southeast Asian Studies.

Ockey, James. 1994. "Political Parties, Factions, and Corruption in Thailand." *Modern Asian Studies* 28 (2): 251–77.

O'Donnell, Guillermo. 1979. "Tensions in the Bureaucratic-Authoritarian State and the Question of Democracy." In *The New Authoritarianism in Latin America*, ed. David Collier. Princeton, NJ: Princeton University Press.

O'Donnell, Guillermo et al. 1986. *Transitions from Authoritarian Rule: Prospects for Democracy.* Baltimore, MD: Johns Hopkins University Press.

Okada, Kunio. 1993. "The Source of Japanese Management." In *Japanese Business: Cultural Perspectives*, ed. Subhash Durlabhji and Norton Marks. Albany, NY: SUNY Press, pp. 19–30.

Organski, A.F.K. 1965. *The Stages of Political Development.* New York: Knopf.

Ozawa, Ichiro. 1994. *Blueprint for a New Japan: The Rethinking of a Nation.* Tokyo: Kodansha.

Palmer, Norman. 1975. *Elections and Political Development.* Durham, NC: Duke University Press.

Parenti, Michael. 1995. *Democracy for the Few.* New York: St. Martin's Press.

———. 1993. *Inventing Reality: The Politics of News Media.* New York: St. Martin's Press.

———. 1978. *Power and the Powerless.* New York: St. Martin's Press.

———. 1974. *Democracy for the Few.* New York: St. Martin's Press.

Park, Insook Han and Lee-Jay Cho. 1995. "Confucianism and the Korean Family." *Journal of Comparative Family Studies* 26: 117–34.

Pateman, Carole. 1970. *Participation and Democratic Theory.* Cambridge: Cambridge University Press.

Przeworski, Adam and Henry Tuene. 1970. *The Logic of Comparative Social Inquiry.* New York: Wiley.

Putnam, Robert. 1976. *The Comparative Study of Political Elites.* Englewood Cliffs, NJ: Prentice-Hall.

Pye, Lucian W. 1985. *Asian Power and Politics.* Cambridge, MA: Belknap Press.

———. 1966a. *Aspects of Political Development.* Boston: Little, Brown.

———. 1966b. "Party Systems and National Development in Asia." In *Political Parties and Political Development*, ed. Myron Weiner and Joseph LaPalombara. Princeton, NJ: Princeton University Press, pp. 369–98.

Quigley, Kevin F.F. 1995. "Towards Consolidating Democracy: The Role of Civil Society Organizations in Thailand." Paper presented at the 1995 Annual Meeting of the American Political Science Association, Chicago.

Rae, Douglas. 1971. *The Consequences of Electoral Laws.* New Haven, CT: Yale University Press.

Ragin, Charles. 1994. *Constructing Social Research: The Unity and Diversity of Method.* Thousand Oaks, CA: Pine Forge Press.

Ranseyer, J. Mark and Frances Rosenbluth. 1993. *Japan's Political Marketplace.* Cambridge, MA: Harvard University Press.

Ree, Jong-Chan. 1994. *The State and Industry in South Korea: The Limits of an Authoritarian State.* London: Routledge.

Reed, Steven R. 1993. *Making Common Sense of Japan.* Pittsburgh, PA: University of Pittsburgh Press.

Reischauer, Edwin. 1983. "Not Westernization But Modernization." In *Japan Ex-*

amined: Perspectives on Modern Japanese Politics, ed. Harry Wray and Hilary
Conroy. Honolulu: University of Hawaii Press, pp. 369–83.

Reischauer, Edwin and Marius Jansen. 1995. *The Japanese Today: Change and Continuity.* Cambridge, MA: Belknap Press.

Rhee, Jong-Chan. 1994. *The State and Industry in South Korea: The Limits of the Authoritarian State.* New York: Routledge.

Riggs, Fred W. 1966. *Thailand: The Modernization of a Bureaucratic Polity.* Honolulu: East-West Center Press.

Robertson, Philip S., Jr. 1996. "The Rise of the Rural Network Politician: Will Thailand's New Elite Endure?" *Asian Survey* 36 (9): 924–41.

Robinson, Michael. 1991. "Perceptions of Confucianism in Twentieth-Century Korea." In *The East Asian Region: Confucian Heritage and Its Modern Adaptation,* ed. Gilbert Rozman. Princeton, NJ: Princeton University Press, pp. 204–25.

Robison, Richard and David S.G. Goodman, eds. 1996. *The New Rich in Asia.* London: Routledge.

Rodan, Gary. 1996. *Political Opposition in Industrializing Asia.* New York: Routledge.

Rohlen, Thomas. 1989. "Order in Japanese Society: Attachment, Authority, and Routine." *Journal of Japanese Studies* 15: 4–40.

Ross, Edward W. 1986. "Taiwan's Armed Forces." In *The Armed Forces in Contemporary Asian Societies,* ed. Edwards A. Olsen and Stephen Jurika, Jr. Boulder, CO: Westview Press, pp. 55–69.

Rostow, W.W. 1960. *The Stages of Economic Growth: A Non-Communist Manifesto.* Cambridge: Cambridge University Press.

Rothacher, Albrecht. 1993. *The Japanese Power Elite.* New York: St. Martin's Press.

Rozman, Gilbert. 1991a. "The East Asian Region in Comparative Perspective." In *The East Asian Region: Confucian Heritage and Its Modern Adaption,* ed. Gilbert Rozman. Princeton, NJ: Princeton University Press, pp. 3–44.

———. 1991b. *The East Asian Region: Confucian Heritage and Its Modern Adaption.* Princeton, NJ: Princeton University Press.

Rummel, R.J. 1967. "Understanding Factor Analysis." *Conflict Resolution* 11: 444–80.

Rustow, Dankwart. 1967. *A World of Nations: Problems of Political Modernization.* Washington, DC: Brookings Institution.

Samudavanija, Chai-Anan. 1989. "Thailand: A Stable Semi-Democracy." In *Democracy in Developing Countries: Asia,* ed. Larry Diamond et al. Boulder, CO: Lynne Rienner.

Sartori, Giovanni. 1976. *Parties and Party Systems.* Binghamton, NY: Vail-Ballou Press.

Scalapino, Robert. 1989. *The Politics of Development: Perspectives on Twentieth-Century Asia.* Cambridge, MA: Harvard University Press.

———. 1968. "Elections and Political Modernization in Prewar Japan." In *Political Development in Modern Japan,* ed. Robert E. Ward. Princeton, NJ: Princeton University Press, pp. 249–92.

Schattschneider, E.E. 1960. *The Semisovereign People: A Realist's View of Democracy in America.* New York: Holt, Rinehart, and Winston.

Schlosstein, Steven. 1991. *Asia's New Little Dragons: The Dynamic Emergence of Indonesia, Thailand, and Malaysia.* Chicago: Contemporary Books.

Schmitter, Philippe. 1979. *Trends toward Corporatist Intermediation.* London: Sage Publications.

Schumpeter, Joseph. 1950. *Capitalism, Socialism, and Democracy.* New York: Harper and Row.

Scott, James C. 1968. *Political Ideology in Malaysia: Reality and the Beliefs of an Elite.* New Haven, CT: Yale University Press.

Shils, Edward. 1982. *The Constitution of Society.* Chicago: University of Chicago Press.

Shively. 1965. "Nishimura Shigeki: A Confucian View of Modernization." In *Changing Japanese Attitudes toward Modernization,* ed. Marius B. Jansen. Princeton, NJ: Princeton University Press, pp. 193–242.

Siffin, William J. 1966. *The Thai Bureaucracy: Institutional Change and Development.* Honolulu: East-West Center Press.

Simone, Vera and Anne Thompson Feraru. 1995. *The Asian Pacific: Political and Economic Development in a Global Context.* White Plains, NY: Longman Publishers.

Sohn, Hak-Kyu. 1989. *Authoritarianism and Opposition in South Korea.* New York: Routledge.

Song, Byung-Nak. 1994. *The Rise of the Korean Economy.* Hong Kong: Oxford University Press.

Soon, Cho. 1994. *The Dynamics of Korean Economic Development.* Washington, DC: Institute for International Economics.

Stevenson, Richard W. 1997. "No Storm in Pacific." *New York Times,* November 26, p. 12.

Stockwin, J.A.A. 1988. *Dynamic and Immobilist Politics in Japan.* Basingstoke: Macmillan.

Taagepera, Rein. 1989. *Seats and Votes: The Effects and Determinants of Electoral Systems.* New Haven, CT: Yale University Press.

Tai, Hung-chao, ed. 1989. *Confucianism and Economic Development: An Oriental Alternative?* Washington, DC: The Washington Institute Press.

Tamney, Joseph. 1991. "Confucianism and Democracy." *Asian Profile* 19: 399–411.

Tanin, O. and E. Yohan. 1934. *Militarism and Fascism in Japan.* London: Martin Lawrence, Ltd.

Tetsuya, Kataoka, ed. 1992. *Japan's Postwar Political System.* Stanford, CA: Hoover Institution Press.

Thak, Chaloemtiarana. 1979. *Thailand: The Politics of Despotic Paternalism.* Bangkok, Thailand: Thammasat University Press.

Tocqueville, Alexis de [1956]. *Democracy in America.* Reprint, ed. Richard D. Heffner. New York: Mentor Books.

Tonkin, Derek. 1990. "The Art of Politics in Thailand." *Asian Affairs* 21 (3): 285–94.

Tonnies, Ferdinand. 1963 [1887]. *Gemeinschaft und Gesellschaft, Grundbegriffe der Reinen.* Darmstadt, Germany: Wissenschaftliche Buchgesellschaft.

Tsurutani, Taketsugu. 1989. "The Paradox of Reform." *International Review of Administrative Sciences* 57: 101–12.

———. 1977. *Political Change in Japan: Response to Postindustrial Challenge.* New York: D. McKay Co.

———. 1974. *The Politics of National Development.* New York: Abelard-Schuman.

———. 1972. "A New Era of Japanese Politics: Tokyo's Gubernatorial Election." *Asian Survey* 12 (5): 429–443.

———. 1968. "Machiavelli and the Problem of Political Development." *Journal of Politics* 30 (3): 316–31.

U.S. Arms Control and Disarmament Agency. 1995. *World Military Expenditures and Arms Transfers, 1981–1991.* Inter-University Consortium for Political and Social Research, no. 6364. Washington, DC: Computer file.

van Wolferen, Karel. 1993. "Japan's Non-Revolution." *Foreign Affairs* 72 (4): 54–65.

———. 1989. *The Enigma of Japanese Power.* New York: Alfred A. Knopf.

Wade, Robert. 1990. *Governing the Market: Economic Theory and the Role of Government in East Asian Industrialization.* Princeton, NJ: Princeton University Press.

Ward, Robert E. 1963. "Political Modernization and Political Culture in Japan." *World Politics* 15: 569–93.

Ware, Alan. 1996. *Political Parties and Party Systems.* Oxford: Oxford University Press.

———. 1979. *The Logic of Party Democracy.* New York: St. Martin's Press.

Weber, Max. 1947. *The Theory of Social and Economic Organization.* Glencoe, IL: Free Press.

Weiner, Myron. 1967a. "Political Integration and Political Development." In *Political Modernization*, ed. Claude Welch. Belmont, CA: Wadsworth Publishing.

Weiner, Myron, ed. 1967b. *Modernization: The Dynamics of Growth.* New York: Basic Books.

Weiner, Myron and Joseph LaPalombara. 1966. "The Impact of Parties on Political Development." In *Political Parties and Political Development*, ed. Myron Weiner and Joseph LaPalombara. Princeton, NJ: Princeton University Press, pp. 399–435.

Welch, Claude E., Jr., ed. 1967. *Political Modernization.* Belmont, CA: Wadsworth Publishing Company.

Werlin, Herbert. 1990. "Political Culture and Political Change." *American Political Science Review* 84: 250–53.

Westholm, Anders and Richard Niemi. 1992. "Political Institutions and Political Socialization: A Cross-National Study." *Comparative Politics* 15: 25–41.

White, Gordon and Robert Wade, eds. 1990. *Developmental States in East Asia.* Gatsby Charitable Foundation Research Report.

White, James. 1970. *The Sokagakkai and Mass Society.* Stanford, CA: Stanford University Press.

Wildavsky, Aaron. 1987. "Choosing Preferences by Constructing Institutions: A Cultural Theory of Preference Formation." *American Political Science Review* 81: 3–21.

Wong, Siu-Lun. 1988. "The Applicability of Asian Family Values to Other Sociocultural Settings." In *In Search of an East Asian Development Model*, ed.

Peter Berger and Hsin-Huang Michael Hsiao. New Brunswick, NJ: Transaction Books.

World Bank. 1995. *World Tables*. Baltimore, MD: Johns Hopkins University Press.

Yanaga, Chitoshi. 1968. *Big Business in Japanese Politics*. New Haven, CT: Yale University Press.

Yoshida, Kumaji. 1931. "European and American Influences in Japanese Education." In *Western Influences in Modern Japan*, ed. Inazo Nitobe et al. Chicago: University of Chicago Press, pp. 25–55.

Yoshida, Shigeru. 1962. *The Yoshida Memoirs: The Story of Japan in Crisis*. Boston: Houghton Mifflin.

Zakaria, Fareed. 1994. "Culture Is Destiny: A Conversation with Lee Kuan Yew." *Foreign Affairs* 73: 9–26.

Zeigler, Harmon. 1988. *Pluralism, Corporatism, and Confucianism*. Philadelphia: Temple University Press.

Index

Amsden, Alice, 61
Asian democracy, 183, 185–87. *See also*
Asian political culture; Democracy;
Political development
Asian Development Model, 71–92, 185;
actors, 78–90; bureaucracy, 85–88;
corporate elite, 88–89; culture and,
71–75; elected officials, 89–90; empirical analysis of, 96–102; government and business relations,
78–79; government spending priori-
ties, 87; military, 81–85; three cases,
107–8, 177–78; three stages, 76–81.
*See also under names of specific coun-
tries*
Asian political culture, 34–48; Asian
democracy and, 183, 185–87; communitarianism, 39–40; Confucianism, 34–43; contemporary youth,
188; democracy, 183, 188; group
orientation, 45–46; patron-client relations, 43–45; traditionalism, 33–36.
See also Asian democracy; Democracy; Political development
Authoritarianism and the military, 81–
85
Authoritarianism and transition to liberal democracy, 3–4

Authoritarianism in Asia, and U.S.
foreign policy, 1

Chun Doo Hwan, 156–58
Confucianism, 34–43; guardian class
origin, 41–42; links to traditionalism, 39–40; as moral code, 38. *See
also under names of specific countries*;
Asian political culture; Democracy
Cotton, James, 70, 80
Cultural theory, 23–46; anthropology
and, 22–33, 57–58; in Asia, 33–47;
social construction, 23–25
Culture and democracy, 5, 16–17, 22–
25, 183–85; and rational choice view
of, 14, 24–26. *See also* Asian political
culture; Democracy; Political development
Culture and developmental state, 63–
65
Culture and economic development,
51–53, 72–75, 184–85

Democracy: and communitarianism,
183, 188; Asian style of, 183, 185–87;
consolidation of, 13, 15–16; culturalist view, 31–32; defined, 53–56, 80–
81; developmental state, impact on,

Mills, C. Wright, 59
Modernization, 2; and growth in Asia, 4–5, 95–96; measurement of, 95–96; party competition and, 100–02; theory of, 21–23; and Westernization, 46–48, 102–03

Neher, Clark, 179 n.9

Occupation of Japan. *See* Japan

Papua New Guinea, 63
Park Chung Hee, 147–51, 154–55; legitimacy problems of, 150; use of Confucianism, 150; Yushin Constitution and, 154–55
Phibul Songgarm, 167–71; and collaboration with Japan, 169; and Thai nationalism, 170–71
Philippines, 63
Political development: alternative approach in conceptualizing, 11–13; Asian democracy and nationalism and, 187; changing values of, 188–89; democratic consolidation and developmental state, 181–82; developmental state and, 12; East vs. West, 108–9; extraparliamentary protest, 51–52, 155–56; in Japan, 117; linked with modernization and party competition, 100–102; through mobilizational leadership, 13; as modernization without Westernization, 46–48, 102–3; political leadership and, 13; in South Korea, 150–51; top-down orientation, 74. *See also* Asian political culture; Culture and democracy; Democracy
Political parties, 7, 54–55, 92; decay of, 8–10; in Japan, 134–39; and political-system competitiveness, 75, 93–95, 97–102; role in Asia, 90; in South Korea, 149–50; in Thailand, 175–77. *See also* Asian political culture; Culture and democracy; Democracy; Extraparliamentary protest

Pridi Phanomyong, 167, 171; authoritarianism and, 170–74
Pye, Lucian, 2, 25–26, 36, 41, 57

Reischauer, Edwin, 48
Rodan, Gary, 55
Rothacher, Gilbert, 131

Sarit, 172–73
Scholsstein, Steven, 164
Singapore, 86–87
South Korea: Asian political development model and, 143; business and government relations in, 151–52; Confucianism in, 150–51; developmental state and nationalism in, 151–53; elite structure, 149–50; feudal Korea, 144–45; imperfect legitimacy, 143–44; increase in corporate power, 158–59; Japanese colonization, of 145–47; Kwangju Massacre, 156–58; labor oppression, 148–49, 151; logic of political parties in, 149–50; military elites, source of, 152–53; Park Chung Hee, 147–56; prospects for democracy, 160; regionalism in, 148; Saemaul Undong, 151; transition to democracy, 157–58; value differences between elites and masses, 156; volatility of politics, 159–60; weakness of political institutions, 155; Yushin Constitution, 154–55

Tanaka, Kakuei, 44
Thailand: accommodation of threats, 166; Asian Development Model in, 163–65; Chinese in, 177; critique of strong state, 179 n.9; developmental state, 174; encounter with modernization, 166–67; impact of rapid modernization, 164–65; parties and the military use of, 176; Phibul Songgram, 168–71; pluralism and political development in, 164; Pridi Phanomyong, 170–74; rural and urban cleavage, 176–78; semi-democ-

racy, 175; tradition in Thailand, 182;
urban elites in, 176; weakness of
political parties, 176; Young Turks,
168–69

Weber, Max, 35
Welch, Claude, 39–40

Yoshida, Shigeru, 3

About the Author

ROBERT W. COMPTON, JR. is Assistant Professor of Government at Western Kentucky University. His main research interests include East Asian democratization and state legitimacy in the context of political culture, politics, and the economy.